Rohinton Mistry

WRITERS OF THE INDIAN DIASPORA

Series Editor
Jasbir Jain

Available Titles in this Series

Jasbir Jain	: WRITERS OF THE INDIAN DIASPORA: INTRODUCTORY VOLUME
R.K. Kaul	: NIRAD C. CHAUDHURI
Manjit I. Singh	: V.S. NAIPAUL
U. Parameswaran	: KAMALA MARKANDAYA
Jameela Begum	: CYRIL DABYDEEN
Mala Pandurang	: VIKRAM SETH
C. Vijayasree	: SUNITI NAMJOSHI
R.K. Kaul & J. Jain	: ATTIA HOSAIN

Forthcoming

Santosh Gupta	: AMITAV GHOSH
Akshaya Kumar	: A.K. RAMANUJAN

Writers of the Indian Diaspora

Rohinton Mistry
Ethnic Enclosures and Transcultural Spaces

NILUFER E. BHARUCHA

Series Editor
Jasbir Jain

RAWAT PUBLICATIONS
Jaipur and New Delhi

ISBN 81-7033-800-X
© Author; Series Editor's Preface, Jasbir Jain, 2003

No part of this book may be reproduced or transmitted in any form or by any means, electronic or mechanical, including photocopying, recording or by any information storage and retrieval system, without permission in writing from the publishers.

Published by
Prem Rawat for *Rawat Publications*
Satyam Apts., Sector 3, Jawahar Nagar, Jaipur 302 004 (India)
Phone: 0141 265 1748 / 7006 Fax: 0141 265 1748
E-mail : info@rawatbooks.com
Website: rawatbooks.com

Delhi Office
4858/24, Ansari Road, Daryaganj, New Delhi 110 002
Phone: 011-23263290

Typeset by Rawat Computers, Jaipur
Printed at Chaman Enterprises, New Delhi

For
my parents
Daisy and Eruch

Contents

Series Editor's Preface   9
Preface   13

1. On the Wings of Fire: Theorising the Parsi Diaspora   19
2. Ethnic Enclosures, Transnational Spaces and Multiculturalisms   47
3. *Tales from Firozsha Baag*: A Return to the Beginning   72
4. *Such a Long Journey*: When Old Tracks Are Lost...   119
5. *A Fine Balance*: Making the Subaltern Speak   142
6. *Family Matters*: About Happiness and Unhappiness   168
7. Conclusion: Transcending the Self and the Other   197

Appendix—Biography: Rohinton Mistry (1952–)   210

Bibliography   216
Index   226

Series Editor's Preface

Diasporic studies have, by and large, integrated themselves into postcolonial approaches. But as one explores and relates to the different kinds of writing by writers who live away from the lands of their origins, a host of new questions come up, questions which demand attention outside the blanket umbrella of postcolonialism. The term has been marked by difference, a difference of all kinds – race, language, nation, culture, history, aesthetics. And has been defined through resistance, subversion and alternity. Power equations have played an important role in it and critics like Homi Bhabha have perceived hybridity to be one of its features.

But with a writer like Rohinton Mistry one is compelled to ask other questions and to reexamine the conjunction between diasporic studies and postcolonialism. Diasporic writing is not necessarily a literature of resistance. It also is not necessarily interested in the category of nation. Its concern becomes one of representation: how the self is represented, seen and remembered against the backdrop of the past. The history of the Jews and their years of living through their language and ritualistic ceremonies is one example of how diasporic communities survive. But the history of the Jews also shows us the violence, the non-belonging and later the construction of a nation, a course of action which other diasporic communities are not interested in and do not look forward to. Instead the new approach needs to locate itself in the politics of belonging –

how ideas of citizenship can be re-formed to include the diaspora. Equality rather than subalternity, acceptance rather than power relations need to be negotiated.

Several writers of the diaspora from various countries are twice-removed. Migrations are no longer one to one. Once begun they have a tendency to continue. There are also 'global citizens' like Pico Iyer and permanent travellers like V.S. Naipaul. A whole group of writers from the Caribbean islands are also twice removed. So what then is so strikingly different with the Parsi community from which Rohinton Mistry hails?

Immediately what comes to my mind is the nature of 'belonging'. At what point does a diasporic community cease to be diasporic? This would apply to the settler colonies like USA, Australia and Canada. It would equally apply to the Moghuls who came to India and settled here. At some point of time the diaspora ceases to be a diaspora: it becomes part of the new nation. Traditional ways of belonging may be perceived as language, lifestyle, shared concerns. But that does not take care of the past which happens to be different in many ways and cannot be altered. Thus it needs to find a place in the new community, to be absorbed and be accepted for itself.

Histories are more time specific than cultures; they are more deeply rooted in political structures than memories and myths. They also have a tendency to be subjectivised by the degree of articulation of the individual. Thus their relationship to new locations can be fairly problematic. It is history which records discriminatory practices, unfair laws and animosities. The remembering of history is not without its problems. It is this which intervenes in the process of belonging.

Another aspect which deserves attention is the relationship of the individual to a community and the manner in which communities cohere through social rituals and practices. Communities often struggle to maintain an identity of their own through 'ethnic' practices and rites related to birth and burial. This aspect gets heightened in a diasporic community as it struggles to retain its distinctive features. But at some point the concerns of the body and the mind, the concerns with materiality and environment push one to recognize the similarities behind the veneer of distinctiveness. Last year two books have appeared which though written by two diasporic writers approach similar themes from within their own cultural practices and, clearly to the extent they share the environment, the works also happen to be a response to their immediate surroundings. These books are Rohinton Mistry's *Family Matters* and Neil Bissoondath's *Doing the Heart Good*. Both are about ageing parents, their loneliness, their physical disabilities and family support structures which move across resistance, aversion and unwillingness to a caring adjustment. This then is the human aspect woven into the social context of the country of adoption, reflective of the cultural practices and environment of the community of origin. This then is a way of belonging.

Rohinton Mistry's work raises a whole lot of other questions specifically related to the 'homeland' and political memory. Neither nostalgia nor memory in itself can account for this rootedness and preoccupation with the homeland and the environment precincts of the city of birth. It is also not merely the fact of being more at home or having a more intimate relationship with the space back there. It is, more than all these, a projection of the individual character, a gesture of expanding the memory to include both the specific and the universal. Bombay (or Mumbai as it is now called) comes to represent both for the author and his protagonists, a stability essential for the travelling self to feel secure. And even as the history of the colonial past is unfolded, the 'universality' of the present in matters of human relationships, in matters of discrimination, construction of religion and racial boundaries, hatred, greed, aversion, love, value of family ties surfaces. This happens in novel after novel as the specific expands to embrace the outside world out there.

In the present volume the location of Mistry's work simultaneously in Parsi history, Indian postcoloniality and the diasporic reality allows the reader to explore the multi-layered meanings of his fiction and moves further into the direction of defining diasporic studies anew. Professor Bharucha, herself a Parsi and a Bombayite, has brought a fine sensibility to work on Mistry's novels and background. We are happy to be making this volume accessible to the reader. It has been in the making for a long time but the wait has been worth it.

Jasbir Jain

Preface

The Indian Diaspora began during the colonial period when the British Empire had spread its tentacles round the globe and the red stain of imperialism had leaked into diverse land masses. Indian labourers and then entrepreneurs followed the Union Jack from the Caribbean islands to Fiji and from Canada to South Africa. Thus were established 'little Indias', now inhabited by second- and third-generation persons of Indian origins, who the Indian Government today have labelled *Pravasi Bharatis* (Non-resident Indians). Among this group are also the diasporics of more recent postcolonial origins. There are millions of *Pravasi Bharatis* scattered round the world with considerable economic and political clout and an awareness of this has probably lead to the official recognition of this phenomenon and the offer of dual citizens to Indians in diaspora.

Apart from their political and socio-economic importance, the diasporic Indians have been performing another important role – they have been imaging India to the world. The earlier generation of diasporic Indian writers included men like V.S. Naipaul, the Nobel Laureate, who has had and continues to have a rather stormy relationship with the land of his ancestors. The more recent among the Indian writers in diaspora are Salman Rushdie, M.G. Vassanji, Bharati Mukherjee and Rohinton Mistry among many others. They too are alternately lauded and reviled in their ancestral homeland. This marks not just the ambivalent relationships these writers have with the motherland but also the feelings of acceptance and rejection manifested towards them by India herself. This is not surprising as prodigal sons or daughters are as often resented for their betrayal of the parental home -- by having left it -- as they are loved for sometimes returning to it or displaying a continuing attachment to it in spite of the thousands of kilometres that stretch between the new home and the old.

In more recent years the diasporic writers of Indian origins have been joined by diasporic film makers and musicians, who like the writers have their muses tethered, even though tenuously in some cases, to India and whose audiences are people in the West who find their books, films and music more accessible than those of writers, film makers and musicians who are based in India. This creates yet another problematic area as it leads to a resentment among the stay-at-homers and the hurling of barbs at the 'dispersed selves', that range from "What do they know about India?" to "They misrepresent India". Distance, temporal and geographic, often lends these works an important insider-outsider perspective on India -- a perspective of value within as well as outside India. These aspects of the creative expressions of the Indian Diaspora have to be negotiated by Indians as their dispersed selves find greater and greater visibility globally and now official recognition within India itself.

Among the diasporic group of Indian writers there are some like Rohinton Mistry who have to grapple with not just one diasporic displacement but multiple displacements. A Parsi Zoroastrian, Mistry immigrated to Canada from Bombay, but in racial terms this was not his first diasporic experience. His peoples had first become diasporic when they had left Iran around the time of the Islamic conquest of the Persian Empire and arriving with their sacred fires had sought refuge in India – a refuge that had seen the highs and lows of the Islamic incursions into Gujarat, the subsequent acceptance during the reign of the eclectic Akbar, the coming out of agricultural spaces into those of commerce and industry during the British colonisation of India, the moving back into ethnic enclosures during the blood-bath of the partitioning of the Indian subcontinent, and the feeling of unease of a very tiny community in postcolonial India. This feeling of unease might be debatable given that Parsi Zoroastrians enjoy a relatively comfortable life in India and have been appointed to the highest posts in independent India, ranging from judges, to elected ministers at the centre and states, to governors of states, to attorney generals of India, to the first field marshal of independent India. Yet, the fact remains that not just Parsis but other minorities also often experience an unease today in the supposedly secular spaces of India. This feeling of unease has realised itself in the move to the West, first to the UK, then to Canada and the USA and more recently to Australia and New Zealand. In these new lands the Parsi Zoroastrians carry with them their ethnic selves, that result in the formation of Zoroastrian Associations not just in the UK, USA, Canada, Australia, New Zealand but also in places as unexpected as Moscow, where it is reported there are all of four Parsi families. These ethnic enclosures notwithstanding the Parsis are an assimilative people who have over the centuries perfected the difficult art of being both global and local at one and the same time – something the rest of the world is beginning to talk about only very recently.

Rohinton Mistry's texts focussed as they are on the Bombay Parsis and their ethnic selves are also books that have a wider appeal. Mistry's first book was a collection of short stories, *Tales from Ferozsha Baag*, which illustrated the Parsi knack of being ethnically conscious and yet of interest to the rest of the world. His first novel, *Such a Long Journey*, though focussed on the Parsi protagonist Gustad Noble, was a book that included the socio-political reality of independent India during the troubled years when India fought two wars with

Pakistan and one with China, to safeguard its borders. The socio-political concern became more pronounced in *A Fine Balance* as did Mistry's belief that Mrs. Indira Gandhi, the then Prime Minister of India, was to be blamed for the condition of the Indian polity. This very dark book foregrounded the traumas suffered by the subaltern sections of Indian society, the Dalits and women during the internal Emergency imposed on the country by Mrs. Gandhi in the mid-1970s. Here Parsi ethnicity collided violently with wider Indian spaces – a collision not always credible, as Mistry's limitations as a Parsi and a diasporic prevented him from having a fuller understanding of the Dalit situation and the complex political forces at work during the Emergency period. Being a Parsi need not necessarily be a disqualification in areas of understanding the wider Indian reality and other Parsi writers, such as Keki Daruwala and Gieve Patel have achieved a synthesis between their Parsi and Indian selves. Mistry, however, is not as successful in writing about a group of people of whom he has little first-hand experience. Political understanding too need not be restricted to those who live in that political space, but in *A Fine Balance*, Mistry's geographic and temporal distance from the Emergency years are all too visible to the informed reader. *Family Matters*, while apparently centred round the aged Nariman Vakeel, is once again a text that reaches out to the world through the pan-universal nature of human actions and their consequences. It is a book that is compassionate and wise in the ways of human emotions such as love, hate and guilt.

Mistry's creative writing has over the years collected a large number of awards and media recognition. Sales figures testify to reader loyalties around the world, as each new novel by the reclusive writer is eagerly consumed by its readers.

This book is an attempt to explore the writings of Mistry within the above outlined context of diverse diasporas and to see how his texts display the apparently contradictory features of ethnicity and transculturalism with such ease.

Long years have intervened between the initial mooting of this project and its realisation. These have been the years in which Mistry wrote one more novel, thereby increasing the scope of this volume. This is not a complaint but merely a statement of fact. They have also been years in which the general editor of this series on "Writers of the Indian Diaspora", Professor Jasbir Jain, displayed great patience and endurance as the deadline for submission was stretched time and again to accommodate her truant contributor. These have also been the years in which students and colleagues around the world have been subjected to snippets from these pages and their reactions -- adverse and complimentary -- ploughed back into the text. These have been the years in which a beloved father, Eruch, who was very interested in his daughter's work on a Parsi novelist died. This book which would have been eagerly and proudly read by him, is therefore dedicated to him and to the mother, Daisy, who had died even earlier, without knowing that her daughter would one day etch her ideas upon a surface other than the blackboard. They have also been the years in which friends and a much younger sibling, Nihaarika, apart from a husband, Sridhar, have with words of encouragement and sometimes screeches of impatience, goaded me into completing this book. Sridhar has also been a sounding-board for the book and its first reader. I thank all of them most sincerely as without them the opportunity to write this preface would never have presented itself.

Nilufer E. Bharucha

1

On the Wings of Fire:
Theorising the Parsi Diaspora

Rohinton Mistry is a writer of the Indian Diaspora that is a result of the colonisation of India by Britain which, beginning with the 1830s, sometimes forcibly and at times voluntarily displaced her peoples throughout the British Empire. This diaspora was sparked off by the official end of slavery, when Indian peasants were transported to the Caribbean and the Fiji islands to fill the gaping holes in the work force on sugar plantations there. Indian labour was also used to construct railways and roads in Africa and to work in the rubber and tea plantations in Mauritius, Sri Lanka and Malaysia. Robin Cohen (1997: 57) calls this the 'labour diaspora'. This diaspora was meant to replace slavery with cheap labour from the colonies. However, there was a difference between the indentured labour from the colonies and the black slaves. The indentured labourers could not be bought or sold like the slaves and at the end of their contract period had to be given a free/sponsored passage back home or given an opportunity to be re-indentured with a promise to be set free at the end of their renewed indentures. Though as V.S. Naipaul has noted (*Darkness* 31), very few of the Indians taken to the Caribbean took the passage back home – for most Indians the journey to Trinidad 'had been final'. It is possible that after having lost caste by crossing the ocean – *Kaala Pani*, the Black Waters – the mainly Hindu indentured labourers would have been reluctant to return home and live as outcastes in their villages.

The forced diaspora was followed by voluntary migrations to these countries by small-time entrepreneurs who followed the imperial flag in search of trade. This marks the transformation of the constitution of the Indian diaspora from labour to the petty bourgeoise. After the end of Empire, the Africanisation programmes of several countries on the African continent and the covert and overt racism practised in the Caribbean islands, led large sections of Indians there to once again migrate, this time to either the 'Mother' country Britain or to Canada. In this context it would be worthwhile to note that the story of race in the original sense is the Manichean opposition of Black and White, analysed by Frantz Fanon (*Black Skin, White Masks*) and Edward Said (*Orientalism*). In India the brown races occupied the position of the Blacks, although they were often called the Natives as well. In the African/Caribbean spaces the opposition was between the White colonisers and the Black Africans/Afro-Caribbeans. The diasporic brown races complicated the situation and were in time treated as a colonial elite by the Europeans and hence earned the ire of the Blacks, who thought of them as colonial stooges. This situation was compounded by the economic power the Indian diasporic people began to acquire. This after decolonisation led first to discrimination and then, as in Uganda, to expulsion of the descendants of the indentured Indian labourers and traders. The expelled Indians and those who voluntarily left the African/Caribbean countries, once again did not exercise the option to return to India. The reasons this time being materialistic rather than related to caste.

From postcolonial India too in the 1950s and 60s there has been a move to the West in search of jobs as well as for higher education. Postcolonial India has also seen a petro-dollar diaspora in which a huge number of Indians, mainly from the Indian state of Kerala, went to the Gulf countries to man their oil rigs and 'woman' their health services. In the Caribbean, African countries, Fiji, Singapore, Malaysia, Kuwait, Bahrain, Dubai, Saudi Arabia, Britain and Canada today there are well established 'Little Indias', with second and third generation persons of Indian ethnic origins. These diverse diasporas which began in the nineteenth century with the first group of indentured labourers being transported to Mauritius in the 1830s are now over a hundred and seventy years old.

So, the Indian diaspora could be broadly classified as colonial and postcolonial with subcategories within each of these broad divisions. In the colonial category there was first the labour and then the entrepreneur diaspora. In the postcolonial category the trajectory of migrations takes in education as well as employment opportunities. Those seeking employment include skilled, semi-skilled labour and professionals.

Almost all these diasporas have been well-represented in creative writing. The Caribbean diaspora has V.S. Naipaul as its figurehead and the tail is brought up by writers such as David Dabydeen. From the African diaspora has emerged M.G. Vassanji. Fiji has given us Sudesh Mishra, Satendra Nandan and Subramani. The postcolonial economic and academic diaspora has its own representative writers in North America – Rohinton Mistry, Vikram Chandra and Bharati Mukherjee. It must be noted however that Mukherjee now aligns herself with the American mainstream and does not consider herself a diasporic Indian writer. In Britain there is the towering figure of Salman Rushdie whose father migrated to the U.K. via Pakistan. Rushdie's *Midnight's Children* sparked off the interest in Indian writing in English and consequently led to the theorisation of postcolonial literatures and the focus on diasporic discourse. There are also other first and second generation Indian writers such as Farrukh Dhondy, Hanif Kureshi, Atima Srivastava, Ravinder Randhawa and Sunetra Gupta. The Petroleum Diaspora has given us the bilingual Vilas Sarang. This is only a representative and not a complete list of Indian diasporic writers.

Living in diaspora means living in forced or voluntary exile and living in exile usually leads to severe identity confusion and problems of identification with and alienation from the old and new cultures and homelands. Therefore, we find most diasporic writing suffused with identitarian consciousness and the continuing problems of living in alien societies. As Salman Rushdie has put it in *Imaginary Homelands*, the position of the 'exile or immigrant' is one of 'profound uncertainties'. The diasporic person is at home neither in the West nor in India and is thus 'unhomed' in the most essential sense of the term. However, as Homi Bhabha has pointed out in *The Location of Culture*, to be 'unhomed is not to be homeless'. When the realisation of being unhomed first strikes one 'the world shrinks and then it expands enormously. The unhomely moment relates the traumatic ambivalence of a personal, psychic history to the wider disjunctions of political existence'. This relation of personal and psychic trauma to the disjunctions of political existence is clearly evident in the work of Rohinton Mistry.

The preferred term used here to describe the Indian writer who lives outside India is 'diasporic' -- the term related to the ancient Jewish diaspora -- as it gives the proper sense of dispersement, loss, nostalgia and is thus more evocative than the terms exile or expatriate. However, as Vijay Mishra has pointed out in his essay "The diasporic imaginary: theorising the Indian diaspora" (*Textual Practice*, X. 3. 1996) the Indian diaspora lacks several important parameters of the Jewish diaspora. The most important one being the searing desire to return to the homeland. There is little of that evident in the Indian diaspora.

There is though a section of the Indian diaspora that does have the notion of 'homeland' writ large in their diasporic existence. These are the Sikhs, who have a strong sense of their homeland. The call for the establishment, as well as most of the funding for Khalistan, a separate Sikh state, came from Sikhs in diaspora and a consul-general's office for the non-existent republic of Khalistan was set up in Canada. This consulate also issued a Khalistani passport and Khalsa currency. The desire for a Sikh homeland was in response to what was seen as Hindu domination in independent India. The descent of the Khalistani movement into international terrorism and the storming of the Golden Temple in Amritsar by the Indian army has led to a progressive distancing of most diasporic Sikhs from the Khalistan movement today.

Even though the Sikhs are/were the only constituents of the Indian diaspora to subscribe to the homeland myth, the rest of the Indian diaspora is not deficient in feelings of attachment and nostalgia for India. Even though V.S. Naipaul in *An Area of Darkness* tells us that as a young man in the West Indies, he had not been much aware of his Indian roots, most diasporic Indians worked hard at keeping their traditions and religions alive. As Parekh has pointed out, Hindus in diaspora kept alive their religion and heritage by inviting holy men and learned speakers from India to speak to them. They also adopted the *Ramayana* as their key religious text.

Diasporic Indians like other diasporic peoples thus have strong links to their homelands but also display a keen desire to assimilate and belong to their present place of abode. This creates counter-pulls in the psyche of the diasporics and is reflected in the literature they produce. As Mordecai Richler has said in *St.Urbain's Horseman*, the diasporic home is both a cage and a haven.

As an Indian who now lives and writes from Canada, Rohinton Mistry is a writer of the Indian Diaspora. However,

Mistry is also a Parsi Zoroastrian and as a person whose ancestors were forced into exile by the Islamic conquest of Iran, he was in a diaspora even in India. This informs his writing with the experience of multiple displacements. Mistry's first novel *Such a Long Journey* is prefaced with three epigraphs that evoke a mystical quest motif like that of the Holy Grail. The Parsis' quest for their roots, their past, their heritage is foregrounded even before the text itself begins. The first epigraph is from Firdausi's *Shah Nama*, the second from T.S. Eliot's "Journey of the Magi" and the third from Rabindranath Tagore's *Gitanjali*. The lines from the *Shah Nama* recall the Persian imperial past of the Zoroastrian Parsi community to which Mistry belongs. The other two quotations focus on the motif of journeying, which is central to the identitarian consciousness of that diasporic community.

The Zoroastrians did have 'such a long journey' from Iran to the Western coast of India. This journey began in the twilight years of the Persian Empire when it was under threat from the fledgling Islamic civilisation. Between 638 A.D. and 641 A.D. the Persian Empire was repeatedly attacked by the Arabs bearing the standard of their new religion. Tottering under its own weight the Persian Empire finally crumbled and with it went an entire civilisation, culture and the ancient monotheistic Zoroastrian religion. When the Arabs consolidated their hold over their newly conquered territories, Islam became the religion of Persia. However, while the new rulers of Persia imposed their religion on its people, they appropriated their language and culture to themselves. So, while the Zoroastrian religion was ousted from the public spaces of Persia, the Persian language and culture continued to flourish under the new dispensation. The vast majority of the Persian people made compromises with this new order and adopted the religion of their overlords, but a tiny minority held out and was pushed out further and further from the centre of the Empire to its coastal margins and mountain fastnesses, from where it made its last grandstand against the Arab conquerors. One such last stand was made at the coastal city of Ormuz but proved futile.

Flight was now the only way open to the Zoroastrians if they were to save their religious identities. So small bands of these people with urns containing their sacred fires, the symbol of their faith, took the sea route to India in search of refuge. The proximity of India to the southern Iranian ports and centuries old trade ties between the two peoples made it a natural choice of refuge. Borne on the wings of their fires, they made landfall at Diu in Gujarat. The exact dates of these landings is disputed by historians and dates as far apart as 756 C.E.. and 936 C.E. have been suggested by different schools of historians. Details on this controversy can be found in Mani Kamerkar, J.J. Mody, K.N. Seervai and K.B. Patel and D.F. Karaka. The actual date of the landfall might be in dispute but what is a constant is that the flight was a direct consequence of the increasing stranglehold of the new religion of Islam over Iran and its appropriation of her civilisation.

In Gujarat, the Iranians came to be called Parsis, probably after the language they spoke – Farsi. In Persian the letters 'p' and 'f' are interchangeable. The name could also have come from Pars, the Southern Iranian province. From Diu the Parsis moved to another coastal town called Sanjan, where they made a pact with the local ruler Jadav Rana and were given permission to settle there provided they agreed to certain conditions:

1. The Parsi high priest would have to explain their religion to the king.
2. The Parsis would have to give up their native Persian language and speak the local language.
3. The women would exchange their Persian robes for Indian costumes.

4. The men would lay down their weapons.
5. The Parsis would hold their wedding processions only in the dark.

The ambivalent feelings of simultaneous identification with and alienation from India can be traced back to this rather oppressive agreement. The second condition meant that the Parsis experienced language loss. In an ironic twist of fate however, the Parsis regained access to Persian with the arrival of the Mughals in India. These Central Asian invaders were descendants of the Islamic Arabs who had overrun the crumbling Persian Empire and forced the ancestors of the Parsis into flight. The Mughals now introduced the Persian language and Persian culture into their Indian Empire. Persian became the official language of India and remained so till the mid-nineteenth century, when it was formally replaced by English, the language of her new colonisers.

The third condition under which the Zoroastrian women had to adopt Hindu dress was honoured right through the duration of the Mughal Empire and it was only with the increasing closeness of the Parsis to the British colonisers that a veneer of Western culture began to overlay the manners and costumes of first the Parsi men and then the Parsi women. This acceptance of Western clothes however was rather slow and restricted to urban metropolitan centres and was often restricted to the 'England-returned' upper classes. The Parsi writer Boman Desai has shown this rural-urban/Hinduised-Westernised divide among Parsis in his novel, *The Memory of Elephants*. Desai's protagonist *Bapaiji* (grandmother) is symbolic of the rural Parsi, faithful to the promises made to Jadav Rana. In contrast, there is her daughter-in-law who wears Western clothes and whose idea of heaven is Scotland.

The language spoken by Parsis today is Gujarati, but at the time that the pact was made, the local language would have been Apabhravnsh/Bhasha or what Grierson, quoted in

Anantrai Rawal has called Old Gujarati. It was from Old Gujarati that Nagar/Gujar was derived between tenth and twelfth centuries A.C. The Gujarati dialect spoken by the Parsis differs from standard Gujarati, as well as other Gujarati dialects and includes Persian and Arabic elements. However, it is closest to the dialect spoken in and around the Southern Gujarat city of Surat

The Parsi diaspora thus predates European colonisation and is a direct result of the outward thrust of Islam from its Arabian desert homeland in the first Christian Millennium. Vijay Mishra has bemoaned the fact that the foundation issue of the journal *Diaspora* devotes a mere twelve lines to the Indian diaspora. However, the Parsi diaspora has not merited even a single line in Mishra's own piece. There is a passing reference to Mistry as a writer of the Indian diaspora. However, this does not contradict my argument as Mistry has not been further identified as a Parsi writer. This elision is rather surprising as some of the most dynamic and well-received Indian English texts of the European Colonial Diaspora have been produced by Parsis such as Rohinton Mistry, Firdaus Kanga, Farrukh Dhondy, Boman Desai and Bapsi Sidhwa, among others. Moreover, in all these texts the *Parsipanu*/Parsiness is the focus around which the discourse revolves. This makes one wonder if this is a continuation of the practice of assimilating 'difference' within the sameness of the self. Maybe Mishra also had the noble intentions of Jadav Rana.

Like most diasporic writers, the Parsis too are obliged to 'deal in broken mirrors some of whose fragments have been lost' (*Imaginary Homelands* 10–11). In their case however, the lost fragments are very large indeed, as vast quantities of historical manuscripts and scriptural material were irrevocably lost when Alexander the Greek burnt the library at Persepolis, the seat of the ancient Persian Empire, in 331 B.C. This had happened centuries before the fall of the Persian Empire to the Arabs. So even the later Persian dynasties were deprived of a considerable section of their heritage. Thus the appropriation of Persian culture and civilisation by the Islamic conquerors is ultimately an incomplete appropriation. It is intriguing to note at this point that with the coming of the Mughals to India and the aforementioned restoration of the Persian language to the Parsis, they made several attempts to reclaim their heritage and salvage at least some of their scriptures but huge chunks remained lost. In 1478, the Parsis had sent an emissary, Nariman Hoshang, to Persia to ascertain the authenticity of their religious practices and rites. More emissaries were sent between the fifteenth and eighteenth centuries C.E. to Persia and the resultant data was collected in the *Rivayats: codes of usages and rituals*.[1]

Thus, unlike the other writers of the Indian Diaspora, Parsis are in diverse diasporas that often run concurrently. These diasporas could be visually represented as under:

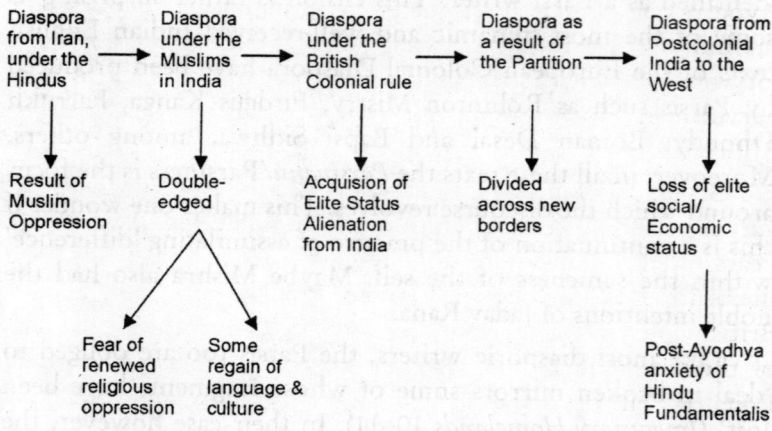

There is first of all the diaspora from Iran to Gujarat, where the Zoroastrians acquired the new identity of Parsis and had to

1. For more details see M.N. Dhalla, *History of Zoroastrianism*, Bombay, 1914, Reprint 1963 and *Zoroastrian Theology from the Earliest Times to the Present Day*, New York, AMS, 1972.

live under a Hindu dispensation. Then came the diaspora spent under the Muslim rulers of India, culminating with the Mughal Empire. After this was the diaspora spent in British Colonial India. The elite status gained by the Parsis under the British rule was acquired at the cost of further alienation from their Indian hosts. Then there is the partition diaspora, where the partitioning of the sub-continent in 1947, into India and Pakistan, found the Parsis on both sides of the blood-drenched border. In this diaspora the Parsis have had to tread very carefully indeed so as not to antagonise either their Hindu or Muslim hosts. In postcolonial India and Pakistan, Parsis have had to contend with the loss of the elite status they had enjoyed in colonial India; this has resulted in the Western/First World Diaspora in which Parsis in the 1950s and 60s have left India/Pakistan to live in Britain, Canada, USA, Australia and New Zealand. The imposition of Hindu hegemony in the 1990s, culminating in the destruction of the Babri Mosque at Ayodhya in Northern India, has generated an anxiety among the minorities and even those Parsis who had thrown in their lot with postcolonial India have begun to display a certain nervousness about their future in a Hindu dominated/BJP-ruled India.

Given the fact that the Parsis have been in diaspora for a very long time now and that their Indian Diaspora is over 1,300 years old, it is intriguing that they have produced such little literature. This is especially true of the period that precedes British colonisation. This could have been the result of the loss of their ancient Persian literature and culture, noted earlier. Equally well, the apparent lack of a literary tradition could be viewed as a natural diasporic phenomenon – where the displaced community has to first come to terms with its new environment, create a space for itself, safeguard its continued existence and only then is it able to turn its attention to creative expressions. This Parsi silence could also be explained as a self-preservation device, a wise decision on the part of a minuscule group, not to in any way anger their hosts. What could have further deepened this silence in pre-colonial India, was the subsequent conquest of Gujarat, where most of the Parsis then lived, by the Muslim Sultans between 1295–1315 A.D. The conquest of their land of refuge by members of the very religious group they had fled from in Iran, created a deep sense of unease among the Parsis.

However, while the Parsis kept a deliberately low profile from the time of their first landing in Gujarat till the arrival of the European colonists, they were not completely silent and they did not go completely unnoticed. By the tenth century A.C. the Parsi presence had spread all around Gujarat and they had established themselves in the five *panthaks* (districts) of Sanjan, Nausari, Godareh-Ankleshwar, Bharuch and Khambat. Parsis are also mentioned in European travelogues beginning with the fourteenth century. The visit of the Parsi priest Dastur Mehrji Rana to the Mughal Emperor Akbar's court and the subsequent influence of Zoroastrianism on Akbar's syncretic religion – *Din-e-Ilahi* – is well documented by historians and travel writers such as Jordanus (1322) and J.J. Modi (1903).[2] Also well documented are the *Rivayats*, the collection of letters exchanged by Iranian and Indian Parsi priests written between 1478 and 1766. These consist mainly of instructions and advice given by the Iranian priests to their Indian co-religionists. There is also the foundational text, *Kissah-e-Sanjan* written in 1600 which praises Parsi courage and bears witness to their arrival in India. The Parsi *Garbo*, based on the Gujarati folk song and dance tradition, records the arrival of the Parsis on

2. See the French monk Jordanus' descriptions of Parsis in Thana and Broach in 1322, quoted in R.E. Enthoven, *Tribes and Castes of Bombay*, Bombay, Government Central Press 1922, Vol.3, 189. See also Odoric in 1323, Garcia d'Orta in 1563, A. Monserrate in 1579, E. Terry in 1615, Thomas Herbert in 1626, H. Lord in 1630, J.A.V. Mandelslo in 1658, J. Ogilby in 1673, J.B. Tavernier in 1681 and J. Fryer in 1697. Also, J.J. Modi, *The Parsees at the Court of Akbar*, Bombay, Bombay Education Society Press, 1903, 85.

Indian soil and their conditional acceptance in Sanjan. So the extant literature, oral and written, of the pre-colonial period is comprised of religious tracts and narratives of valour. These texts display some of the classic features of diasporic discourse noted by William Safran (1991: 83-99) – the fostering of the motherland myth, insecurity and a sense of alienation from the host country. However, these texts lack some of the other diasporic features detailed by Safran, particularly the belief in the restoration of the homeland and the definition of self in terms of this lost homeland.

The way back to Iran was effectively sealed off by the consolidation of Islamic rule there and return to Iran has never been a central part of the Parsi consciousness. Instead there are, as noted by Kulke (1978), some other parameters of identity construction – the Zoroastrian faith, a shared history of flight from Iran and refuge in India, an elite consciousness and feeling of unease in the adopted homeland. It is through such centre-staging of religion and construction of a distinct Parsi identity, that the community has managed to retain a separate presence in India for over 1,300 years. A more detailed discussion of the issue of ethnicity has been attempted in the next chapter.

With the establishment of British colonialism we find the Parsi voice raised for the first time in documented creative expression – both in Gujarati and English. Why did this happen? Was it because in the colonial space – neither Hindu nor Muslim – the Parsis for the first time felt confident enough to write in a creative mode? In *On Colonialism* Karl Marx has pointed out the contradictory strains in colonialism. Colonialism enables as well as disables. British colonialism ruined the indigenous economy of India but it also created wealth – for instance, in the form of the industrial empire constructed by the Parsi industrialist Jamshedji Tata. Socially and culturally if the British Imperialists downplayed or even downgraded Indian society and culture, they also sparked off the internal reform of this society and the renewed flowering of this culture -- here we have the case of the Arya Samaj and the Bengal Renaissance.

The Parsi identification with the colonial ruling class has been documented in considerable detail by Parsi as well as non-Parsi historians, sociologists and anthropologists. The latest in this long list of books comes from T.H. Luhrmann (1996), who in the introduction to her book on Parsis asserts that 'The story of the Parsis is the agony of the long-delayed recognition of the emptiness of [the] promise that they might one day be Englishmen'. That the Parsis were one of the most Westernised communities in British India and that they identified to a considerable extent with the colonisers is a fact. However, what needs to be examined are the psychological motives and socio-political realities behind such an identification. Given the conditions imposed by Jadav Rana, the Parsis had no opportunity in India to crystallise their 'otherness'. So, while in Hindu Gujarat they had identified with the Hindus and had very reluctantly lived under the Muslim dispensation, in British India they once again identified with the dominant group.

Even before the arrival of the British, the Parsis had made their mark as middlemen for the Portuguese, the French and the Dutch traders in India. Prior to European colonisation, the Parsis had focussed on agriculture and petty trade. Under the European imperial order they moved rapidly into trade – especially ship-building, which was so essential to the Europeans who depended on ships to keep the colonial economy alive.

Further, the Parsis were not the only elite group in colonial India that identified with the ruling class, nor were the British the only colonising culture, to have created mirror images of themselves in their colonies. The French in Algeria, the Portuguese in Goa and Macao spring to mind, as do the words of Frantz Fanon, the Black psychoanalyst from the South American French Colony of Martinique, who had settled in French colonial Algeria. In *Black Skin, White Masks* (1956), he has articulated the trauma and dilemma of the colonised – especially the elite groups: 'For the Black man there is only one destiny. And it is white' (10). But the black man can never really be white and that ultimate 'othering' is what leads to what Homi Bhabha (1990, 1994) calls the 'ambivalence' found in the discourse of the colonised. It is from the complexities of such ambivalent reactions to colonial rule that we have the paradoxical rise of the Nationalist movements in colonial societies, movements which are initiated, nurtured and brought to fruition by the colonial elites.

So if there was identification with the Raj, among the Parsis, there was also a strong spirit of nationalism and in some cases even revolutionary radicalism. Parsis such as Dadabhai Naoroji and Pherozshah Mehta spearheaded India's Nationalist movement. Madame Bhikaji Cama, who is credited with designing and unfurling India's first national flag, was a radical and was exiled by the colonial regime. Further, while a Parsi, Jamsetjee Jeejeebhoy was the first Indian baronet, there was also Jamsetjee Nusserwanji Tata, who laid the foundations of modern Indian industry, and met with opposition from the colonial administration. Tata was denied a knighthood for his pro-Indian stand. This is not to imply that the first Baronet was anti-Indian. The diverse charities, for the benefit of all Indians, instituted by Jeejeebhoy, range from the J.J. Hospital and J.J. School of Art and Architecture in Bombay (where Rudyard Kipling was born when his father was Principal of the school), to the construction of the Mahim Causeway in Mumbai and waterworks in Pune, would challenge such a view. However, the pro-Indian, pro-nationalist attitudes of several Parsis in the colonial period does not negate the fact that by the end of the nineteenth century, well-to-do Parsi families had become greatly anglicised. Their homes had become cluttered with heavy carved rosewood and teak furniture and Victorian *bric a brac*. Parsi girls from rich families were blessed with English governesses. The Parsi historian D.F. Karaka (1884: 329) writes approvingly of how Parsi girls and boys learnt to play the piano and the violin, and how they preferred Western music and dances to 'the ugly and absurd *natches* of native dancing girls'.

In these sentiments we see what Stuart Hall (1990) has called the positioning and the construction of identities within the discourses of history and culture. Here we have a classic example of what Fanon in *The Wretched of the Earth* (1963: 170) has termed the colonial strategy: 'Colonisation is not satisfied merely with holding a people in its grip and emptying the native's brain of all form and content. By a kind of perverted logic, it turns to the past of the oppressed people, and distorts, disfigures and destroys it'. A further twist to Fanon's contention, within the Parsi context, is that the Parsis' Persian past is once removed, and what the coloniser's Orientalist project, detailed by Edward Said in *Orientalism* (1978) and *Culture and Imperialism* (1994), distorted was not so much the Iranian past as their adopted Indian past.

Anglicised though the nineteenth century Parsis were becoming, they were not insensitive to what many among them called the danger of over-identification with the British. There was also considerable debate among the Parsis about the widening gulf between the Gujarati-speaking rural Parsis, still under the influence of Hindu society and culture, and the English-speaking, Westernised, urban Parsis. There was also the very real danger of Westernised Parsi youth becoming attracted to Christianity and abandoning their Zoroastrian religion. Dr. John Wilson, the missionary-scholar, after whom the Wilson College in Bombay is named, had a strong impact on Parsi youth and his influence was sought to be countered by the Parsi reformers such as Dadabhai Naoroji, Naoroji Furdoonji, S.S. Bengali, K.N. Cama and Ardesher Framjee Moos. The Gujarati newspaper, *Rast Goftar* (Herald of Truth), established under the leadership of Dadabhai Naoroji in 1851, became the mouthpiece of Parsi reforms such as female education, free association of women with men at public functions and social gatherings, abolition of child marriages and widow remarriages. Under the influence of the reformists, the scientific, natural aspects of Zoroastrianism were stressed and its monotheistic nature showcased. This magnified the self-esteem of the Parsis and enabled them at one and the same time to identify with the colonial rulers' social norms and religion, maintain their elite status and yet retain their distinct Parsiness and Zoroastrian faith. Further, the Parsi reformists included within their ambit, not just their co-religionists but also their Hindu brethren. While at one level this might be seen as illustrative of Parsi identification with their Hindu hosts, it was also often interpreted, by factions among the Hindu community, as uncalled for interference. This was particularly so in the case of the writings of Behram Malabari.

Behram Malabari (1853–1912) was a bi-lingual poet (Gujarati and English), a journalist, a travel writer and above all a social reformer. Malabari's poetry was as much influenced by Wordsworth and Tennyson, as it was by the Gujarati poets Premanand and Akha. Malabari called himself a 'Parsee Hindu'. This identification with the Hindu aspect of his identity – at that point in time the umbrella 'Indian' identity was still being formulated by nascent Nationalism, hence the pre-Nationalist 'Hindu' tag. *Nitivinod* was Malabari's first collection of poems. They were written in Gujarati. He brought these poems to Bombay and showed them to Dr. Wilson – the Christian missionary and founder-Principal of Bombay's Wilson College. Wilson was impressed by the young man's talents and got him a job as a journalist with *The Times of India*, which was then being edited by Martin Wood. He also arranged for Malabari's poems to be published and the book appeared in 1875. After this marvellous start, Malabari's diverse careers as poet and journalist went from strength to strength. His career as a journalist stabilised with the editorship of *The Indian Spectator*. Under Malabari the *IS* was recognised as a newspaper of merit. For more than forty years, Malabari was the premier journalist of India. He used his 'Round and About' column to write about his travels around India. He authored the much appreciated *Gujarat and Gujaratis* in 1882. Malabari also travelled extensively in England. His impressions of those trips have been recorded in *The Indian Eye on English Life* (1885), which went into three editions and *The Sunday Review* compared it to the writing of Kipling. Theorists on colonial travel writing have commented on how the 'Imperial Gaze' identified with the force and contempt of colonial authority (Pratt, 1992; Spurr, 1993; Thomas, 1986). Malabari's 'Gaze', however, is that of the colonised, viewing the coloniser's home. Though in a subject position, Malabari's discourse does not flinch from recording what he observed to be the shortcomings of the Master Race. His reformist heart was particularly wrenched by the poverty of the working classes in the East End of London and in the other industrial cities of Britain. Malabari also took up cudgels for English women. He wrote that he was pained that in the Westminster Abbey, there was not a single bust of a woman, nor did any of the cathedrals honour a woman. He concluded that this was not accidental. As for the Englishman's criticism of the Indian's English, Malabari fumed that the English may poke fun at 'Babu English', but how many of them could speak Bengali half as well as the Bengalis spoke English? Here we have Malabari very strongly identifying with the 'Indian' side of his self. Even when in India, Malabari never advocated the acceptance of European ideals, as was suggested by those who took exception, to his 'meddling' with Hindu affairs. Malabari's identification with the plight of Indian women who were married at 10 and often widowed at 12 was at an emotional level. He agitated for the raising the Age of Consent for Indian girls from 10 to 12.

Such a comprehensive understanding of the issues of race, class and gender from the insider-outsider position, needless to emphasise, attracted criticism from the dominant groups. The Hindu society rejected Malabari's vision and he was branded a heretic and an infidel. It was said that his critique was not based on Hindu *Shastraic* versions, nor could he quote chapter and verse to fortify his arguments. In trying to reach his goal, Malabari therefore had not only the apathy of a colonial government to overcome, but also the active opposition of some of his countrymen. Malabari did not allow either to dishearten him and in 1891 he finally succeeded in getting the marriageable age of Indian girls raised from 10 to 12. This was the Age of Consent Bill passed by the Government of Lord Lansdowne in 1891. In postcolonial times, social reforms undertaken by colonial regimes are often viewed as imposition of an alien disposition on native peoples. In the case of the banning of *sati* in an earlier period too, there had been much opposition. However, the advocates of that reform had been Hindus themselves. With Malabari, his Parsiness and the fact that the Parsis were seen to be very close to the colonisers, vitiated matters even more. Malabari staunchly defended his reforms against attacks from orthodox Hindu circles in Bengal and Maharashtra. To the 'Hinduism in Danger' cry raised by Bal Gangadhar Tilak (the Nationalist from Maharashtra), in his newspapers *Mahratta* and *Kesari*, Malabari countered with his articles in the *IS* (September 28, 1884): 'If my Hindu friends take this line of argument -- that I am "only a Parsi", I will be forced to reply that I am as good a Hindu as any of them, that India, is as much my country as theirs, and that if they do not give me a *locus standi*, in the case, I will take my stand on the higher ground of humanity...'. Malabari's stand was supported by many influential nationalists and reformers – Vidyasagar in

Bengal, Sir T. Muthuswamy Iyer in Madras and Justice Govind Ranade in Bombay.

Among the other colonial writers of the Parsi diaspora in India are Cornelia Sorabji, the social reformer and novelist, Fredoon Kabarji and A.F. Khabardar, who were poets – all of whom wrote in English. There are also Jamshedji N. Petit and Jehangir B. Marazban who wrote poetry in Gujarati. The playwrights, C.S. Nazir: *The First Parsi Baronet*, 1866, D.M. Wadia: *The Indian Heroine*, 1877 and P.P. Mehrjee: *Dolly Parsen*, 1918, also belong to this period. The Parsi theatre, operated mainly in Gujarati and Hindi and as Gopal Shastri (1995) in his book on the Parsi theatre has put it, it had a foundational impact on Indian theatre and cinema.

Cornelia Sorabji, like Malabari, was also a crusading Parsi. She was the daughter of a Parsi who had converted to Christianity, but had been brought up to respect all religions. Sorabji was the first woman graduate of the University of Bombay. A first class degree made her eligible for a Government of India scholarship to Britain, but her gender debarred her from this award. She finally used her savings and supported by her English friends, went to Somerville Hall, Oxford in 1889. Here too she was the first woman student to take the Bachelorship of Civil Law examination. She was not allowed to write the examination in the same room as the men and although she got the degree, her femaleness prevented her from taking the solicitor's examination. It would be pertinent here to observe that the Metropolitan Centre was in the case of Sorabji in a backward state and the Periphery, i.e., the Indian colony, was more progressive. This is also true of the Irish colony, where the women had achieved a higher degree of autonomy and participation in public/political life than had their sisters in Britain in late nineteenth and early twentieth centuries.

It was only in 1922 when the Bar in Britain finally admitted women, that Sorabji became a full-fledged member of Lincoln's Inn and was called to the Bar. Sorabji, however, did join the solicitor's firm of Lee and Pemberton at Lincoln's Inn but soon returned to India where she made the cause of Indian women, who were confined to the veil, her life-time's work. Her literary career is inextricably tied up with her reform work. In 1901 she wrote *Love and Life Behind the Purdah*. Sorabji's reformist agenda was, however, less radical than Malabari's. She did not call for an abolition of the Purdah system, instead she asked for the betterment of women who had to lead such lives. Working in women's spaces made it primary for Sorabji to look at the questions of health care and education. Both areas being neglected by the male order in general. The fact that imperialism itself has been seen by Fanon (1956) and Said (1978) as a projection of extreme maleness, makes Sorabji's mission even more important. She lobbied the Government of India for the provision of educational and medical facilities for these women. *Sun Babies* (1904), is a delightful collection of short-stories, focussed on children. *Between the Twilights* (1908) is a further collection of short fiction. *India Calling* (1935) and *India Recalled* (1936) are her autobiographies, which she wrote in Britain where she had returned in 1929. She lived there till her death in 1954.

In this sense Sorabji is the first Parsi writer to have written out of a double diaspora, Indian and British. The fire and empathy found in Malabari's work is missing in her writing. Her Christian religion and British education further distanced her from India and this is reflected in her work. Did geographical distance lead to ideological weakness? Did her location in Britain dilute her Reformist position? However, Sorabji herself has noted in her autobiographies that, her heart always remained with her *purdanasheen* – veiled – women in India. Can this be seen as sentimentalisation? If so, would such a 'judgement' be applicable to all postcolonial Indian diasporic writers – Parsi or otherwise? Would we be able to say this of Mistry's texts too? This shall be investigated in detail in the chapters that deal with his texts.

Like Sorabji, Fredoon Kabarji too identified with Britain but when it came to the crunch, he was very Indian. His collection of poems *A Minor Georgian's Swan Song* contains poems written mainly in the 1920s, but was published only in 1944. 'A Pianoforte Recital' (1922) is very quietly elegant and has no pro-India or ideological agenda. But in 'The Patriots', written when three young Indian radical Nationalists, Bhagat Singh, Rajguru and Sukhdev were hanged, Kabarji says, '.....fathers, mothers, sweethearts of three young/Sons of India.../The shame, the horror was not theirs/....They were not too weak to die:/but we were too weak to live/who would have saved their lives../ours but the shame and sorrow..'. Kabarji's love and admiration for England did not blind him to the faults of the British in India. In *I Look Upon Simla*, he wrote: 'Simla so English/Where the offensive poverty of India is shut out by/English gentry, by English gaiety, by English health...'.Kabarji was educated in England and lived there for long periods of time. He too was in a double diaspora.

With the end of colonial rule in India on the 15th of August 1947, the Parsi muse once again went into a kind of hibernation. The independence of India was won at a high cost – the country was divided into India and Pakistan. While Pakistan came into being as a result of the 'two-nation theory' – one nation for the Hindus and the other for the Muslims, India made its debut as a secular democracy. However, this did not prevent the horrible bloodshed which took place on both sides of the new border, as massive exchange of Hindu and Muslim populations were effected in both nations. This carnage once again made the tiny Parsi minority feel extremely insecure. The colonial presence which had been a buffer between the Parsis and their Indian hosts, was removed and the Parsis retreated into prudent silence.

This silence was at times punctuated by stray stories and novels, written by writers such as D.F. Karaka Jr. and B.K. Karanjia, but was broken in a major way only in the 1980s. This literature written by Bapsi Sidhwa, Farrukh Dhondy, Rohinton Mistry, Firdaus Kanga, Dina Mehta and Boman Desai was not only a part of the resurgence of Indian English Writing led by Salman Rushdie, but also, displayed ethno-religious attributes that had not been evident in the writing of the colonial Parsis, but had been centrestaged in the writing of the pre-colonial Parsis.

The Euro-American academia and publishing houses tend to lump together all writers from former colonies in the category of 'postcolonials' and consider their discourse in the light of current postcolonial theories. While the writing of the 'postcolonials' does foreground 'fractures' and 'subversions' such hegemonising is ultimately reductive. For instance, the all-encompassing label of 'postcolonial' elides the fact that texts by the Parsi writers might display the above-mentioned features of postcolonialist writing, but they are also engaged in creating their own spaces within the dominant Indian cultural space. As Arun Prabha Mukherjee (1990) puts it, postcolonial theories focus only on those texts that subvert or resist the coloniser and overlook the fact that 'a large number of these texts speak of other matters'. These 'other matters' of ethnicity, gender and religious differences are not sub-textual in the Parsi texts, or for that matter in the texts of the other Indian English writers of the 1980s. Postcolonial theories tend to suppress these differences. Ethnicity especially is an almost pejorative term for those who think in terms of post-nationalism and the global order. Yet it is as central to the discourse of many postcolonial writers as are subversion and resistance. Salman Rushdie's Indo-Islamic roots inform his texts as much as does Parsi Zoroastrianism the novels of Rohinton Mistry. The next chapter has discussed ethnicity and ethnocentric writing in greater detail, as in the case of the Parsi writers of the post-1980s, the focus on ethnic and religious matters, needs special attention given the fact that Malabari had called himself a 'Parsi Hindu' and Sorabji had said her 'heart was forever with India', even though the Parsis were an elite community in the colonial period. Notwithstanding the nationalist credentials of a Dadabhai Naoroji, or a Pherozshah Mehta, or the radicalism of a Madame Cama, the majority of the Parsis had very ambivalent feelings about India's nationalist agenda.

Also, in decolonised India, the exalted position enjoyed by the Parsis during the Raj has been eroded and increasing dominance by the majority Hindu community has marginalised them. Parsis today are trying to reorient themselves to this new much reduced role. Some seek to assimilate themselves into the Indian mainstream, while others in a bid to escape this changed status, move to the West. In both cases the Parsi identity is a casualty. A retention of this identity is crucial if Parsis are to survive even the twenty-first century. According to the 2001 Census of India, Parsis number less than 70,000 in India. There are another 5,000 in Europe, mainly in Britain. Exact figures for Canada and the U.S.A. are not available. Nor is it there much data about the Parsis in Australia and New Zealand. There are also some Parsis in Africa, especially East Africa, where they were part of the wider Indian diaspora. Once again, although most of these countries have Zoroastrian Associations, including a tiny one with four families as members in Moscow, reliable data is not easily available. In addition to these diasporic Parsis, there are still Zoroastrians in Iran. During the reign of the last Shah, the Zoroastrian past of Iran was stressed and Indian Parsis were actively encouraged to migrate or at least work in Iran. However, under the Ayotollahs, Zoroastrians in Iran maintain a low profile. Parsi sources in India usually quote the figure of 25,000 for Zoroastrians in Iran. So worldwide there would be approximately a hundred thousand Zoroastrians. Late marriages, marriages outside the Parsi community by Parsi women, whose children are not accepted into the faith, and a low birth rate have resulted in a situation where the laws of statistics dictate the eventual annihilation of the race.

This adds a particularly piquant element to Parsi diasporic discourse -- that of 'last witness'. The texts of Rohinton Mistry, Bapsi Sidhwa, Boman Desai and others are written within this 'life and death' context. As Mistry has said, 'There are only 120,000 Parsees in the world. So it is not a threat or a delusion that they are on the verge of disappearance. What is 60,000 in a city [Bombay] of 12 million? And it is a pity when anything disappears from this world, any species, man, animal or insect' (Interview with Dirk Bennett, www.artsworld.com). These texts as such are making a 'last grand stand', asserting the glorious Persian past, the Indian connection and finally dealing with the more recent Western experience. This discourse also deals with the increasing tension between the Parsi minority and the dominant sections of Indian society. These tensions have not erupted into violent confrontation as have those between the Hindus and Muslims, but the covert animosity is ever present.

Those Parsis who have gone into a Western Diaspora also face problems. In the land of the white races, they hold no unique position and are lumped together with the other brown races -- the Asians. This is an identity the Parsis were trying to avoid in India and it creates confusion and delays assimilation into the new Western context.

It is in the light of these inferences that Rohinton Mistry is being read in this text. Mistry is interesting as a writer if he assumes a significant niche to enable the exploration of the core areas of critical concern in this study. Mistry needs to be read not just as a postcolonial Indian writer, or as a South Asian Canadian writer, or as a Diasporic Indian writer, he needs to be deconstructed as a Parsi writer too. The chapters in this book are structured so as to reflect these multivalent readings.

To state the bald facts as a frame of reference – Rohinton Mistry is a Parsi writer who writes from the West. He went into a Canadian diaspora in the 1970s, when he was in his 20s. His first book a collection of short stories, *Tales from Firozsha Baag* (1987), was followed by his first novel *Such a Long Journey* (1991), *A Fine Balance* (1995) and *Family Matters* (2002).[3] The earlier texts deal with Bombay of the 1970s and only the last with the city in the 1990s. Like many diasporic texts, they display a sense of time warp. What agitates Mistry most is not the genesis of the modern Indian nation or its current degeneration into warring rival fundamentalist/casteist camps – as it does Rushdie – but the rise of Indira Gandhi and the culmination of her brand of power politics in India's declaration of an internal 'Emergency' in 1975. The ostensible reason for the declaration of Emergency was that there was a threat to the security of the Indian nation. The threat, however, was more to Mrs. Gandhi's government than to the Nation. A fact little known in the West and increasingly forgotten in India is that Mrs. Indira Gandhi's husband Feroze Gandhi was a Parsi from her hometown of Allahabad. This makes her children Parsi according to the Parsi law of male descent. However, neither Sanjay nor Rajiv were formally received into the Parsi religion and Mrs. Gandhi drifted away from her husband, who died in his forties. In spite of this, Mrs. Gandhi maintained her Parsi link and was particularly close to her husband's aunts who lived in Bombay. During the 1971 war with Pakistan, which resulted in the creation of Bangladesh,

---

3. Rohinton Mistry, *Tales from Firozsha Baag*, 1987, Rupa & Co., Calcutta, 1993, all quotations from 1993 edition. *A Fine Balance*, 1995, First Vintage International Edition, 1996, all quotations from 1996 edition. *Family Matters*, Faber and Faber, London, 2002, all quotations from these editions.

there was a major financial scandal that involved Mrs. Indira Gandhi and the Parsi chief cashier of the State Bank of India. Mistry's *Such a Long Journey* is a factional narrative that focusses on this event.

During the Emergency, the fundamental freedoms guaranteed by the Indian Constitution were suspended and Mrs. Gandhi's faithful ministers declared that this included the right to life. These were also the years which saw Mrs. Gandhi's younger son, Sanjay, becoming increasingly powerful. Sanjay in effect ruled India and unleashed a reign of terror, especially in Northern India where his acolytes bent over backwards to implement his pet project, the birth control programme, through the forcible sterilisation of Indian males. The sterilisation programme was supposed to target married men who already had two or more children. But inevitably it was misused to settle old scores and several unmarried youths were sterilised, especially in the villages. Almost all of them belonged to the lower/lowest castes and had usually done something to annoy the upper castes in the villages. Those dark days are showcased in *A Fine Balance*. If *A Fine Balance*, centrestages the Emergency, *Tales from Ferozsha Baag* and *Such a Long Journey*, focus on the Parsi identity and the challenges it faces from the rise of regional chauvinism in the form of the political party, the Shiv Sena. *Family Matters* too is a text that is about Parsis but not about *Parsipanu*. The ethno-religious details of these texts put them in the 'last witness' category. As Mistry has said when the Parsis have disappeared from the face of the earth, his writing will 'preserve a record of how they lived'. However he has added that that is not the central focus of his writing. Notwithstanding this denial, Mistry's collection of short-stories do revolve around the detailing of *Parsipanu*-Parsiness. Mistry's texts are quintessential diasporic discourse asserting ethno-religious difference. Homi Bhabha (1994: 2) has called such writing, 'the social articulation of difference, from the minority perspective'. What adds further value to Bhabha's words is that his own critique is not just Indian diasporic but also Parsi – Bhabha himself being a Parsi from Bombay whose current US diaspora was arrived at via a long stay in Britain.

In spite of this overt detailing of racial and religious characteristics in Mistry's texts, few of the protagonists are prisoners of their ethnicities or religion. Most of them try to move beyond these constructs, to wider spaces free of intra-group domination, as well as hegemonic pressures from dominant groups in postcolonial India and Pakistan. As for the West, many Parsis have succeeded, like the protagonist in 'Swimming Lessons' (*Tales from Firozsha Baag*), to open their eyes under water and enjoy a 'periscopic view' of both the East and the West. As a diasporic people, they have perfected the art of existing on boundaries, partaking of different cultures and yet retaining that ultimate ethnoreligious retreat. So while ethnocentric, these texts are not ethnic enclosures. This aspect of Parsi writing in general and Mistry's writing in particular, is detailed in the following chapter.

2

Ethnic Enclosures, Transnational Spaces and Multiculturalisms

The current explosion of ethno-religious politics in the Indian sub-continent, Yugoslavia, Rwanda and Sudan and the continuing racial/religious conflicts in Ireland and Spain, has forced the recognition that racial/religious identities cannot be easily subordinated to indices of 'secular' modernity or postmodernist post-nationalisms. In the face of global market-economies and the cultural hegemony of satellite communication, ethnicity is often the last refuge into which great masses all over the world are retreating. It appears that in a postcolonial, postmodernist, post-Marxist world, there are millions of human beings who have retreated into what Harold R. Isaacs (1971) calls the 'House of Mumbi', the home of the progenital mother of the Kikuyu tribe in Kenya.

Samuel P. Huntington (1996) has said that ethnic identities are very dangerous and have led to major military conflicts today. He has said that while 'nation-states remain the principal actors in world affairs, their behaviour is shaped as in the past by the pursuit of power and wealth, but it is also shaped by cultural preferences, commonalities and differences (21). Huntington has called the post-cold war, post-Marxist world 'The World of Civilisations' and identified nine major world civilisations -- Western, Latin American, African, Islamic, Sinic, Hindu, Orthodox, Buddhist and Japanese. He feels that the real danger to world peace today is not clashes between nations but clashes between civilisations. Huntington sees the fault line between the Western and Islamic civilisations as the most dangerous flash point for such clashes.

However, Huntington elides the role played by materialist forces, the capitalist order and the military-industrial complex in these so-called 'civilisational clashes'. While the Yugoslavian conflict could be seen as either a clash between modern and orthodox or Western and Islamic civilisations, there was also the Iraq-Kuwait conflict. This was an intra-Islamic conflict in which, because of Kuwait's oil-wealth and hence importance to the West, the civilisational lines were blurred. The West solidly supported Kuwait during this war in an attempt to safeguard its capitalist investments and the interests of its military-industrial complexes. The terrorist attack on New York's Trade Centre Twin Towers, has also been seen as a civilisational clash. President Bush of the USA, called it 'an attack on civilisation', thereby meaning Western civilisation, but in the fashion of orientalist discourse, not using a marker -- the privileged civilisation never being marked like for instance 'Islamic civilisation'. Elided in the consequent bombings in Afghanistan, where the attackers were allegedly holed up, was the importance of Afghanistan as a conduit through which the natural gases from the Central Asian Republics would find their way to the ports of Pakistan, yet another strange bedfellow in the 'clash of civilisations', the earlier one having been Kuwait. E. San Juan Jr. (1998) too has a theory that effectively counters Huntington's culture-based world view. Juan has posited the idea that 'recent US intervention into Central America, the Middle East, Africa, Bosnia, and other flashpoints...confirms the ascendancy of the Hobbesian principle (the Realpolitik of free trade) in international affairs' (11).

There is also a further complication in the case of some ethnic groups such as the Parsi Zoroastrians who have an ethnic identity but have no civilisation today. The Persian/Iranian civilisation which was part of the wider Aryan civilisation was taken over by the Islamic civilisation. In the case of the nation state of Israel too there is the problem of the lost Judaeic civilisation. After the fall of the Judaeic state to the Roman Empire and subsequent diasporic dispersal of the Jews, the vacant space was subsequently occupied by the Islamic civilisation. The Israelis today might ethnically be called a Semitic people, but they belong to a different civilisation from their Arab neighbours. The Parsi Zoroastrians in Indian or Western diaspora, might nominally belong to the same ethnic group as the present-day Islamic Iranians, but they are separated by their religions and different civilisations. Parsis are culturally closer to their Aryan Indian hosts than they are to the Islamic Iranians. In this matter Huntington (1996: 42) is right when he says that 'people of the same race can be deeply divided by civilisation'.

One of the standard sociological definitions of ethnicity is 'a collectivity within a larger society having real or putative common ancestry, memories of a shared past, and cultural focus on one or more symbolic elements which define the group's identity, such as kinship, religion, language, shared territory, nationality or physical appearance' (Blumer 1986:54). Ethnic identity is fundamental and primordial. All other identities are acquired later. It is an identity that cannot be shrugged off like that of religion or nationality, both of which can be changed.

At this point it would be pertinent to note that the West today considers ethnicity to be a kind of bias. It is even more pertinent to note that the West does not think of itself as having an ethnic identity. Being the dominant group it ceases to be 'ethnic' and becomes the 'universal norm'. So British and American Literatures in Britain or the USA, or even in the Non-Western academia, are not ethnic. Black Writing, or Asian Writing however is marked ethnic. Given the economic and political power enjoyed by Britain in the imperial period, its national culture, especially its literature transcended its national boundaries and attained the status of a universal literature. The sole superpower status of the USA today has guaranteed a similar privileged position for its culture and values. The ethnic marker therefore generally means the marginal or the subaltern.

Jenny Bourne (1987: 1) takes a rather anti-ethnic politics stance and says that "identity politics is all the rage. Exploitation is out (it is extrinsically determinist). Oppression is in (it is intrinsically personal). What is to be done has been replaced by who am I". Bourne takes exception to ethnic politics because they subsume ideological stances (Marxist/Feminist) and thus weaken ideology based movements and identities. Her essay has been written in the context of the construct of Jewish Feminism, within the framework of Zionism, which she feels encourages ethnic divisions in the area of feminist solidarity and female bonding. She has also taken exception to the sub-division of feminism into black feminism.

Bourne might have a point but within the hegemonic world order ethnic identities provide visibility. As a White, middle class woman, even if Jewish, Bourne does not have to contend with 'invisibility' and elision in the same way in which her Black or Asian sisters do.

The politics of ethnicity also operates within postcolonial spaces. In postcolonial societies, the dominant group becomes the norm and the ethnic minorities become marked. So postcolonial texts do not merely foreground resistance to the colonial past or resultant psychic traumas but also focus on indigenous domination and marginalisation within the new national spaces. In independent India, even in secular Nehruvian India and not just in today's BJP Hindu dominated India, the term "Indian" generally meant and means Hindu. When one wishes to speak of Muslim, Christian, Jewish or

Parsi culture, one has to specifically say one is doing this. During India's independence movement, Gandhi and Nehru sought to play down the ethno-religious divide but it flared up in the resentments -- real or imagined – of Mohammed Ali Jinnah and resulted in the division of India into India and Pakistan. Nehruvian India however stubbornly clung to secular politics, but even in those days India's huge hydro-electric projects were inaugurated with the chanting of Hindu prayers and the breaking of the auspicious coconut. In those early euphoric years this was not challenged by India's minorities. However, by the time Nehru died in 1964, minority disenchantment with Delhi's Hindu, Hindi-speaking, upper caste domination had expressed itself in language riots, caste unrest and greater assertion of distinct identities by religious minority groups. Since then, the chanting of Sanskrit hymns has been downplayed in favour of multi-denominational prayers to mark state events such as the death anniversaries of Gandhi, Nehru and other national leaders.

Notwithstanding this "political correctness", ethnic minorities in India have been subjected to increasing domination by the Hindu majority. Approximately 80 per cent of the Indian population is Hindu. Of the remaining 20 per cent, about 15 per cent are Muslims and the rest are Christians, Jews and Parsi Zoroastrians – in that descending order. Thanks to their dominance during the 500 years of Muslim Kingdoms and Empires in India, as well as the Muslim-friendly, divide and rule policies practised by the British Raj, the Muslims in India have always had a strong sense of ethno-religious identity. The Hindu-Muslim riots which flared up before and after the partitioning of India, further intensified the Muslim's sense of 'otherness'. One of the many other parameters of this 'othering' of the Muslims is their positioning within the economic strata which keeps them poor. This was however not so in the case of the other religious/racial minorities.

The British Raj had for very practical reasons, discouraged missionary activities in British India. The majority of Christians in India are the Goan Catholics, who became a part of India only in the 1960s, when Goa was liberated from Portuguese rule. So in the first two decades of its postcolonial existence India did not have to contend with an assertion or otherwise of a Christian Indian identity.

As for the Jews, the Jewish presence on the Western coast of India goes back nearly two thousand years in the case of the Bene-Israeli Jews and over two hundred years in the case of the Baghdadi Jews. Jews in India have adopted the local languages and costumes and given the fact that there has been no anti-semitism in India, they have not felt the need to assert their identities as Jews elsewhere did. This is reflected in their literary and non-literary discourse. The Indian English poet, Nissim Ezekiel is a Bene-Israeli Jew but in his poetry has never identified himself as such. The majority of Ezekiel's poetry however dates back to the more idealistic years when India's minorities did not feel threatened. The Jewish community in India today has dwindled considerably, as in the 1960s, and 70s, very large numbers of young Jews migrated to Israel in search of better economic conditions. Interestingly, some diasporic discourse in Marathi (the language adopted by the Jews in India) has been emerging in recent years from among this community in Israel.

Current ethno-religious discourse in India is in direct response to her increasing engagement with Hindu fundamentalism. The inner disputes within the Congress party and the discrediting of its 'secular', pro-lower caste image has meant that the political arena in India is being dominated by the extreme right wing Hindu party, the BJP (Bhartiya Janata Party) and regional parties with strong lower-caste affiliations. This has alarmed the smaller minorities in India who saw the nominally secular politics practised by the Congress party as a protection and guarantee of their rights and freedoms. They feel threatened by the militant Hinduism of the BJP and even though they are currently not the targets of their anger, they do feel disturbed by their slogans of Hindu India and their anti-Muslim rhetoric.

Even the Parsi Zoroastrians who as noted earlier number under 70,000 in India and approximately 1,00,000 worldwide, feel threatened enough to produce distinctly ethno-religious discourse. In order to preserve their ethnic identity in India the Parsis practised strict rules of endogamy and a ban on conversion to Zoroastrianism. You cannot become a Parsi, you can only be born one. The ban on conversion to Zoroastrianism, does not apply in modern day Iran which still has a small number of Zoroastrians -- approximately 25,000. However, converts to Zoroastrianism in Iran or any other part of the world, cannot legally be defined as Parsis in India. The promises made at the time of refuge in India, detailed in Chapter 1, are today observed more for economic reasons than theological. Historically, these promises and self-imposed conditions were a means of self-protection and self-definition. However, today, there are other, not often voiced, reasons for the ban on proselytisation. During the British colonial period, the Parsis prospered tremendously in economic terms and today the Parsi Panchayat Trust Funds are very rich indeed in terms of property, bonds, shares even liquid cash. Given the sky-high property prices in Bombay and other metros in India, conversion to Zoroastrianism would give the new converts the right to reside in the sprawling housing complexes owned by the Parsi Panchayats and claim rights also to their other welfare schemes. This is a scenario not too many Parsis would welcome with open arms.

The reasons for the wealth the Parsis amassed during the British colonial period can be traced back to the fact that the Parsis became mediators between the imperial power and the Indian peoples. However, while the majority of Parsis continued to foster close links with the colonial rulers, as has been mentioned in the earlier chapter, a small but very powerful number of Parsis became active in India's anti-colonial freedom struggle. Dadabhai Naoroji and M.M. Bhownugree became the first Indian members of the British Parliament and represented India's interests there. Naoroji was also one of the founder members of the Indian National Congress. Phirozsha Mehta became the Mayor of Bombay and took the British administration head on in several well documented and colourful conflicts. Bhikaji Cama was a radical revolutionary who was exiled by the Raj. She had the distinction of unfurling India's first national flag at an international forum. Thus, in the colonial period, while many Parsis aligned themselves with the British, some began to image themselves as nationalist Indians.

This nationalist tag stood most Parsis in good stead in postcolonial India, where while some Indians recalled the Parsis' 'colonial stooge' status, most were prepared to forgive and accept the Parsis as Indians, thanks to the nationalist reputations of Parsis like Naoroji and Cama. Even if the Parsis in postcolonial India do not enjoy the status they did as a colonial elite, they are not exactly a subaltern group. The fabled status of Parsis as one on the wealthiest Indian communities has declined and there is some real poverty among them today, but there is still the cushion of very substantial Trust Funds administered by the Parsis Panchayat in the form of welfare schemes, grants to widows, scholarships for students and subsidised housing estates – like the eponymous Firozshah Baag of Mistry's collection of short-stories.

Given this background can Parsis claim an ethnic identity? If being ethnic means being oppressed, means living within the culture of victims, can Parsis be called an ethnic minority? From a purely racial point of view, Parsis in India or in the West, are an ethnic minority. But as Sander L. Gilman (1998:23) has put it 'Can successful ethnics still be ethnic? Do ethnics have to be subalterns? Or can they be good bourgeois..?'. Then again can a successful minority like the Parsis in India be ethnocentric in India but try to 'pass' in the West as part of the White mainstream? This is not as far-fetched as it might sound. Given their pale colouring and Caucasian features-courtesy their Central Asian origins – many Parsis in the West do not like to reveal their Indian/Parsi Zoroastrian identities. Can ethnicity be flaunted in one context and denied/hidden in another? Can the same people occupy ethnic space in Postcolonial India and transcend ethnicity/nationality in the West? Can ethnicity and transnationalism co-exist?

Does living in diaspora automatically elide national boundaries and national/ethnic identities? Does the 'irremovable strangeness of being different' ever disappear in transnational spaces? Homi Bhabha (1998) in his paper of the same title, which he has borrowed from Clifford Greetz (1986) has also asked several pertinent questions in the matter of ethnicity and location of culture. Bhabha, who is also himself as noted earlier a Parsi Zoroastrian, dislocated first in Britain and now in USA, takes recourse to Jaques Derrida but recommends that one reads Derrida 'against the grain'.

Derrida (1994) says that in postmodern times the tele-media and the network of information and communication accelerates and dislocates the assumption of national ontology. Bhabha (1998:34) then goes on to relate this dislocation to 'the specific conjecture of identity, location, and locution that most commonly defines the particularity of an ethnic culture. Derrida also points out that 'the nation is rooted first of all in the memory or anxiety of a displaced -- or displacable – population. It is not only time that is out of joint, but space, space in time, spacing' (83). Bhabha contends that 'The anxiety of displacement that troubles national rootedness transforms ethnicity or cultural difference into an ethical relation that serves as a subtle corrective to valiant attempts to achieve representativeness and moral equivalence in the matter of minorities. For too often these efforts result in hyphenated attempts to include all multiple subject positions -- race, gender, class, geopolitical location, generation -- in an overburdened juggernaut that rides roughshod over the singularities and individuations of difference' (34).

If transcultural agendas thus come to represent 'juggernauts', is ethnicity, especially as related to minorities, a corrective? Where there is anxiety about elision can there be neutral transnational spaces? In such a situation can minorities in diaspora or otherwise ever come out of the enclosures of ethnicity? Greetz goes as far to say that 'Foreignness does not start at the water's edge but at the skin's (112). Given such a scenario are we going to move into smaller and smaller 'House of Mumbi'? Will the 'Parsi Hindu' envisaged by Behram Malabari in Colonial India, remain unrealisable? Will the postmodern breaking down of barriers and boundaries remain a Western majority/hegemonic myth? Bhabha ends his essay by allowing us to hope that the frontiers of the skin may someday be breached, but not within the context of 'universal frames or synchronous knowledges...' (39).

This would however require the non-West to first become truly postmodern and this brings to the fore the question whether as in the case of modernity, a non-Western country like India is merely simulating a postmodern state or even more important can it ever be postmodern? Do the social inequity, material conditions, class and caste politics and gender considerations make the wide open spaces of postmodernity a possibility in such a context?

Moreover, postmodern/transnational spaces have to be truly outside the ambit of national cultures/civilisations. They should not be euphemisms for Western cultural/civilisational hegemony. Appealing though ethnicity and 'castles of the skin' might seem to be, once ethnicity is deconstructed, it cannot remain an essential truth. As Werner Sollers (1989) has said: 'By calling ethnicity -- that is belonging and being perceived by others as belonging to an ethnic group – an 'invention', one signals an interpretation in a modern and a postmodern context' (xiii). Sollers has an intriguing manner of deconstructing ethnicity, which moves it from enclosures into vaster spaces: 'Ethnicity is not so much a deep-seated force striving from the historical past, but rather the modern and modernizing feature of a contrasting strategy...It marks an acquired modern sense of belonging that replaces visible, concrete communities...It is not a thing but a process-and it requires constant detective work from readers' (xiv-xv).

By going along with Sollers' argument one is able to feel 'at home', even when not at 'home'. It has earlier been pointed out how Bhabha has called the moment of the first realisation of being 'unhomed' and thus 'made strange', a moment of immense liberation. Does this indicate that the homed/unhomed, victim/exploiter-oppressor dichotomies could be overcome when one slips through the spaces between these constructs? And if so how does one slip though? In modernist discourse, such as that of Kafka's *The Trial*, the differences between the judge and the accused ultimately collapses. In the feminist space, Julia Kristeva (1986:210) suggests that 'the habitual and increasingly explicit attempt to fabricate a scapegoat victim as a foundress of a society or a counter-society be replaced by the analysis of the potentialities of victim/executioner which characterize each identity, each subject, each sex'.

Is this a utopian dream or a postmodern dystopian hegemonic ploy? Can writing/creative texts help the realisation of this dream? Can ethnocentric discourse be 'read against the grain' to move beyond ethnic enclosures? Or is ethnic anxiety going to prove unbreachable? However, before one even begins to consider a 'contrapuntal reading' (Said, 1978) or otherwise of Mistry's ethnocentric texts, one need to come to grips with the notion of transnationalisms and in the Canadian context within which Mistry's texts have been produced, the concept of multiculturalisms.

Ethnocentricity need not get fossilised and inward-looking. It can be that starting point from which through the past, through shared history, the present can be grasped and the future envisioned. The enclosures of ethnicity can be the borders which can be crossed into wider transnational spaces. The minute detailing of a particular culture need not become a bind, it can become a lead into the arena of multiculturalism. This of course, could raise the questions of why should ethnicity be transcended? Who needs multiculturalism or why transnationalism?

At the risk of inviting the anger of the Nativists it needs to be said that whenever any culture or ethnic group or civilisation has privileged itself over all others, their agendas of self-glorification have usually led to destruction of not just that ethnic group or civilisation but also that of the others who have been drawn into that vortex of mass annihilation. Ethnic enclosures often lead to the gateways of brutality and even bestiality. The mind closes upon itself in a fit of self-destruction. The syncretic worldview of the Mughal Emperor Akbar when herded into the Islamic spaces of his descendent Aurangzeb, resulted in the crumbling of the Mughal power and opened India up to the forces of European imperialism. The ethnocentric pride of the Nazis and the ethnic cleansing practised by them is an apt illustration of ethnic privileging gone mad. Too much of a focus on ethnic identity can lead to fetishisation and essentialisation of identity.

Identities should ideally operate in ever-widening circles of belonging. Assertions of ethnicity come within the ambit of the first/primary circle and is only one of the parameters of identitarian consciousness. For Parsis in the Indian diaspora, the fact of being a Parsi Zoroastrian is a racial and religious identity; then comes the Nationalist identity; then the wider transnational identity. None of these identities need cancel out the other. Since we do not live in a perfect world, however, they could come in conflict with one another, but they could equally well complement one another. Also, these identities could be placed within private and public spaces. Having said that there could be overlaps within these spaces and private and public histories could clash. But it is precisely the sites of such clashes that result in what Bhabha (1994:9) has called 'the literature of recognition'. It is these liminal moments which throw up challenges and resistances to the hegemony of ethnicities/nations/civilisations. It is at such moments of what the Greeks called 'kairos' -- when the eternal meets the temporal -- that ethnocentric discourse moves into the realms of transnational textuality. It is when the particular becomes the general that we traverse from labelling a text ethnocentric to calling it an example of world literature.

This is where contrapuntal readings or readings against the grain come into their own. One could as well view Mistry's texts as narrow and dealing with the Parsi experience alone or read them as having been written in those in-between spaces, the Derridean interstices, through which they cross the borders between ethnicity and transnationality. Similarly feminist texts could be penned within feminist spaces or else through a contrapuntal reading let out into cross-border worlds.

In fact, the more ethnic, more particular, more feminist, more Black a text, the greater its potential for displacement into other spaces. Such texts could be read as identity politics texts or victim texts but they could also be seen as texts that hover around the crossroads of histories, peoples, cultures and civilisations. Contrapuntal readings become the responsibility of the literary/cultural critic. While the interaction between a text and its reader takes place within private spaces, in the home, in the study, its interpretation/analysis happens in more public realms. The critic uses the fora of the literary review and increasingly the media to formulate public opinion on a book. In a satellite-savvy and information-highway order, the 'world' intrudes into the 'home' and it would be futile to talk about the sanctity of the reader-text relationship or the reading of a book for pleasure. A book belongs to the public space and is packaged and marketed in this space. The moment a book finds itself in the market-place it becomes a commodity that is bought and sold.

Depending on the language in which it is produced, a text comes under the sway of ethnic, religious, national or transnational materialist pressures. Being translated into a language of wider communication such as English, overrides the above provisions for a text produced in any language. Texts thus become part of a global phenomenon. Within such a dispensation is it possible to speak of ethnic literatures or even national literatures? Are we then in the realms of World Literatures?

The concept of World Literatures is not new. As early as 1830, in his 'Note on World Literature', Wolfgang Von Goethe had suggested that disruption of cultural continuities could lead to the construct of World Literature. Homogenous cultures could be challenged through terrible wars between combative nations. Peoples of these warring nations 'could not return to their settled and independent life again without noticing that they had learned many foreign ideas and ways, which they had unconsciously adopted, and come to feel here and there previously unrecognised spiritual and intellectual needs'. Goethe's reference was to the Napoleonic wars but in our times the awareness of difference could be related to the aftermath of extensive European colonisation and the resultant displacements and disjunctures in both the postcolonial as well as post-imperial worlds.

No matter how much critics of a Nativist hue, argue that colonisation was but a small episode in the long histories of the colonised countries, it is true that the colonial experience was a transforming moment. The evolving of the former colonies into modern nations, along Western lines was a direct result of colonisation. The postcolonial nations in many ways continue to be the mimetic other of their former colonisers. The hegemony of imperialism has made possible the evolution of the current global order. The collapse of the Communist world and the subsequent end of the Cold War has brought nearer the possibility of a Unipolar world. However, if the hegemony of the West, or to be precise that of the USA in its representing role of the western civilisation has created new cultural representations and power structures, it has also created clashes along what Huntington (1996) has called the 'fault-lines' of cultures. For Goethe 'the inner nature of a whole nation as well as the individual man works all unconsciously'. He also believed that the cultural life of a nation was 'unconsciously lived'. Placing the unconscious lives of nations and peoples alongside one another, the notion of world literature could be as Homi Bhabha has put it be seen as 'an emergent, prefigurative category that is concerned with a form of cultural dissensus and alterity, where non-consensual terms of affiliation may be established on the grounds of historical' (1994).

Considered thus world literature could become the agent through which cultures come to terms with complex constructs of the self and the other. World literature could transcend national projections of selfhood and otherness and move into transnational spaces where also the old hierarchies of centre and margins, the empowered and the powerless could be replaced by the open terrains of world discourse. Such a world literature could also stand the traditional concepts of home and abroad, the homed and the unhomed on their respective heads. So the literatures of the enslaved, the socially, ethnically, politically and sexually underprivileged, the migrant, the diasporic and the colonised could all claim an equal stake in the hitherto hegemonic spaces occupied by the literatures and cultures of the empowered nations and ethnic groups in Europe and Northern America.

The boundaries of literature would then expand tremendously and the houses of fiction would be built not within boundaries but beyond them. There would be a realisation that 'a boundary is not that at which something stops but, as the Greeks realised, the boundary is that from which something begins its presencing' (Heidegger).

However, one cannot overstress the fact that World Literature should not become a covert means of privileging Euro-American centricism. Also, dwelling in the House of World Literature would presuppose that the inhabitants comprehended one another and did not lapse into a Tower of Babel situation. This would make the act of translation central to a transcultural society. Translations, however, would need to be multi-directional and not restricted to the translation of the literatures of the hitherto empowered, into the languages of the disempowered. Only then would literatures cease to represent nations and begin to represent the world. This could sort out some of the problems the Nativists have with the concepts of World Literature and Cosmopolitanism.

Hence do Rohinton Mistry's texts exist in the corrals of Ethnic discourse or do they leak into transnational spaces? However, before we begin to answer this question, there is also the matter of these texts having been produced in the officially 'Multicultural' spaces of Canada. What is Canada's policy of Multiculturalism? How does it or does it not fit in with ethnic discourse and world literature? More importantly, how does Mistry, a Parsi, an Indian, a South Asian fit into a 'multicultural' Canada?

Canada began its modernist existence when it was 'discovered' by Cabot in 1497. It was occupied by the French in 1534 and then ceded to Britain by the Treaty of Paris in 1763, when it became a part of Britain's overseas Empire. In the hierarchy of Empire and its colonies, Canada had enjoyed a superior status of a Settler Colony as opposed to the countries of South Asia -- India, Ceylon, Burma -- which were conquered colonies. Also, by virtue of the predominantly Caucasian make-up of its population (the original inhabitants, until very recently, were dismissed from Canadian consciousness), Canada, in a colour-conscious Empire, constructed predominantly on psuedo-scientific Darwinian notions of the superiority of the White races, scored over the colonies populated by the darker races. However, as far as the Postcolonial scenario is concerned, the South Asian multilingual, multiracial, multicultural, multireligious giant, India, is the senior partner. India became an independent republic in 1950, while Canada severed its constitutional ties with Britain only in 1982 and still retains as its titular head, the Queen of England. Even in colonial times, India became a single political entity in 1858, under the Act for the Better Government of India -- by which the East India Company had transferred the rule of India to the British Crown. The federal state of Canada united only in 1867, under the British North American Act. Also, India has been in the vanguard in the area of the study of Comparative Literatures, which involves rethinking of 'cultural systems' as 'nations' in the nineteenth century terms. Such rethinking involves the setting up of dynamic and interactive frames of semiotics and anthropology to respond to the cultural complexity and diversity of nation states which are composed of different linguistic and ethnic groups. Such an approach is diametrically opposed to the traditional European centrist mode. A comparative approach does not permit the privileging of a single literature over others but views all literatures emanating from the nation-state space as independent expressions of the various ethnic and linguistic groups who inhabit this space (Dev 1991). This cuts loose the conventional European tie between literature and national territory and allows the 'cultural intertext', to cross over national boundaries and exist in the interstices between monolithic national cultures and notions of global culture (Goddard 1990).

Canada has only recently begun to engage with its multicultural and multi-ethnic selves. Officially, Canada is a bilingual country – English and French. However, this bilingual space is today increasingly being challenged by minority discourse. There is much debate in Canada today about categories of aesthetic value and legitimacy claims of the ethnic minorities to the Canadian cultural space. For in spite of having a long history of immigration, the terms of reference of the Royal Commission on Bilingualism and Biculturalism established a clear hierarchy between 'the two founding races' (English and French) and 'other ethnic groups' (Report I: xxi). Bill C-18, which established the Department of Multiculturalism and Citizenship Act has also been severely critiqued within Canada by writers and critics. Nourbese Philip (1992: 185) has said that 'multiculturalism...has no answers for the problems of racism, or white supremacy – unless it is combined with a clearly articulated policy of anti-racism, directed at rooting out the effects of racist and white supremacist thinking'. Others like Scott MacFarlane (1995) challenge the fiction of Canada as protecting multicultural respect, development and participation. MacFarlane has also strongly indicted the Act for excluding the First Nations thereby perpetuating the myth that 'the liberal nation was born elsewhere', rather than through colonialist negotiations with First Nations over land rights. The emphasis on the discourse of rights traces the origins of the nation through the development of European Constitutional Law placing it within the formalism of Canadian and international rights legislation rather than with the colonialist history of Europeans in Canada. This act works to homogenise Canadianness as Whiteness. Thus the Canadian ideal of 'multiculture' exists within a system of signs in which race refers to people of colour and First Nations, as opposed to white individuals, who are dominant and hence raceless. This is fiercely resented by the minorities and is reflected not just in their discourse, but also in the bitter battles they have to wage in order to get their books published and to find representation on bodies such as the League of Canadian Poets, the Writers Union of Canada and PEN. Nourbese Philip's (1992: 160–61) caustic comment on the 'white-washing of cultural values', sums up the situation most such writers of the visible minorities find themselves in – 'Canadian writers of African, Asian or Native backgrounds have a difficult time getting their work published because of the small size of their respective ethnic audiences, except if their works are 'good' enough to appeal to a white audience'. This in spite of the fact that almost all this discourse is produced in the dominant Canadian languages – English and/or French. This is true as much of South Asian Canadians, as of Black and First Nations Canadians.

The story of Indian (South Asian is the preferred label in Canada) immigrants in Canada has two distinct phases. The first phase of immigrants settled in Canada during the British Raj. They were part of the Imperial Labour diaspora, which has been discussed in the first chapter, and in effect filled in the empty spaces vacated by the Africans at the end of slavery. A second wave of South Asians followed these labourers and were shop-keepers and traders who went out to Canada to service the settlements of their countrymen there. The second wave of South Asians swept into Canada from the 1950s to the 1970s, in the wake of decolonisation. These men and women were of a different class from the first wave of immigrants. They were in the main well educated and from the middle-classes. They were in Canada to improve their economic prospects or had taken the route to Canada via the African continent. Rohinton Mistry was part of this second diasporic wave, to which belong Uma Parmeswaran, Michael Ondaatje, M.G. Vassanji and at one time also Bharati Mukherjee.

As Uma Parmeswaran (1996: 142) has put it, the 'real literature of South Asian Canadians lies in a treasure-house that has not been tapped to advantage as yet -- it lies in the memories of the pioneer (s)...arrived in Canada at the turn of the century'. These were soldiers of the Sikh regiments who passed through Canada on their way back from representing the Raj at Queen Victoria's Diamond Jubilee celebrations in London in 1897. Some of these men stayed back and were soon joined by their womenfolk. In 1907, there were nearly two thousand Indians in British Columbia and these included the 700 who had been expelled from Washington state in the USA. By 1910 Canada had passed 'orders-in-council' that strictly controlled the immigration of Asians into Canada. Asian immigrants had to now pay two hundred dollars as head-tax. Racism and xenophobia were the rule of the day and White Canadians were generally united in their resolve to keep Asian immigrants out of Canada. These were also the years in which the 'Koma Gata Maru' incident took place. This Japanese ship had been hired by one Gurdeep Singh to ferry 376 Indians to Canada. When the ship reached Vancouver harbour on 23 May 1914, it was quarantined off the coast. The Government then discussed how to get rid of the 'Brown Peril'. The ship was sent back and only those passengers who were already immigrants in Canada and had been visiting in India, were allowed back into Canada (Dodiya 1998:12–13).

Uma Parmeswaran feels that this history of the Indian pioneers in Canada has to be excavated. She is also of the opinion that theses histories of the early South Asian Canadians has to take female oral narratives into account. Moreover, such narratives would of necessity be constructed in languages other than English and French. The present state of South Asian Canadian literature does not truly reflect female experiences nor does it include non-English discourse. With the exception of writers like Parmeswaran herself and women like Himani Banerjee, Surjeet Kalsy, Suniti Namjoshi and Nilambri Ghai, most other writers are male and even the women write only in English.

The reason for an inadequate representation of women among these writers can be traced to the stifling patriarchal Indian sub-continental tradition that silences the female voice. This situation is further complicated by the fact that in a strange, and often hostile, environment, where these South Asian women are almost entirely dependent on their men, it would be extremely difficult to take autonomous, feminist stances. Race thus takes precedence over gender.

As for the predominance of English in their texts, the colonial past, in which post-primary level education was almost exclusively imparted through the English language, has ensured that for most South Asians, English is, as Raja Rao had put it in the foreword to *Kanthapura* (1938), 'the language of our intellectual make-up'. In postcolonial India, as in Pakistan and Sri Lanka, English continues to be a prestige language and is taught at a compulsory level to all school-going children. It is also almost exclusively the language of higher education, business and commerce. However, English is rarely the language of the emotions and South Asian writers face the problem of conveying their thoughts and ideas in an alien medium. Notwithstanding these handicaps, South Asian Writers in Canada have utilised English to construct their texts.

However, not too many of their texts engage with the ground-realities of life in 'multi-cultural' Canada. Most of these texts deal with the past -- this is not unusual as 'exiles, or emigrants or expatriates, are haunted by some sense of loss, some urge to look back...' (Salman Rushdie 1991). Also many expatriate/diasporic writers hesitate to write about their new homeland, as if they did, they would write as outsiders -- persons who did not belong. Till date, Salman Rushdie's major novels have looked back and tried to recapture the past. Each time this has happened, he has expressed the hope that that would be the last Bombay book he would write, but then the hold of the past has reasserted itself.

Rohinton Mistry's first collection of short stories, *Tales from Firozsha Baag* (1987), is set almost exclusively in Bombay. But there are three stories in this collection which are either partially or wholly set in Canada – 'Squatter', 'Lend Me Your Light' and 'Swimming Lessons'. These have been discussed in detail in the next chapter which is focussed on Mistry's short stories and hence they have not been elaborated upon here. Bharati Mukherjee's novels *Wife* (1975) and *The Tiger's Daughter* (1972), which she wrote while still in Canada, have Indian settings. However, her collection of short-stories, which she wrote after she had moved to the USA, has several stories with Canadian settings. Michael Ondaatje's Booker Prize winning novel *The English Patient* (1992), does not have a Canadian setting, but it does have a Canadian character – the nurse Hana. However, Ondaatje's earlier autobiographical novel *Running in the Family* (1982), has the Canadian author going back to his Sri Lankan roots in an attempt to understand his Canadian present. Uma Parmeswaran's poems, plays and fiction tries to draw links between the Indian roots and the Canadian present. In her dance drama *Sita's Promise* (1981), she has made connections between the Indian epic *Ramayana* and Inuit children in Canada. By and large though, since this discourse tends to focus on pre-Canadian experience, as the critic Diane McGifford (1992) has said, the 'Canadian society goes unscathed, and Canadians are free to savour the edifying cultural distinctiveness of these works and to shake their liberal Canadian heads, aghast at the barbarous racist policies of South Africa and amused by the quaint Bombay Parsi community'.

However, the one writer who does not let Canadians get off scot-free is Bharati Mukherjee. In her introduction to her collection of short-stories, *Darkness* (1985), she writes: 'In the years that I spent in Canada – 1966 to 1980 – I discovered that the country is hostile to its citizens who had been born in the hot, moist continents like Asia; that the country proudly boasts of its opposition to the whole concept of cultural assimilation'. Mukherjee was actively unhappy in Canada where she claims that she was 'frequently taken for a prostitute or shoplifter, frequently assumed to be a domestic, praised by astonished auditor that [she] didn't have a "sing-song" accent' (ibid). It is not the intention to belittle Mukherjee's suffering or trauma, but it is a little difficult to imagine how an upper-caste, English educated woman like her, with a White husband and moreover, one coming from a privileged socio-economic background like hers could have had the type of experiences she narrates about herself.

Moreover, racism and what Mukherjee has called 'crippling assumptions' about one's identity, are not restricted to Canada. Rohinton Mistry, when asked in an interview about racism in Canada has said that he found the racism that went on around him in Bombay 'so much more offensive and hurtful, coming as it did from my own community...the community in Bombay, people who were my classmate, neighbours, my fellow country men, lets go that far, let's say my fellow Indians. I am thinking about, first of the whole caste system, the insidious form of racism, I am thinking about all the embarassment that went on in schools of the majority [Hindu] community towards the others...who were in a minority.. ('The Long Journey of Rohinton Mistry', interviewed by Ali Lakhani at the Vancouver International Writer's Festival). Mukherjee being neither a member of the lower castes nor one who belonged to the minority community, would not have experienced this racism in India. This is not to imply that Mistry is not critical of the overt and covert racism practised in Canada, but that he places it in its right perspective and does not react to it with the kind of manner in which Mukherjee does. In the autobiographical 'Swimming Lessons' (*Tales from Firozsha Baag*), Mistry writes of how as he entered the showers, 'three young boys..from a previous class...hold [their] breath and hum..under [their] breath: Paki Paki, smell like curry.' The universally-hated Multicultural Department also comes in for its share of some delightfully wicked, scatalogical humour, in 'Squatter' (ibid). Here the constipated immigrant is advised to seek financial assistance from the said department to have a small device 'Crappus Non Interruptus, or CNI' implanted in his bowels. For the uninitiated Mistry has elaborated upon the Multicultural Department – it is 'a Canadian invention. It is supposed to ensure that ethnic cultures are able to flourish, so that Canadian society will consist of a mosaic of cultures – that's their favourite word, mosaic – instead of one uniform mix, like the American melting pot. If you ask me, mosaic and melting pot are both nonsense, and ethnic is a polite way of saying bloody foreigner' (ibid).

Moyez Vassanji, the author of *The Gunny Sack* (1989) and *No New Land* (1991), has lived in Canada since 1978. Of Indian ethnic origins, his route to Canada was via Dar es Salaam, Tanzania, in East Africa. *The Gunny Sack* in fact had won the Commonwealth Prize in the African section. Unlike Rohinton Mistry and Bharati Mukherjee his move to Canada was not a matter of choice. The question of choice was taken out of his hands, like it was for most of his compatriots, when they found themselves discriminated against in postcolonial Africa. Belonging as they did to the Indian diaspora of colonial lineage, they were the truly dislocated, who perforce had to relocate in countries like Canada. For the Westernised Indians in East Africa, the only route out of Africa was in Britain, Canada or the United States. For the more traditional Islamic communities the road led to Iran or some of the Arab countries. In *The Gunny Sack*, Vassanji had looked back on his Afro-Indian origins and tried to work out his past. In *No New Land*, the setting is Canadian. This text deals with an Asian,

Muslim family who had gone to Canada from Africa. Here they find themselves in that Mecca of all immigrants to Canada, the Toronto suburb of Don Mills. The family's problems of relocating are compounded by the accusations levelled against its head, Nurdin Lalani, of having attacked a girl. Vassanji has presented a wonderful gallery of diverse characters who live in the high-rise of Rosecliffe Park, along with the Lalanis. All of them face problems of racism and sheer survival -- but in a true pioneer spirit, they survive all that is flung at them. Unlike, the Mukherjees of this world, the Lalanis do not have the luxury of leaving Canada. Nurdin's future lay in Canada, as did that of his children. Also, by facing the past, it was 'vivid, devoid of mystery. Now it was all over you. And with this past before you, all around you, you take on the future more evenly matched' (*No New Land*).

As for Michael Ondaatje, in *Running in the Family*, he sets out on 'quests to discover places, people, histories, and personas which might provide a sense of belonging, strength, and psychic peace' (Leahy 1992). In this text, Ondaatje has grappled not just with his father's dipsomania but also with Sri Lanka's colonial past. By doing so he wishes to come to terms with his Canadian present.

In spite of the physical and psychic struggle involved in being dislocated and relocating across boundaries, the ultimate feeling one gets about these works is its positive nature. These texts are not merely of being dislocated or being unhomed, but embody discourse that tries to move beyond boundaries.

3

Tales from Firozsha Baag:
A Return to the Beginning

Rohinton Mistry left Bombay for Canada in 1975. It is not generally known that before he left Bombay he had begun to make a name for himself as a folk singer and accompanied himself with guitar and harmonica. Polydor had brought out an EP, *Ronnie Mistry*, on which he has sung his own songs, some traditional folk songs and some cover versions too. In an interview with Adil Jussawalla (1988), Mistry has said that he left for Canada because he wanted to become famous in the music world. Unfortunately, however, he found it difficult to survive in the field of music in Canada too and took up a job in a bank. While working at this job, enrolled for a course in literature and as a result, after seven years in the new land, came his first story 'One Sunday' in 1983. Mistry has said that he wrote this story because a friend rang up and told him about the Hart House literary prize and that there would be 'a cash prize with the added incentive of seeing your story bound in leather' (Jussawalla, 1988). Mistry's story won the prize that year and the next year he followed it up by winning the prize again for his story 'Lend Me Your Light'. In 1985 'Auspicious Occasion' was published in *Canadian Fiction* and won the contributor's award. His collection of short stories, *Tales from Firozsha Baag* was published by Penguin Canada in 1987 and Mistry now found himself being wooed by publishers and in that year was short-listed for the Governor-General's Award. Except for a year spent in Long Beach, California – 1986–87 – Mistry has lived in Toronto since his arrival there in 1975.

Tales from Firozsha Baag marks a journey back to the beginning. The locale of these short stories is a Parsi housing complex in Bombay. They could thus be termed 'Nostalgia Writing'. Mistry however refutes this and has said in an interview that 'nostalgia is interesting as an emotion, but for a writer to write out of a feeling of nostalgia is debilitating because it makes the writing too sentimental' (Lakhani). Yet he admits further on in the same interview that 'I think in Bombay and India, my imagination is engaged by that place still after all these years...' (ibid.). Even though *Tales from Ferozsha Baag* might not be nostalgic discourse, they are definitely stories that use memory and remembering as a narrative technique. Craig Tapping has said that in *Tales from Ferozsha Baag*, Mistry is engaged in identity construction through the location of the present in the past (Tapping 1992: 39). The seeing of the past as present is common to most diasporic writers, who as Rushdie has put it tend to live in imaginary homelands.

Having said this it must be admitted that the buildings in Firozsha Baag have very little of the airy-fairy imaginary about them. There is also little sentimentalising of the locale or its inhabitants. They are presented to us peeling paint, peculiarities and all, what could be termed as nostalgia conjured as re-memory. In a recent interview Edward Said has said that 'exile is punishing but also rewarding. Once you have lost your homeland, it cannot be recovered as paradise'.[1]

The first story in the Firozsha Baag collection is 'Auspicious Occasion' and is immediately engaged in identity construction. Ethnicity, Zoroastrian religious rituals, Parsi customs, costumes and cuisine, we-consciousness among the

[1]. Interview with Nikhil Padgaonkar, Doordarshan's Metro Channel, December 6, 1998.

Parsis, alienation from the majority, dominant community and downgrading of status in postcolonial India all find a place in this text. This makes it 'show-window' discourse for the expression of Parsiness or *Parsipanu* as Parsis themselves would put it in the Gujarati language. The Parsis in this story are presented warts and all without any attempt at airbrushing. What is also significant is that not only does this story not sentimentalise the Parsis but that it also is in a sense a myth-buster. Parsis thanks to their colonial closeness to the Master race and their industrial barons reputation, continue to be perceived as rich and prosperous. The Parsis in Firozsha Baag are middle class and like other middle class persons in Bombay have to engage in daily battle with intermittent water-supply, dilapidated homes, peeling paint, falling plaster and leaking WCs.

'Auspicious Occasion' in fact opens with the male protagonist Rustomji emerging from the WC. This sets the tone for the no-holds barred, often scatological language that the characters in Mistry's stories use. Rustomji's language is generously peppered with Gujarati phrases and choice abuses. A character like that of Rustomji could easily descend into the realms of the farcical. Such stock characters of the abusive, comic Parsi are to be found in the Parsi theatre and Hindi cinema.

Mistry's characters might appear to teeter on the edge of the farcical, but they then make the existentialist leap across the chasm. Rustomji and his wife Mehroo are not stock comic Parsis, they are real human beings who at the end of the story almost become tragic characters.

Rustomji also expresses the general Parsi view of most Indians being 'uneducated, filthy, ignorant barbarians' (15). His encounter with the 'ghaatis' [a derogatory term for Indians from the Western Ghats (hills) in the state of Maharashtra] at the bus stop, focusses on the confrontation between the Parsi identity and the Indian identity. In this encounter Rustomji has to resort to playing the clown to escape being physically assaulted by the crowd. This is a pointer to the downgrading of the Parsi elite in postcolonial India.

There are several other tropes that this story deals with, which makes it a good one to introduce the collection to the readers. The first of these deals with the general Parsi feeling that the Parsi Panchayat in Bombay is either inefficient or dishonest, or both, in handling the huge trust funds and properties entrusted to them. As a result the housing estates owned and managed by them are in an extremely dilapidated condition and there are constant battles between the Panchayat and the tenants about putting up the money required for urgent repairs to the buildings. While Mehroo feels that they should undertake the repairs themselves, as the workmen engaged by the trustees would do shoddy work, Rustomji refuses to pay for the repairs: 'I will not spend one paisa of my hard-earned earnings! Those scoundrels sitting with piles of trust money hidden under their arses should pay for it!' (5). The reason why the Firozsha Baag buildings, like other Parsi Trust properties in Bombay, were in such a sad condition was that 'the flats had been erected in an incredibly short time and with very little money. Cheap materials had been used...Now during the monsoon season beads of moisture trickled down the walls, like sweat down a coolie's back, which considerably hastened the crumbling of paint and plaster' (7).

Another aspect of this story which finds an echo in other stories too is the relationship between Parsis and mainstream Hindus. Most Parsis are rather isolationist and living in ethnic ghettoes like Firozsha Baag only excebrate this tendency. About the only contact most of them have had with their Hindu co-nationals, is through the domestic servants who work in their homes. This restricted contact at times intensifies their sense of superiority vis-à-vis the Hindus. However, as Mistry is careful to point out most Parsis treat their servants well and Mehroo is no exception to this rule. She feels extremely sorry for her servant Tanoo who is old and whose deteriorating eyesight leads to breakage of dishes. 'Rustomji too would have like to feel sorrow and compassion. But he was afraid. He had decided long ago that this was no country for sorrow or compassion or pity -- these were worthless and, at best, inappropriate' (8). Rustomji had not always been like this, in his college days he had attempted to identify with India and had joined the social service league in his college and gone on camps to distant villages and had built roads, constructed wells, etc. For the villagers. However he had put all that behind him and now concentrated on living his own life.

It would be unfair to castigate middle-class, urban Parsis alone for such an attitude. Most middle class, urban Indians belonging to other majority and minority ethnic groups also experience this sense of futility of ever changing the condition of rural India. However, here as in his later novel, *A Fine Balance*, Mistry misses out on the chance to elaborate upon the difference between what Dickens in *Bleak House* has called 'individual do-gooding' and an ideological, organised, concerted attempt to deal with what are after all systemic evils that require systemic solutions.

Apart from a feeling of compassion mingled with helplessness, Parsis also objectify their Hindu other. This is especially true of Parsi men and Hindu women. The Parsi men tend to see the young Hindu women who sweep and mop their home as objects of covert sexual lust. This objectification of the 'Gangas' (a generic name bestowed by Parsis on all their women servants), is not again restricted to Parsi males, as women servants who work for other Indians too, often find themselves sexually exploited, but while that exploitation is on the basis of gender and caste, it is in the case of the Parsis and their 'Gangas', intertwined with colonial notions of racial superiority and the rights of the 'Master Race', which the

Parsis, as a colonial elite, had appropriated from their White Masters.

Important though these aspects of Parsi existence in India are, what is even more important is the Parsi consciousness and observance of ethno-religious rituals and customs. It is these that have enabled the Parsis to retain their 'we-consciousness' and distinct identity in the all-consuming ethos of India. And it is this that Mistry has meticulously detailed in those rituals and customs, from the observance of certain holy days (such as Behram-roj), to the decoration of the main entrance doors with chains of fragrant flowers, to the adornment of the threshold with auspicious chalk designs -- studded with coloured powders -- to the cooking of special dishes, to the tying and untying of the sacred thread, to the wafting of sacred smoke around the home from small hand-held fire-containers, to visits to the fire temples and other such endlessly recalled minutiae.

In spite of all this nostalgia and reconstruction of memory, there is little sentimentalisation in Mistry's text. He is very clear eyed about how much or how little these rituals mean to the Parsis. He is also fairly critical about the Parsi priests, who he sees as rather human and consequently as often lascivious men. This would not be a common view point and would be considered subversive by most Parsis, who would rather prescribe to Mehroo's belief in Dustoor Dhunjisha being a rather holy man.

This 'holy man' or 'old goat', depending on how much or how little credence you give to the piousness of priesthood, is murdered half-way through the story and this traumatises Mehroo. It also impacts upon the more secular Rustomji who while on his way to the agiary -- fire temple -- to join his wife is inadvertently sprayed with betel-nut juice by a fellow commuter. Rustomji forgetting that he no longer belonged to an elite section of society, protected by their closeness to the colonisers, shouts at the paan-chewer. This turns the other commuters rather nasty and they gang up on Rustomji and he is saved from a severe beating only by playing the clown -- 'He reached his fingers into his mouth, dislodged his dentures, and spat them out onto his palm....With much effort and spittle he sputtered: "Look, such an old man, no teeth even" (18). This feeds into the crowd's stereotypical notions of Parsis as 'mad bawajis' – crazy old men and Rustomji gets away unscathed.

Behind Rustomji's self-directed joke lies the trauma of the realisation that in spite of the Parsis' continued belief in their superior status, in postcolonial India they have been downgraded to the unenviable status of a has-been community of eccentric old men and women. Thus, for Rustomji and his co-religionists, the coming of freedom for India has meant a lowering of lifestyle and consequent despair of the possibility of any future in independent India. This disillusionment and despair informs not just this story, but most others in this collection and it is this that has led not just Mistry's protagonists, but himself too, to take the route out of India and into a Western diaspora.

It is this tragedy of shattered dreams and socio-political downgrading that lurks beneath Rustomji's comic mask and scatalogical humour, that ultimately makes the story come across as tender and sensitive discourse. The delicately etched and dignified character of Mehroo also contributes to raising the story above the level of the farcical.

The second story in the collection, 'One Sunday', deals with the notion of Parsis as subalterns, but seen as elites, by those even more subaltern in the Indian social order. Contrary to general Indian perceptions, the majority of the Parsis are not rich. Not all of them have access to upper middle class domestic conveniences like refrigerators let alone the privilege of owning a car. This was especially true in the 1960s and 70s -- the period in which Mistry has set his stories and novels. The general economic trends and the socialist ethos, that then pervaded India, did not favour imported goods and luxury items. Hence, consumer items were scarce and expensive. This meant that very few of the tenants of Firozsha Baag owned a refrigerator. The lucky owners to their credit usually allowed their not so fortunate neighbours to use their fridges. This was not an entirely altruistic decision, as this sharing led to the acquisition of a certain cachet and meant that the fridge-owner enjoyed several special privileges and services in the building.

One such fortunate fridge-owner was Najamai. She could leave her flat locked and unattended for a whole day, secure in the knowledge that Tehmina and the Boyce family who used her fridge, would with their ingress and egress, to and from the flat in her absence, give the impression that it was occupied.

Tehmina, who lived alone, mainly used the fridge as a ready source of ice cubes for her midday drink of chilled lemonade and her evening scotch and soda. The Boyce family, blessed with two growing boys, made a more substantial use of the fridge and stored their weekly supply of beef in the freezer compartment, neatly divided into seven packets. Unlike the Hindus most Parsis eat beef, even though the cow is sacred to both the religions. Also, beef is cheaper than mutton and hence more within the reach of poorer Parsis like the Boyces.

In return for the use of the fridge, Najamai borrowed the newspaper every evening from the Boyces. The Boyce boys, Kersi and Percy, whenever called upon, rid Najamai's flat of invading rats, by swinging at them with their cricket bats.

On the eponymous Sunday, the boys were called upon to swing the bat at more than a rat. In Najamai's absence, Tehmina whose eyes were troubled by cataracts, had not locked the flat door properly, after her usual collection of ice-cubes. As a result Francis, a destitute boy, who earned his living by doing odd jobs for the tenants of Ferozsha Baag, had slipped into the flat. His motive was probably some petty thievery but Najamai's return frightened him and he hid behind a door, where he was soon discovered. Najamai's scream brought the Boyces to her aid and even Tehmina put her head outside her door. The Boyce boys, armed with their cricket bats, were despatched to Tar Gully (Lane), where it was believed that Francis was hiding out.

In Tar Gully, where the really destitute of Bombay lived, the bat-wielding Parsi boys were unwelcome. They were resented as representing the race that considered itself superior to them. The boys were taunted with – 'Parsi bawaji! Cricket at night? Parsi bawaji! What will you hit, boundary or sixer?' (35). The boys retaliated with.. 'bloody ghatis'. The term *ghaati* is a descriptive term for people who live in the Western Ghats, but as used by the Parsis, acquires a pejorative sense and generally means an uncouth, barbaric person.

When the boys spotted Francis, they cried out, 'Chor! Chor!' and the cry was soon taken up by the till recently hostile Tar Gully inhabitants. Francis was pursued and caught by three men. He was beaten, spat upon and abused so severely that it made the Boyce boys quite ill. Francis was led back to Ferozsha Baag and brought before Najamai. Najamai was heart-broken that Francis had abused her trust and tried to burgle her flat. After several more kicks and blows, Francis was let off and the crowd dispersed.

At the end of this story too, the noise and action is resolved in quiet disgust and pathos. Najamai discovers a pool of urine behind the door, where Francis had been hiding. So the prospective prey realises that the predator had probably been more frightened than her. Kersi, the brave rat killer, retches his innards out in the bathroom and comes to the conclusion that smashing a man's head is rather different from killing a rat. In a frenzy, he rips off the rubber grip and cord from his bat: 'Soon the cord lay on the floor in a black and tangled heap and the handle looked bald, exposed, defenceless. Never before had

Kersi seen his cricket bat in this flayed and naked state. He stood up, grasped the handle with both hands, rested the blade at an angle to the floor, then smashed his foot down upon it. There was a loud crack as the handle snapped' (38–39).

In the context of the history of Parsis in postcolonial India, this empathising with the even more subaltern group, cannot but be seen in a psychological light. However, the emotions experienced by Kersi and his destroying of the weapon used to berate the unfortunate Francis, can also be seen as the ultimate inability of the 'elite' group to align with the truer subalterns and this becomes even clearer in the following story.

'The Ghost of Firozsha Baag' has a non-Parsi narrator. This change of voice means a change of perspective and leads to an external perspective on the Parsis of Ferozsha Baag. The narrator here is a Goan woman, Jacqueline – known as Jaaykalee to her Parsi bosses. Before the supply of women servants from Goa dried up – it was diverted to the Gulf countries from the 1970s onwards – it was almost *de rigeur* for Parsis to have what they called 'Goanese' ayahs for their 'Baby and Babas'. This was part of the heritage of having been a colonial elite. In the words of Jaaykaylee herself: 'They thought they were like British only, ruling India, side by side' (46). The 'Ghaati' women – the 'Gungas' – were good enough for the rough work, but the children could not be entrusted to them. For that the English-speaking ayah had to be imported from the Portuguese enclave of Goa. As children my sister and I had our Goan Ayah, called Rosie, and my father's half-brothers, considerably younger than him, had earlier an ayah called Jacky, who after my half-uncles had grown up, married a John, who made a huge sum of money as a supplier of bootleg liquor. Jacky visited us often and was sometimes even accompanied by her John.

Our Rosie, however, did not display such sterling qualities of loyalty and vanished one day with her steel trunk. However, like Mistry's Jaakaylee, she too used to concoct delicious Goan curries, for which she herself ground the necessary spices on the grinding stone in our kitchen. This was before the time when the electric grinder mixer became a ubiquitous feature of most middle-class Indian kitchen equipment. Our Rosie, was employed only to look after us 'babies', so cooking curries was not part of her job description, but if she was in a particularly good mood, she would share her curry with my parents. We 'babies' were considered too young to eat her spicy curries and were deprived of the pleasure.

Mistry's Jaaykaylee's duties included being a cook, so her Seth, whom she had looked after ever since he was a baba, and his wife were able to justly partake of the curries whipped up by her. These curries and the spices ground for them, are the leit motif that run through this story. They are sort of interludes and are marked by italicised script. The act of grinding the masalas, cooking the curry and then eating it are very obvious sexual symbols of sensuality and satiation. The sexual undercurrent linked to cooking and eating is projected onto the so-called 'The Ghost of Ferozsha Baag'.

This ghost can be viewed as an overt projection of Jaaykaylee's suppressed sexuality and resultant sexual frustration. This frustration was further fuelled by Jaaykaylee's unvoiced resentment of the way in which her Bai and Seth had mangled her name. The mangling of Jacqueline's name is just one more example of how Parsis had domesticated English. Jaaykaylee herself admits that her Bai says 'igeechur' for easy chair and 'ferach beech' for french beans. This is an indication that the Parsi acceptance of British/European mores was not unproblematic and very often the strange was familiarised before it was accepted.

Domestication of that which is foreign is a common ploy employed by the colonised subject to subvert the essentialising power of the coloniser. In the context of India, its not just the

Parsis who Indianised English but also other Indians, as is amply evident in the texts of Rushdie and his band of midnight's children. However, when a colonial elite like the Parsis, who were so closely associated with the ruling class, subverts it points to an ambiguity in the accepted world view of their proximity to the coloniser and problematises the entire construct of the 'Colonial Elite' itself. How much of a collaborator was Ariel in *The Tempest* and how much of a subverter of Prospero's designs on Sycorax's island? Also, the fact that this observation regarding the domestication of English by the Parsis, is made by Jaaykaylee, a subject of another colonising power -- the Portuguese in Goa – further muddies the waters here.

Jaaykaylee's dull existence -- grinding spices, cooking curries and sleeping on the floor at night -- was spiced up suddenly by the appearance of the ghost. The ghost put in an appearance on the night of Christmas Eve, when Jaakaylee returned home from the midnight mass. She was afraid he would roll her down the stairs, if she slept outside her Bai and Seth's flat -- this was expected of her as her late return from the mass would disturb her employers.

Jaaykaylee thought it would be less dangerous to wake up Bai and Seth, than take chances with the ghost. Their reaction to her story was anger on the part of Bai and hilarity on the part of the Seth. This hurt her as she had sung Konkani songs for Seth when he was a Baba and he had been very fond of her. All the same she was glad to have a job in Bombay as there was nothing to do in Panjim. Also, she felt that she was lucky to have been accepted by a Parsi household as they normally preferred lighter-skinned ayahs from Mangalore. The colour prejudice exhibited by the Parsis was also echoed by the subalterns from Tar Gully and cries of 'Blackie, blackie..' (46) followed Jaakaylee whenever she went shopping there. Although the Maharashtrians are not as fair as the true North

Indians they have by virtue of their membership in the Indo-Aryan grouping – racially and linguistically – considered themselves superior to their Indo-Dravidian brethren and sorority. The irony here is that the ayah, as a Goan, also technically belongs to this non-Dravidian grouping, in spite of the even more southern location of Goa. However, the colonising Portuguese, unlike the British in India, but like the Spanish elsewhere, did not shy away from miscegenation. In fact, they revelled in the creation of a new mixed race which were often the privileged elite whether in Goa or in Mexico. Yet, colour and class prejudices did operate in those colonial situations too and generally the colonisers mixed their seed only with the fairer upper caste/class natives of Goa. The racial mixture resultant in the lower classes/castes generally came from the mating of the locals with the Black African slaves imported by the Portuguese into their Goan colony. This was probably the reason why the poor ayah was darker than the average Indian from Goa and hence the but of the colour-conscious 'Ghaatis' of Tar Gully, who in an ironic reversal of roles would be called 'Blackie' themselves by the fairer, equally colour-conscious Parsis of Ferozshah Baag.

The appearance of the ghost made Jaaykaylee's life even more difficult. Now added to the colour prejudice, she had to contend with loud, lewd jokes about the *Bhoot*. She bore all this stoically and decided to keep quiet when the ghost made a re-appearance at Easter time. This time he sat on her chest and bounced up and down, in an apparent parody of the sex act. Jaakaylee, weakened by her fasting during the Lent period, before Easter, was barely able to push the Bhoot away.

The children in 'C' block, where Jaakaylee lived, thought up various games to tease her about her *Bhoot* and the adolescent boys used the opportunity to tease the girls in the building too. This led the adults to ban further *Bhoot* games. This dying down of the high-jinks surrounding the *Bhoot*, also changed his nature and he now lay down quietly next to Jaakaylee and put his head on her chest. The ghost is clearly a Freudian symbol of Jaakaylee's barren sex life. As she half-heartedly pushes away his wandering hands, she is reminded of 'Cajetan back in Panjim always trying to do same thing with girls at the cinema or beach' (48). The guilt regarding what she had allowed Cajetan to do to her -- 'he came to my bed, lay down with me, tried to touch me' (49) -- resurfaces forty-nine years later in the ghost and his caresses. Cajetan had been kept a secret pleasure and Jacqueline had not confessed about him to the priest in Goa.

Jaaykaylee, however, decides to exorcise the disturbing ghost by making a confession to the priest in her church in Bombay. After that the ghost absented himself -- and the author keeps the reader in as much ignorance about the ghost's whereabouts as he does Jaaykaylee. The ayah at first attributes this absence to the ghost being afraid of the Father in the church: 'How scared men are of fathers' (50). Later though Jaaykaylee begins to miss her ghost and his comforting presence in her bedding.

As for the ayah's hypothesis that the ghost was scared of the priest -- the Father -- just as most men are scared of their biological fathers is a tempting analogy to extend to the rest of the stories in this collection and it is even more tempting to extend the same to Mistry himself. In several stories we have young male characters who are closely attached to their mothers -- this is especially true of Jehangir Bulsara, who features in 'The Collectors' and 'Exercisers'. Bulsara the bookworm, as he is known is at once repelled and fascinated by the macho young boys in the colony. This fascination also spills over into homoeroticism in both the stories.

Interest in the ghost revives though when Jaaykaylee's Bai sees him late one night when she and her husband are returning home from a New Year's party. Bai's word for having seen a spectral creature, being more weighty than Jaaykaylee's could ever be, serious measures are taken to rid 'C' block of the apparition. Parsi priests are summoned and Zoroastrian prayers chanted to scare away the evil spirit.

The ghost does not re-appear but he now seems to have captivated the Bai as much as he had earlier the ayah. So, the story takes a bizaare turn with the two women exhibiting female solidarity and trying to summon the ghost by using a cane winnower, in an interesting combination of Parsi and Goan folk lore and superstition. The women in a rather muddled fashion manage to entice the spirit into their *soopra* and thereby enclosing him there – maybe for future invocation, whenever needed. This 'exorcism' rite fuels the appetite, in a mimic activity of sexual passion, and Jaaykaylee's fire-hot curry is used to douse the flames of unrequited passion.

The ethno-religious detailing in this collection of stories, which began with Behram-roj and visits to *agiaries* is now extended to funeral rites in the story entitled 'Condolence Visit'. After the loud and often lewd earlier stories, this is a quiet little gem, as dignified and truly tragic in its tone as its main protagonist, the newly widowed Daulat Mirza. Although this story is set fully in India, the immigrant experience puts in a guest-appearance in the form of a reference to Daulat's nephew Sarosh, known as Sid in Canada. Sarosh/Sid has an entire story to himself in 'Squatter', in which the diasporic experience of alienation and inability to belong to either the old or new order, is the focus of the text. Sid had brought the gift of a tape-recorder for his aunt and uncle, which Daulat had refused to accept, saying 'Poor Minocher sick in bed and I listen to music? Never' (60), provides momentary relief, through black humour in her grief.

Following the Parsi custom, friends and relations were expected to pay a condolence visit to the bereaved family. These visits in the time-honoured manner would begin after the *dusmoo* or the tenth day ceremonies in honour of the departed soul. Some more tactful persons would hold back till after the *masisa* or the first month anniversary. However, the majority would start streaming in after the *dusmoo*. So, Daulat in a very pragmatic fashion begins to prepare for this influx. She steels herself for the thousands of questions the visitors would ask and the pain she would have to endure in repeating and thereby re-living the trauma and tragedy of the last days of her husband Minocher. With bitter cynicism she half-jocularly wishes that she had accepted the Sid's gift as she could have then taped the story and played it to the visitors whenever they asked for the details of Minocher's illness and death.

Daulat's neighbour Najamai -- she of the refrigerator fame -- offers to help out by lending her chairs and glasses to cope with the flow of visitors. Daulat is annoyed but restrains her anger by reminding herself how lonely Najamai was and how she usually meant well. Najamai like several ageing Parsis in Bombay had children who lived abroad and rarely visited home. Najamai's two daughters Vera and Dolly had gone abroad for higher studies leaving her absolutely alone. Mistry tells us that for some time her refrigerator had helped her socialise but after the time when Tehmina had left her door open and the servant boy Francis had slipped into Najamai's flat, the neighbours were wary of using her fridge, in case they were blamed for any burglary.

This carry over of characters from one story to another provides a commonality between them. There are also other features that link the stories in this collection to one another -- ethnic detailing, alienation from postcolonial India, immigration to the West -- especially Canada, lonely old men and women and identity-confusion among the young.

Another common trope deals with the question of superstition and blind dogma that besets the Parsi Zoroastrian community. This matter had been considered within the context of the supernatural in 'The Ghost of Firozsha Baag', here in 'Condolence Visit', the focus is on superstitions and rituals connected with death and funeral rites.

Daulat Mirza in spite of her grief-stricken condition stands up bravely to the demands made upon her by dogma and ritual as prescribed by 'concerned' relations and neighbours. With reference to the oil lamp she had lit by the bedside of her late husband, Daulat takes evasive measures to evade the criticism of her neighbour Najamai. According to Parsi orthodoxy, the lamp should be extinguished after the fourth day -- *charam* -- ceremonies. This would enable the soul to sever ties with this world and go 'quickly, quickly to the Next World. With the lamp burning the soul will be attracted to two different place: here and the Next World. So you must put it out, you are confusing the soul' (64), advised Najamai. Daulat gets around this objection by shutting the bedroom door so that the burning lamp would not offend the eyes of the orthodox. The little lamp shining in the dark had become a comfort for her and she was loathe to let it go out. As long as the flame flickered in the small glass, memories of Minocher could be recalled with ease. The moments that Daulat cherished were small ones, the minutiae of a long married life -- the monthly de-bugging of their furniture that Minocher used to supervise, or more poignantly the last months of his life when he used to squirrel away his dinner in a tin he kept under his bed and fool Daulat into thinking he had eaten it.

Intertwined in the narrative of the unwelcome condolence visits Daulat has to put up with, are the ways in which she deals with the letting go of her memories. While on the one hand she does not put out the contentious lamp, she sorts out Minocher's clothes for giving away to charity. Among the items she sorts out is Minocher's *pugree*, the tall, black hat worn by Parsi men on ceremonial occasions such as weddings and *navjotes*. Minocher's *pugree* was a particularly splendid specimen and well preserved. Young Parsi men no long wore *pugrees* at their weddings and new ones were thus not manufactured any more. This made Minocher's *pugree* an antique piece and rather valuable. So, instead of letting it rot away and then have it thrown out after her own death, Daulat decides to give it away to someone who would value it. The opportune reading of a small advertisement in the Parsi newspaper – *Jam-e-Jamshed* -- where the advertiser wanted just such a *pugree*, made Daulat call him up, in the hope that Minocher's *pugree* would find a fitting home. This little by-play allows Mistry to offer his usual understated comment on the jettisoning of traditions and traditional garb by present-day Parsis.

The visit by the prospective buyer of the pugree also gives Daulat a respite from her oversympathetic first 'condolence visitor'. In a melodramatic and almost mock-tragic manner this woman -- Moti -- falls upon Daulat's neck reeking of eau de cologne, uttering loud cries of distress. The eau de cologne is incidentally an almost inseparable part of the toilette of Parsi women of a certain age. This cologne is normally associated with the sick room and death in the Parsi psyche. A Parsi patient is often soothed by the discreet application of a little eau de cologne on his/her forehead. A Parsi corpse is kept smelling fragrant by liberal sprinklings of this perfumed water. At Parsi funerals, a corpse bearer or junior priest sits by the corpse with a big bottle of eau de cologne, and his only role in the ceremony is to periodically sprinkle it over the body. In the colonial period and immediate postcolonial times, the eau de cologne used was the original No. 4711 imported from Germany. But during the stringent socialisation of the Indian economy in the 1960s and 70s, most Parsis were reduced to using the Indian substitute manufactured by the house of Tatas, itself a Parsi concern. Hence, it was the most appropriate fragrance to be worn on a condolence visit.

To Daulat's relief, Moti's fragrant histrionics were interrupted by the arrival of the young man in search of a *pugree*. This horrified both Moti and the ubiquitous Najamai: 'Minocher's *pugree* being sold and the man barely digested by vultures at the Towers of Silence!' (74). They both tried to influence the young buyer into leaving but Daulat was adamant and not only does she make him try on the pugree but also refuses to accept payment for it: 'It is yours, wear it in good health. And take good care of it for my Minocher' (76).

The story ends in a touchingly dignified way with Daulat alone in the flat and finding the strength to finally put out the lamp and let Minocher go.

'The Collectors' tells the story of Dr. Burjor Mody's splendid stamp collection and his attempts at initiating young Jehangir Bulsara into the mysteries and pleasures of philately. Dr. Mody was a new tenant at Ferozsha Baag. He had been transferred to Bombay from Mysore, to take up the Principalship of the Bombay Veterinary College. In spite of his recent antecedents Dr. Mody soon became an integral part of the Baag and pitched in to fight the crooked trustees on the one hand and the rapacious Municipal Corporation on the other. So, the battle for setting right broken lifts was carried on simultaneously with the battle for preventing the Municipal Corporation from appropriating Baag property during a road-widening exercise.

Dr. Mody's altruism was in contrast with the goonish behaviour of his only son Pesi, who had been given the grand sounding name of Peshotan, drawn from the Persian epic *Shah Nama*. The original Peshotan was a noble general and a lover of art. Dr. Mody's Pesi (an abbreviated form of Peshotan) was far from noble and not even his worst enemy could accuse him of having an aesthetic sensibility. His wild ways and irreverence for his elders, was the bane of his father's existence. About the only talent young Pesi had exhibited so far was an ability to break wind in a way that resulted in diverse interesting sounds. So when the bookish Jehangir Bulsara had been roughed up by Pesi, the vet had sought to make amends by inviting the boy home on a sunday morning. This was the beginning of Jehangir's interest in stamp collection.

The stamp album that Dr. Mody showed the shy young boy, opened up huge new vistas for him from Antigua, through Russia to Togo and Zanzibar. He was initiated into the world of stamp-collection, but his limited funds could not buy him too many stamps and the new hobby soon had the shy Bulsara boy teetering on the verge of a homosexual experience and being implicated in the stealing of stamps from the road-side vendor outside his school.

The homosexual episode is dealt with considerable sensitivity as Jehangir is asked to manually satisfy the class bully Eric's erotic impulses, in return for Eric swiping stamps for him. What started out as a duty soon became a pleasure and 'when the school week started, Jehangir found himself looking forward to Thursday' (93), the day on which the boys had a visual period, in which they saw films in a darkened room. The darkness provided the right opportunity for Eric to be pleasured and then Jehangir. These 'under-cover' activities meant that Jehangir's stamp collection grew by leaps and bounds as the pleased Eric threw discretion to the winds and swiped the stamps in a rather careless manner. Like all good things, these happy times came to an end when the vendors complained to the school authorities. Eric's tenderness and indulgent manner evaporated and he demanded that Jehangir return all the stamps. The idyll with Dr. Mody was also winding down.

Although the return of the stamps had meant that Jehangir's collection was much leaner now, he did take it the next Sunday to Dr. Mody, who to cheer him up showed him his special treasure – a Spanish stamp showing a dancer.

However, he had to leave the boy with the stamp when his wife summoned him. Dr. Mody's wife was jealous of the fact that her husband spent so much time with the Bulsara boy and ignored their own son. When Mrs. Mody's loud screams penetrated through to Mrs. Bulsara's flat she took away her son but the embarrassed Dr. Mody insisted the boy returned the following Sunday, he had no option but to do so. On that occasion the vet told Jehangir that the Spanish stamp had gone missing from the previous Sunday and the last person to have seen it was Jehangir himself. The boy could sense that he was the prime suspect but keeping the stamp swiping episodes in mind, he chose not to defend himself – 'he did not mind this undeserved blame. In fact, it served to equilibriate his scales of justice' (97).

Mistry's narrative now moves two years ahead in time and takes in changes both at the microcosmic level as well as at that of the macrocosm. At the latter, Indira Gandhi's 'Garibi Hatao', gets a sly mention: 'The Bombay police, in a misinterpretation of the nation's mandate: garibi hatao – eradicate poverty, conducted periodic round ups of pavement dwellers, sweeping into their vans beggars and street vendors, cripples and alcoholics, the homeless and the hungry, and dumped them somewhere outside the city limits...' (98). This 'human detritus' mentioned only in passing here gets a very detailed treatment in *A Fine Balance*.

'The Collectors' ends with the sudden death of Dr. Mody. A year after this event a much chastened Mrs. Mody extends the olive branch to Jehangir's mother and invites Jehangir to her flat to take away her late husband's stamp collection. 'I wanted to give you something of Burjor Uncle's. I thought about it for many days. Pesi is not interested, and I don't know anything about it. Will you take his collection?' (100). A contrite Mrs. Mody also confessed that the valuable Spanish stamp had not been lost, she had destroyed it so as to make her husband suspect Jehangir.

Jehangir takes the collection home but cannot not summon up much interest in it and pushes all the stamps into a trunk and puts it under his bed. Soon cockroaches and white ants infest the trunk and destroy the entire collection. The boy strangely feels no sense of loss or pain -- only relief. After all his foray into the world of 'collectors' had at least briefly traumatised his young life to a considerable extent.

'Of White Hairs and Cricket' is a story that weaves within itself several recurring motifs in the collection. First of all is the liet motif of the Parsis as an ageing and dying race; then there is the time warp that informs all the stories; the motif of cricket stands for notions of honour, valour and manliness that had been inculcated into the Parsis by the British during the colonial period; the remembered past leads to alienation from postcolonial India; this in turn leads to immigration to the West; this immigration mainly by the young leaves behind old parents; loneliness and age is thus the other motif; related to this loneliness of the old Parsis in India, is the loneliness and lack of acceptance of the Parsis in the West; such alienation and loneliness often leads to dysfunctional and aberrant behaviour both within the Indian as well as the Western contexts.

Also intertwined into these multiple and complex motifs is the one other motif that is foregrounded in most of Mistry's stories, the father-son relationship and the construction of a masculine identity. 'Of White Hairs and Cricket' opens with young Kersi resentfully pulling out the grey hairs from his father's head. Kersi had featured earlier on in the collection in the form of the rat-killer in the story 'One Sunday' and put in several other 'guest appearances' in other stories too. Kersi hero-worships his debonair father who used to play cricket with the boys from the Baag on Chowpatty beach every Sunday and quite happily pulls out the stray grey hairs from his father's head, so that the latter could cling a little longer to the illusion of youth.

These hair-pulling activities are however a source of conflict between Kersi's father and his grandmother. The grandmother like most Parsis was firmly convinced that hair was a thing of evil and could be used for purposes of black-magic. This is the reason why most orthodox Parsis keep their heads covered with a white cloth (in the case of women) and with a cap (in the case of men). So by making the boy pull out his grey hairs, Kersi's father was in the eyes of his grandmother committing a sin: 'Sunday dawns and he makes the child do that *duleendar* thing again. It will only bring bad luck' (109). Kersi's *Mamaiji* was not only superstitious about matters concerning hair, but was also a rather devout woman who spun wool for *kustis* -- the sacred thread worn by Parsi men and women around their waists -- and wove them herself. This spinning activity fascinates young Kersi, who stares spell-bound at the rotating spindle descending into an optical vortex. This fascination with rotations, grooves and vortexes spilled over into the observation of records spinning on the old gramophone they had at home. These grooves and vortexes could be seen as metaphors for interlocking narratives and criss-crossing trajectories in Mistry's discourse. This is of further interest as in the last story of the collection -- the self-reflexive 'Swimming Lessons' -- Kersi is cast in the role of the writer of stories and one is tempted to see him as Mistry's alter ego.

The feeling of warmth and comfort that Kersi derives from this sometimes also carried over to the culinary delights his grandmother feeds him on the sly. Kersi was supposed to have a delicate stomach and the spicy delights whipped up by *Mamaiji* often irritated his tummy.

Kersi's upset tummy is not the only false note that is struck in the melody of the family idyll, the failure of his father to deliver on the promises he has made to his wife about finding a better paying job, were leading to a certain degree of unhappiness at home. When he speaks of buying her a fridge and a new stove, she asks him to stop day dreaming: 'All your *shaik-chullee* thoughts are flying again. Nothing happens when you plan too much. Leave it to the hands of God' (113). This lack of belief in Daddy's abilities, soon begin to influence Kersi's opinion of his father too.

Kersi begins to resent the time he has to spend plucking out the grey hairs from his father's head every Sunday morning: 'All my friends had fathers whose hair was greying. Surely they did not spend Sunday mornings doing what I did, or they would have said something' (115). The cricket matches on Chowpatty beach too became rarer and rarer as Kersi's father loses interest in them and the boys have to resort to playing in the Baag itself, but this too soon has to stop as too many windows were being smashed.

Kersi now has to depend on his friend Viraf for companionship on Sundays but one Sunday even this was not possible as Viraf's father is taken seriously ill and the doctor has to be summoned to attend to him. This makes Kersi realise how much he cares for his own father and wishes he hadn't been so rude to him over the white hairs.

It is however too late to make amends, to recall the words he had spoken, so Kersi can only cry for all the shattered dreams, the physical weaknesses associated with ageing and the distances bred by pride.

The theme of loneliness and despair is repeated in 'The Paying Guests'. Here the loneliness of the elderly couple Ardesar and Khorshedbai is most directly linked to their only son having immigrated to Canada. Their tale enables Mistry to foreground the desperate situation of old parents who are reduced to almost penury, after having scrimped and saved to send their sons to the West. The parents in this story have had to resort to becoming paying guests in the flat of the young couple Kashmira and Boman.

The paying guest situation is peculiar to space-strapped Bombay, where an antiquated rent act coupled with extremely high real estate prices, makes it almost impossible for the average person to either rent or own a flat. The rent act has the rents pegged at an unrealistically low 1940s level, so that landlords are loathe to rent out their premises without a hefty 'consideration' – called *pugree* in Bombay lingo. Another aspect of renting a flat in Bombay is that once you are a tenant or even a sub-tenant/paying guest, almost nobody, not even God himself can throw you out, so even if you as a tenant or landlord wish to let/sub-let your flat you do not do so because of the fear that you would never be able to get rid of your tenant/sub-tenant/paying-guest or even increase their rent. There have been several attempts to amend the Rent Act and bring it in line with the actual value of real estate in Bombay, but till date these attempts have been frustrated by politicians, who see tenants paying the old rent as vote banks they can depend on if they in turn frustrate all efforts to revise these rents. As for owning a flat in Bombay, the per square feet price rivals that in Manhattan, New York and given the difference in the rupee/dollar exchange rate, this makes ownership accommodation a distant dream for most middle-class Bombayites.

It is within such a context that one has to read the double-helplessness of both the old and the young couple in the story. Both are equally caught in an aporia. The old people have nowhere to go and the younger ones cannot get them to leave but must try to recover their room as they too have only that flat to call their own and cannot even hope to find another rented one. The ugliness and sordidness that invests this story is the direct result of this no-win situation. The ultimate denouement is almost Balzacian and in a microcosmic manner foreshadows the horrorscape of *A Fine Balance*.

In 'The Paying Guest' Khorshedbai's descent into insanity and bizarre behaviour begins with the ritual scattering of first garbage and then excreta outside her landlady Kashmira's door and culminates in the horror of abducting Kashmira's baby

Adil and shutting him up in the empty cage of her beloved dead parrot Pestonjee. Mistry maintains his own 'fine balance' in this story regarding authorial sympathy for the two women. Both helpless and traumatised in their own fashions. The reader too would find it difficult to favour only one of them.

Khorshedbai's aberrant behaviour is triggered off by the court notice that is served on her and her husband to vacate the room they occupy in Kashmira and Boman's flat. After the birth of their baby Adil, the younger couple decide they needed the room they had sub-let to Khorshedbai and her husband. At first they politely request them to leave but when that does not work, the recourse to law is adopted and the relationship deteriorates: 'Six months of futile and wearying procedures then began' (133). These were also the months in which the regular episodes of littering by Khorshedbai began: 'Khorshedbai littered in the morning and Kashmira swept in the evening...' (134). At the end of this time the final verdict came -- it was in favour of the paying guests. The young couple is crushed and this emboldenes Khorshedbai.

The older woman sees this as a divine dispensation to intensify her war against Kashmira and Boman. After a visit to the *agiary* and the appeasement of all her forefathers, by lighting *agarbattis* before their framed photos in her room, Khorshedbai winds up her old gramophone and loudly plays her one and only record -- *Sukhi Sooraj*, 'a paen to the rising sun' (135). That night Khorshedbai's beloved deceased parrot appears in her dream. She sees him sitting in his cage and throwing the peanut shells and long green chillies out of the cage. These gestures are interpreted by the old woman as a message from the parrot, Pestonjee, to litter Kashmira's doorstep.

Between the littering and the loud playing of *Sukhi Sooraj*, Kashmira and Boman get little sleep. They also soon find out that while their neighbours sympathised with their predicament, they were not willing to go to court and testify against Khorshedbai. One by one the neighbours refuse. Mr. Karani claimed that he followed the three-monkey principle – see no evil, hear no evil, speak no evil. Rustomjee was no help either and Najamai said: 'Me a widow, living all alone, how can I go falling in the middle of a court *lufraa*?' (138). Boman is desperate and knows that the only person who would speak up in court was the Muslim who lived in the next flat. 'But desperate as Boman was, he would not stoop to that, to ask him to testify against a fellow Parsi'.

There are two interesting things happening in this refusal to approach, one is the fact that the Parsis like most minority communities have a 'closing-of-rank' approach to their problems. A minority does not invite attention to one's self or expose one's internal weaknesses, to the communal other. Moreover, there would also be the question of the inherent distrust that most Parsis still harbour towards Muslims because of the expulsion from Iran of their forefathers by the Muslim Arabs. The other interesting matter connected to the Muslim tenant of Ferozsha Baag is a more practical one. Given the fact that Ferozsha Baag was a property managed by a Parsi Trust – the trustees are reviled often in most of the stories -- it is surprising to find a Muslim in such a housing estate. Parsi Trust funded housing is available for Parsis only and even those Parsi men who marry non-Parsi women and whose children have been admitted into the Parsi religion find themselves served with legal notices to vacate their flats in Parsi baags and colonies.

In the midst of all these troubles Kashmira delivers her baby and after returning home decides that she is not going to cower in her room all day. The baby requires fresh air and she needs to stretch her legs too. So, she sallies forth with little Adil to the verandah, at about the same time that Khorshedbai has taken to littering it. This does not daunt the paying guest, but she 'was careful to skirt Kashmira's immediate vicinity' (139). One morning Kashmira goes to the verandah to collect her mail and is beckoned further out by a friendly Najamai who was on her way to the shops. The two women stand talking to one another for some time and then Kashmira returns to her room. What follows next is the tragic denouement of the story.

Once little Adil is rescued from Pestonjee's cage in which Khorshedbai had put him, there is no shortage of neighbours willing to testify against the paying guests. However there is no need for that: 'The paying guests went quietly: Khorshedbai first, by ambulance, everyone knew where; then Ardeshar, no one knew where, by taxi' (139).

The rest of the four stories in the collection are even more inter-related than the others before them. 'Squatter', 'Lend Me Your Light' and 'Swimming Lessons' are the three Canadian stories, set wholly or partially in Canada and which display to the maximum extent the 'periscopic vision' of the diasporic writer foregrounded by Salman Rushdie in his critical essays, *Imaginary Homelands*. 'Exercisers' though set in Bombay is linked to 'Swimming Lessons', through the concern with the erotic and sexual which has informed even some of the earlier stories 'The Ghost of Ferozsha Baag' and 'The Collectors'. Yet another commonality is the focus on narrative devices and self-reflexion which makes 'Squatter' and 'Swimming Lessons', not just examples of diasoric Parsi/Indian writing, but also places them in the mainstream of postmodernist fiction. Above all what strings these stories together is the all pervading tone of irony, scatalogical humour and self-mockery, which is typical of Parsi discourse, especially Parsi drama. The Parsi dramatist most closely associated with this style was Adi Marzban, whose plays were replete with broad humour and the double entendre. However, what sets Mistry apart from Marzban is the fact that Mistry's texts are ultimately tragic texts and the scatalogical humour and irony are most often resolved in the tragic which elevates them to a dignified status not available to Marzban's *naataks*.

Although 'Exercisers' is sandwiched between two Canadian stories, its being considered earlier here, as then the three Canadian stories can be considered as a group. 'Exercisers' picks up the story of Jehangir Bulsara -- he of the bookworm, stamp-stealing and homo-erotic fame, who had featured in the earlier stories too. Here Jehangir's sexuality is once again the focus of the narrative. However, the object of his affection is now not a man but a woman – a rather unsuitable girl in his parents' opinion. The story opens with Mr. and Mrs. Bulsara seeking the aid of their family guru, Bhagwan Baba, to convince Jehangir of how unsuitable the girl was for him. Here we have the Hindu element of a personal guru introduced into the text – an element which is alien to Zoroastrianism which does not allow mediation between the believer and his/her God. However, centuries of living in India has obviously meant that some of the dominant community's beliefs have leaked into the Parsi way of life. Along with a belief in gurus, there are also the largely Hindu rituals at Parsi weddings and Sanskrit *shlokas* in Zoroastrian prayers which have been some of the results of a cultural collision between the two groups of Aryans on Indian soil – the Zoroastrians and the Hindus.

Jehangir's 'unsuitable girl' was his first girlfriend and even this rather late romantic interest (Jehangir was already in his third year at college), is frowned upon by his parents, who still insist on imposing rather strict curfew hours on their grown-up son. This, however, does not stop Jehangir's interest in girls from blooming. He had earlier been in the habit of going to the Hanging Gardens and admiring the young men who used to gather there to exercise together. The sight of the rippling muscles used to excite the young boy: 'Jehangir, hidden behind a bush or tree, watched the exercisers. They fascinated him. Their rippling, sweating muscles were magnified versions of the bodies of the boys in the school gym. Watching their powerful torsos and limbs had a strange effect on his own skinny body, it sometimes triggered a longing for brawn and sinew in his slender arms and legs' (203). Once he joins college Jehangir's latent homosexuality is diverted into more heterosexual channels and he takes to frequenting cinema houses, where in the darkness he could slyly press his arm against that of the girl in the seat next to him or else graze the back of her legs with his knees, when she slides past him to get to her seat. Such activities are of course not restricted to strictly brought up Parsi boys alone, but are common experience for most Indian youth, whose sexuality is sought to be controlled by parental dictat and moralistic societal norms. In fact it could be such control that is the reason for the latent homosexuality that seem to afflict a large section of Indian youth and to which Mistry has made ample mention in these stories.

When after two years at college, Jehangir finally succeeds in making contact with a girl in the choir group, his parents disapprove of her as too 'modern' and his mother even suggests that she showed interest in Jehangir only because 'she knows you will go to study in America one day and settle there' (207). To wean their son away from this girl, the Bulsaras drag him to see their guru who lived in a distant suburb in Bombay. The train journey to the guru's house provides Mistry with an opportunity to include some more local colour in his text.

The guru's reply to the Bulsara's anxious query vis-à-vis the suitability of the girl, is rather cryptic in the best mystic tradition. So, the Baba's words: 'Life is a trap, full of webs, but no one can do anything about it' (213), is interpreted in the most negative manner by Mr. Bulsara as a dire warning against the girl, but Jehangir himself reads a certain inevitability in the words and the inability of anyone to change anything.

Yet, in spite of himself Jehangir is a little worried by the Baba's message and begins to wonder if Behroze had really set out to trap him. Unsure about the meaning of Baba's words,

Jehangir begins to avoid Behroze and once more visits the Hanging Gardens and starts watching the Excercisers 'he rediscovered what he had always found strangely enticing, and remembered the days in the gym at St. Xavier's..' (216). Jehangir had once taken Behroze to Hanging Gardens too, but when she had tried to initiate physical contact, he had shrunk away from her. This in spite of the fact that there were several couples around them engaged in far greater intimacies. Troubled by the Baba's prophecy, Jehangir decides to throw in his lot with the male fraternity of the exercisers and make a clean break with Behroze.

Jehangir's plans however misfired when he finally goes to Behroze's place. He finds her alone at home and ends up making love to her. This unscheduled love-making means that Jehangir was not going to make it home in time for his mother's eight o'clock curfew. As the girl stares at him 'in stark disbelief' he transforms before her eyes 'from man to cowering child' (224) and he 'rushed through the streets like a madman, shivering, tormented and confused' (224), but it was still eight thirty before he rang his doorbell. The inevitable happens and his mother shuts the door in his face and he has to reconcile himself to spending the night outside his flat. The humility is thus complete but the mother-son bonding is re-established when 'the soft clanking of the chain being removed from the door woke him up' (225).

Mistry's focus here on the near Oedipal nature of the mother-son bonding is once again not peculiar to the Parsi community in India, but manifests itself in the mainstream Hindu society, as well as among the Muslims. The near obsession that most Indians have about having a male child, when a son is finally born, leads to a tremendous privileging of that male child. This is especially true of the mother, whose status within the family is tied up with being the producer of the desired male child and this results in an almost unhealthily close relationship between mother and son. Among the

Hindus, the desire for a male child was linked to inheritance laws, wherein only the male heir could inherit his parents' property and to funeral rites which again could only be performed by a son. Although, this has changed now and Hindu women have more equal rights in their father's estate, they are usually fobbed off with a dowry at the time of their marriage, instead of an equal share. Also, very few Hindu women assert their right to light the funeral pyre of their father or widowed mother. The Muslims too have male-favouring inheritance laws. All of these above mentioned reasons do not apply to Parsis and yet they too by virtue of being as patriarchal in their orientations as other Indians, also favour their male children. A blatant example of this male domination is the fact that male Parsis, when they marry non-Parsi women, can have their children admitted into the Zoroastrian religion and they can then claim all the benefits and privileges of other Parsi Zoroastrians – except rights of residence in a Parsi housing estate. However, a similar privilege is denied to Parsi women who marry outside the Parsi community.

'Squatter' – the first story in the Canadian group – is narrated by the master story-teller of Ferozsha Baag, Nariman Hansotia. This also places the story in the orature tradition of the East – a tradition further exploited by Mistry in *Such a Long Journey*, which has Scherazadic features of the Arabian Nights' narrative techniques. The Scherazadic narrative mode has been used by other Indian postcolonial writers too – notably Salman Rushdie, particularly in *Haroun and the Sea of Stories* and by Githa Hariharan in *When Dreams Travel* (1998). 'Squatter' also uses tongue-in-cheek labels instead of names for several characters like does Rushdie in most of his texts.

Nariman Hansotia begins the story of the squatter by framing it within the story of the valourous Savuksha the mighty cricketer and hunter. The shame and ignominy of the contemporary Parsi immigrant to the West is thus off-set by the swashbuckling Parsi of yore. Savuksha had single-handedly salvaged the prestige of the touring Indian cricket team by whacking whatever the English bowlers sent him, all around the field with complete impunity. One of Savuksha's shots hit an English fielder on the hand he had put out to stop the ball and the impact had caused him to howl: 'Never at any English stadium was a howl heard like that one, not in the whole history of cricket... The hand that he had reached out to stop it, he now held up for all to see, and *dhur-dhur, dhur-dhur* the blood was gushing like a fountain in an Italian Piazza, like a burst water-main from the Vihar-Powai reservoir, dripping onto his shirt...' (149). As for the ball itself, it lay past the boundary line: 'Rent asunder. Into two perfect leather hemispheres' (149). Savuksha would have led the Indian team to victory but for the rain which had resulted in a draw. This tale of derring-do filled Hansotia's young listeners -- all male -- with pride in their lineage. This has for long been one of the reasons for story-telling, mangnifying the self-esteem of the tribe.

Savuksha's exploits were not restricted to the cricket playing-field, he was also a hunter. Hansotia embroiders the tale of Savukshaw the hunter with delicate details of the culinary expertise of Mrs. Savukshaw, especially in the cooking of the favourite Parsi dish – *dhansaak*. It is these little details that keep Mistry's texts squarely within the ambit of Realistic fiction, in spite of their flirtations with Postmodernist techniques. The merits of Mrs. S's dhansaak have been almost lovingly described and a Parsi reader can almost smell the aroma that wafted around Mr. S's camp-fire as he heated up his chicken *dhansaak* dinner. Maybe, it was the heavenly aroma that lured the tiger out of the forest and made him lick his chops as Mr. Savukshaw lifted the first morsel of his dinner to his lips. As Hansotia, like any good story-teller spun out the suspense and asked: 'What do you think happened next?' (151), his young listeners cried out: 'What, what, Nariman Uncle?' (151). Alas, for them as well as for the young-at-heart reader,

Hansotia does not complete the tale nor does he take it up at another story-telling session.

The story he narrates instead is that of the squatter, a cautionary tale for young Parsis enarmoured of the West and seeking emigration out of India. However, before he begins this story, he quizzes his listeners and wants to know what they had learnt from the story of Savukshaw. The answer is provided by the bookish Jehangir Bulsara -- of the homoerotic and stamp collection fame: 'He was a man searching for happiness, by trying all kinds of different things' (153). Hansotia uses this answer to say: 'Remember this, success alone does not bring happiness. Nor does failure have to bring unhappiness. Keep it in mind when you listen to today's story' (153). This not only provides a lead-in for the squatter's tale but also stresses the traditional role of the story-teller as a teacher, the role that Chinua Achebe has taken upon himself within the context of the Nigerian novel. So begins the tragi-comic story of Sarosh/Sid, who had put in a guest-appearance in 'The Condolence Visit', as the nephew who had wished to gift a tape-recorder to his aunt and uncle in Ferozsha Baag. Sarosh is further contextualised within the story of Najamai's daughters Vera and Dolly who went 'abroad for studies many years ago, and never came back. They settled there happily' -- like them 'Sarosh also went abroad, to Toronto, but did not find happiness there' (153).

The glorious opening of Savukshaw's story is contrasted with the pathetic posture adopted by Sid -- as he climbs up onto the toilet seat in his Canadian home every morning to void his bowels. The recalcitrant bowels refuse to keep pace with the metamorphosis of Sarosh into Sid, and insist on the squatting position before emptying themselves out. This scatological opening is an ironic comment on the immigrant's identity-construction and identity-confusion. S/he may at the surface level mimic the Western mores and picture him/herself in the mirror of the White world, but the inner self is often reluctant to keep pace with the outward, cosmetic changes and masks adopted to conform to a new identity.

Almost ten years in Canada, Sarosh cannot get his bowels to perform in a seated position. This causes him endless trauma, as before leaving for Canada, he had grandly promised himself, his family and friends that 'if I do not become completely Canadian in exactly ten years from the time I land there, then I will come back..' (155). This promise now haunts him as he strains every morning on the seat and finally hops on it to finish the job. But as the end of the ten years approached, in increasing despair Sarosh refuses to adopt the squatting position and this delays his reporting to work in the morning. Also, throughout the day, the faintest twinge in his abdomen would drive the wretched Sarosh to the toilet to try his luck, but the job could only be accomplished in the squatting position. This however, leads to considerable embarrassment: 'The absence of feet below the stall door, the smell of faeces, the rustle of paper, glimpses caught through the narrow crack between the stall door and jamb -- all these added up to only one thing: a foreign presence in the stall, not doing things in the conventional way. And if the one outside could receive the fetor of Sarosh's business wafting through the door, poor unhappy Sarosh too could detect something malodorous in the air: the presence of xenophobia and hostility' (156). It is at such moments that Mistry's critique of his host society rings out sharply and without the least hint of a 'slave mentality'.

Irony is the other weapon employed by Mistry to hit out at the hollowness of Canada's claims of being a multicultural and fair society. Sarosh's supervisor at work finally summons him and asks for an explanation for the late-coming and frequent absences from his seat during office hours. Sarosh tries to pass it off as 'an immigration-related problem' (157), the supervisor 'who must have had experience with other immigrants, because right away he tells Sarosh, "No problem. Just contact your Immigrant Aid Society. They should be able to help you. Every ethnic group has one: Vietnamese, Chinese -- I'm certain that one exists for Indians"...' (157).

Sarosh decides to take this advice and contacts the Indian Immigrant Aid Society and makes an appointment to meet 'Mrs. Maha-Lepate' at the society's office. Hansotia's listeners appreciate this inclusion of a label for the society's officer, and look meaningfully at one another: 'Nariman Uncle had a nerve, there was more *lepate* in his own stories than any where else' (158). A touch of inter-textuality is also introduced into the story at this point as Hansotia elaborates upon Mrs. Meha-Lepate's reference to 'Wonder Bread'. He tells his audience that 'Wonder Bread is a Canadian bread which all happy families eat to be happy in the same way; the unhappy families are unhappy in their own fashion by eating other brands' (158). Only Bookworm Jehangir Bulsara catches the sly reference to Tolstoy in these sentences -- Hansotia notices this and is pleased.

Mrs. Maha-Lepate rattles off several cases of immigrant problems which the society's Dr. No-Ilaaz had reportedly cured. Sarosh's cure however has to be deferred to the next instalment of the story as Jehangir is called away for dinner by his irate mother and Hansotia reluctant to carry on without his best interlocutor, closes the session. The following evening the story-teller and his listeners re-convene and Sarosh is traced back to Dr. No-Ilaaz's office. The good doctor assures the protagonist of the story within a story that there is a remedy for Sarosh's problem: 'It involves a minor operation which was developed with financial assistance from the Multicultural Department. A small device, *Crappus Non Interruptus*, or CNI as we call it, is implanted in the bowel. The device is controlled by an external handheld transmitter similar to the ones used for automatic garage door-openers -- you may have seen them in hardware stores' (160).

To ease his young listeners' bewilderment vis-à-vis the grand sounding 'Multicultural Department', the micro-story teller Hansotia offers an explanation and as noted earlier in this book, provides the Master story-teller Mistry with the opportunity to take further pot-shots at Canada's much vaunted multicultural order: 'The Multicultural Department is a Canadian invention. It is supposed to ensure that ethnic cultures are able to flourish, so that Canadian society will consist of a mosaic of cultures – that's their favourite word, mosaic – instead of one uniform mix, like the American melting pot. If you ask me, mosaic and melting pot are both nonsense, and ethnic is a polite way of saying bloody foreigner' (160).

Sarosh, however, decides that he would rather go back to India, defeated by his bowels and the Indian squatting habit, than get a CNI embedded in his large intestine. So the trajectory from Dr. No-Hope's office leads him to a travel agent's office, rather than to the Multicultural Department. In the travel agent's office with his last ladder gone, Sarosh is able to finally lie down metaphorically speaking in the foul rag and bone shop of his innermost being.

In the four weeks left before his departure, Sarosh keeps trying to evacuate his bowels without having to resort to the squatting position, his supervisor at work who had kept a strict record of Sarosh's continued late-coming, finally fires him. This gives Sarosh more time to coax his insides to perform in the Western mode, but to no avail and the appointed hour finds him boarding the aircraft for Bombay. Just as the plane is beginning to move down the runway, Sarosh feels 'A tiny rumble. Inside him' (164). Ignoring the 'Please return to your seat and fasten your seatbelt' sign, Sarosh labours in the washroom. As the plane rolls down the runway, Sarosh's past life flashes before his eyes and just as rain started falling with a huge thunderclap outside, inside the cramped aircraft toilet,

Sarosh for the first time in ten years is able to perform without squatting. It is however too late for Sarosh to leave the plane and he is escorted back to his seat.

Hansotia, the story-teller, winds up this section of the story but there is more to come. After the jubilations and celebrations organised by his mother for his return to the fold, Sarosh finds himself as lonely as he used to be in Canada. This is the quintessential condition of the immigrant, at home neither in the East nor in the West – like Rushdie's creations, Mistry's men and women are also in a sense people who live on the margins and peripheries of their chosen locations. This in spite of these persons being ethno-religiously rooted Parsis.

The pitiable figure of Sarosh who had hitherto raised only risque laughter among Hansotia's interlocutors, now begins to put on the mantle of dignity and pathos and almost strives to reach tragic proportions as he broods over his condition on Bombay's sea-fronting Marine Drive. The story-teller now writes himself into the narrative and speaks directly to his protagonist: 'Hello, Sid, what are you doing here on your lonesome?' (167). Sarosh responds first of all by repudiating the Western identity of 'Sid' and then tells Hansotia the sad tale that he had just narrated to his young audience. The story-teller would have his listeners believe that Sarosh had given him a message for them: 'Tell them that the world can be a bewildering place, and dreams and ambitions are often paths to the most pernicious of traps...I pray you in your stories, when you shall these unlucky deeds relate, speak of me as I am; nothing extenuate, nor set down aught in malice: tell them that in Toronto once there lived a Parsi boy as best as he could. Set you down this; and say, besides, that for some it was good and for some it was bad, but for me life in the land of milk and honey was just a pain in the posterior' (168). The mythic mode of narration here, which almost bordered on high tragedy and has echoes from earlier literary texts, dissipates itself in self-mocking laughter so typical of Mistry's texts.

'Lend Me Your Light' begins with an epigraph taken from Rabindranath Tagore's *Gitanjali*: '...your lights are all lit -- then where do you go with your lamp? My house is all dark and lonesome, -- lend me your light'. This is one more story which *a la* Rushdie offers a 'periscopic vision', of both India and Canada. Here are also the tropes of identification and alienation from the older and newer diasporic contexts. In the character of Jamshed, Mistry has given us the alienated Parsi in the Indian context, who in the postcolonial period longs for the elite status that colonialism had bestowed on his forefathers. Like many westernised rich Parsis, Jamshed's life as a boy had revolved around imported model-airplane kits, records of Mantovani and Broadway musicals and later classical music 'from Bach to Poulenc' (175). Kersi's brother Percy and Jamshed were friends when they were at school, but later their paths had diverged, when Jamshed's obsession with all things western, had led him to migrate to the U.S., while Percy had sought greater assimilation within the Indian diasporic situation through work in the Indian villages.

Jamshed's 'Absolutely no future in this stupid place...bloody corruption, everywhere. And you can't even buy any of the things you want, don't even get to see a decent English movie. First chance I get, I'm going abroad. Preferably the US' (178), is now echoed in Kersi's attempts to emigrate to Canada. This aspiration is fully supported by his parents and as they had predicted given his 'education and ...westernised background, and ...fluency in the English language' (178), he did have no difficulties in having his application approved by the Canadian Consulate in Delhi. Kersi's decision in getting away from the 'ghaatis', has the tacit of most of the residents of Firozsha Baag, from the story-teller Hansotia to 'Rustomji-the-curmudgeon' (179).

However, the night before Kersi is to fly to Toronto, he is awakened by a searing pain in his eyes and he wonders if he is being punished for 'the sin of hubris for seeking emigration out of the land of my birth, and paying the price in burnt-out eyes: I Tiresias, blind and throbbing between two lives, the one in Bombay and the one to come in Toronto..' (180). The reference to the ancient Greek prophet Tieresias, is a direct result of the English education, replete with classical European myths and legends, that the British colonisers had inflicted on their Indian subjects, and which continues to have a stranglehold on Postcolonial Indian education too. So, the ironic note is struck here with the future immigrant leaving like a blind prophet – unable to 'see' either the past or the future.

The stage is thus set for the conflict between the Indian 'roots' and the Canadian space. The introduction of guilt is an intriguing motif here, especially in the context of the Parsi alienation from India. This also provides for the duality or double vision that critics have commented upon.

The story now focusses upon the idealistic stay-at-home Percy and the pragmatic Jamshed who had got away to the U.S. Caught between the two is Kersi, who finds himself increasingly drawn to his brother's point of view and who starts seeing Jamshed as somebody whose point of view he does not share. Jamshed reviles all things Indian and thinks that Kersi, who was a fellow-escapee from the mess of postcolonial India, would sympathise with him. Instead, Kersi in a rather contrary fashion conveys to him that even though he might have 'abandoned' India -- the land which had given refuge to his ancestors -- he did not share Jamshed's anti-Indian sentiments. The sub-text to this assertion is the tacit support he thus extends to his idealistic brother Percy's work in India.

Like most immigrants, Kersi congregrates with his own kind in Toronto and becomes a member of the Toronto Zoroastrian Society. The Toronto Parsis are at the receiving end of Mistry's caustic comments and with unsparing irony he delineates their obsession with their annual flight back to Bombay, their shopping sprees in India and their continuing reviling of the 'ghaatis'. In this world of nostalgia and self-complacency, Percy's letters about his work in the Indian villages, usher in a sense of the brutal reality of poverty and exploitation, that Parsis like Kersi are trying to leave behind them, when they migrate to the West: '...my brother [was] waging battles against corruption and evil, while I was watching sitcoms on my rented Granada TV..' (184). Percy's letters also reveal that the gulf between him and his boyhood friend Jamshed is now unbridgeable.

When Kersi makes his first visit back home, he collects gifts for everybody and wonders why he was doing this: 'I felt like one of those soldiers who, in wartime, accumulates strange things to use as currency for barter. What was I hoping to barter them for? Attention? Gratitude? Balm to soothe guilt or some other malady of the conscience?' (186). Like most returnees, Kersi experiences culture-shock when he reaches Bombay the contrast between the lush greenery of the West and 'the parched land: brown, weary, and unhappy' (186) is striking. The city also seemed dirtier and more crowded. Kersi's reaction to a crowded railway station is given in a highly wrought passage. Mistry has here used the device of the morality play to portray Kersi's horror: 'All the players were there: Fate and Reality, and the latter's offspring, the New Reality, and also Poverty and Hunger, Virtue and Vice, Apathy and Corruption' (187).

Such a treatment removes the Indian social order from the realms of reality and places it within mythic spaces. Such mythic treatment and magical realism techniques -- Rushdie's fiction -- could also be seen within the larger context of exile, migration and diaspora, all leading to decentering and displacement of the reality of what has been left behind. This could on the one hand provide the distance from which to objectively view this world without descent into sentimentality or bathos, on the other hand it denies it historicity and immediacy and robs it of meaning. For Kersi, the distancing from India is evident when he forgoes the option of boarding a running bus and the realisation hits him that 'I was a tourist here, and not committed to life in the combat zone' (188). This is a moot point -- for most diasporic writers visit their 'imaginary homelands' and live in the 'presentness of their pasts', but are no longer members of the 'combat zone', that is life in India.

Life in the combat zone is not only uncomfortable but downright hazardous as Kersi finds out when his brother tells him that his associate Navjeet was killed by moneylenders in the village where they had been trying to better the lot of the villagers. While this leaves Kersi and his mother speechless, Jamshed who was visiting them from New York, takes this opportunity to harangue Percy about the uselessness of trying to change things for the better in India. This is ignored by Percy and Kersi and Jamshed return to their respective hidey-holes from the dangers of India.

What makes this story very intriguing are the autobiographical echoes and self-mockery in the narrative -- the writer who 'sees' both the East and the West, feels guilty about leaving India, empathises with Percy but cannot be like him. In spite of the critique of Jamshed, Mistry's location in the West makes him closer to him, than to the idealistic Percy. This story could thus be the key to the self-hatred and unrelenting darkness of Mistry's discourse.

The last story in the collection, 'Swimming Lessons', is yet another self-reflexive story, not only in the sense of being somewhat autobiographical, but also in the context of the process of creative writing itself, which gives it an ontological orientation. This story serves as a sort of self-reflexive postscript to the collection as well, as a self-critique that pre-empts Parsi annoyance at far from flattering portrayals.

This is also the only story in the collection to be set wholly in Canada. Here we have the maximum impact of displacement and alienation. The vexed question of identity in the Indian diaspora is further complicated in the context of Canada. As Atwood has put it in *Survival* (1972), Canada seems a strange land even to Canadians. There is also the question of the vastness of the Canadian space and the severity of the Canadian winter, which leads to a battle with geography and weather that also informs the Canadian imagination and impacts most immediately on the immigrant psyche.

Further in the White, Western spaces of Canada the elitist status of the Parsi immigrant takes a severe beating and in the multi-ethnic, immigrant ghetto of Don Mills, the Parsi self-esteem is in even greater peril than it is in Postcolonial India. Yet, even this lowered status is to be preferred to the real or perceived threat and intimidation of Parsis in a post-Shiv Sena Bombay: 'The postman rang the doorbell the way he always did, long and continuous; Mother went to open it, wanting to give him a piece of her mind but thought better of it, she did not want to risk the vengeance of postmen, it was so easy for them to destroy letters; workers, nowadays thought no end of themselves, strutting around like peacocks, ever since all this Shiv Sena agitation about Maharashtra for Maharashtrians, threatening strikes and Bombay bundh all the time...' (231).

The problem here is not just being a religious minority, but being seen and seeing oneself as a social elite, and fearing a more level playing field in a changing social order. Also, its not just the Parsi youth who have fled the 'take over' by '*ghaatis*', but also the middle classes and thus by definition the upper castes, of even the dominant Hindu group, who have chosen to immigrate -- usually to the USA. The term *ghaatis* is not just a pejorative tag for a Marathi speaking person, it has several other connotations of class and caste attached to it and generally denotes a lower-caste and class Marathi speaker. The fact that this 'take over' has not really come to pass, nearly twenty years after this story was written and fifty years after the Indian

Constitution advocated positive discrimination towards the lower castes, designated the scheduled castes because they appeared in the schedule of the constitution, and tribes of India and post the Mandal Commission, which in the mid-1980s recommended the addition of 'Other Backward Castes' (OBCs), this in spite of some lower caste chief ministers of Indian states, is an irony that Mistry has taken note of neither in this collection or in his later texts. India still pays lip-service to the notion of social equity as it does to gender equity -- both these constructs being enshrined in the Indian Constitution but yet to be transferred to the Indian social order and this in spite of one of the recent Indian Presidents -- Mr. K.R. Narayanan -- being a member of the scheduled castes.

This is not to deny the very real threat experienced by the religious minorities in India -- especially in a post-Ayodhya India, but to point out that the *ghaatis* are not really much better off today than they were in the 1970s, nor more empowered. The Shiv Sena might have enjoyed power in Maharashtra -- albeit in coalition with the Bharatiya Janata Party: BJP -- but neither the Dalits nor women were the beneficiaries of this empowerment of the Shiv Sena. The lumping together of all *ghaatis* and *ghaatans* -- the female variant of *ghaati* -- is thus redolent of reductiveness.

As for 'Swimming Lessons' the trauma of finding an identity and location in a Western space is linked to sexuality, in a trajectory that is a deliberate or inadvertent mirroring of the manner in which imperialism itself saw itself in sexual terms -- the male West and the female East and also in the way in which current postcolonial theorists image colonisation as a rape of the non-West by the West. However, even this sexuality tantalises Kersi only to eventually disappoint him. The women he sees sunbathing from his upper floor window, upon closer inspection turn out to be rather unattractive with 'wrinkled skin, aging hands, sagging bottoms, varicose veins. The lustrous trick of sun and lotion and distance has ended' (233). This is as true of the lure of the West as it is of these sunbathing women. The next disillusionment for the immigrant comes when the woman in the swimming pool reveals her pubic hair only to hide them during subsequent encounters.

The swimming pool and the eponymous swimming lessons provide Mistry with the opportunity to elaborate upon water as the symbol of life. Water is here the primal amionitic fluid, the medium in which Kersi is finally reborn into his new life. The failure to learn swimming in Canada is linked to the earlier inability to master the sea on the Chowpatty beach in Bombay. These failures could symbolise the failure of Kersi, and through him most Parsis, to assimilate in either Indian or Western diasporas. However, by the end of the story, Kersi is able to open his eyes underwater in his bath-tub and see life in a double-perspective -- Indian and Western.

However, before this happens, Kersi has to go through the trials most immigrants have to face -- racism and the bitter Canadian winters. Racism hits him when some young boys at the swimming pool hold their noses at the sight of him and one says 'Paki Paki, smell like curry', while another says 'pretty soon all the water's going to taste of curry' (238). Mistry does not record his protagonist's reactions to these racist remarks -- of anger or otherwise -- at this point or elsewhere in the story. The reader has to be content with the bland two word sentence that follows these remarks: 'They leave' (238). As for the winter and the cold -- Mistry tells us the snowscape makes his hero feel alienated as for him 'it is already too late for snowmen and snowball fights' (244). These sentiments feed into Margaret Atwood's notorious justification for having left out immigrant writers from her anthology of Canadian literature -- you cannot be a Canadian unless you have played in the snow as a child.

The self-relexive element in the story is routed through the reactions of Kersi's parents to his stories. The diasporic writer's need to write about the homeland left behind is dealt with in the father's evaluation of his son's work, especially the story that dealt with Canada – i.e. 'Swimming Lessons': 'if he continues to write about such things he will become popular because I am sure they are interested in reading about life through the eyes of an immigrant, it provides a different viewpoint; the only danger is if he changes and becomes so much like them that he will write like one of them and lose the important difference' (248). Till date, there has not been much danger of Mistry losing this important difference – his subsequent novels have not touched upon his Canadian experience and are entirely set in and concerned with India from the 1970s to the 1990s -- Mrs. Indira Gandhi's India of the 1971 war with Pakistan, the Emergency of 1975 and the post-Babri Masjid India. Unlike Rushdie, Mistry is not given to making public pronouncements about his latest book being the last set in Bombay.

A rather intriguing aspect to the question of Canadian setting is that 'Swimming Lessons' as well as the other Canadian stories provide an unrelentingly dark and gloomy picture of Canada and even caution readers/listeners against the act of immigration – yet return too becomes impossible. Once the journey West has been undertaken, as has been said earlier, there can be no return -- this is so not just in the Parsi diaspora but also in other Indian diasporas, where the equivalent cry of 'Next Year Jerusalem', which typified the Jewish diaspora, never rings out.

At another level, what can also be seen as an absence in Mistry's discourse is the positive aspect of the hybrid condition much celebrated by Rushdie in *Imaginary Homelands* and reiterated in almost all his books. The immigrant in Rushdie's texts is in the fortunate position of having done what most home-bound people only dream of doing and are hence detested by them -- 'the act all men anciently dream ...we have flown'. There is only sadness in the eyes of Mistry's characters as they look back on the world they had left behind. There is only despair when they look forward to life in the cold, inhospitable Canadian world. There is none of the exuberance of Rushdie's Saladin Chamcha (*The Satanic Verses*, or the comfortable hybridity of Rai (*The Ground Beneath her Feet*), or the insouciant indifference to nations, races and borders of his old friend and rival Ormus Cama, in Mistry's creations.

This is not to suggest that the immigrant experience need be a positive one or that hybridity always leads to a magnified vision, but that Mistry's protagonists almost always see the world in unrelieved shades of black and grey -- this is true of both the short stories as well as of the novels. Again, a dark world view is not necessarily inferior to a less unhappy one, but what niggles here is that this view is being offered on behalf of a people who in spite of their falling numbers, downgraded economic and social status in post-independent India still hold on as tenaciously to a positive world view, as they hold on to their this-worldly, positive religion. Mistry's protagonists display all the ethno-religious details of *navjotes*, *behram roj* celebrations, *agiary*-goings, *kusti*-weavings, etc., but none of the positive thinking that kept this tiny community going through 1,300 odd years in an Indian sub-continental space, which has been sequentially and sometimes even simultaneously ruled by rival monarchs belonging to squabbling races, religions and even ideologies.

4

Such a Long Journey:
When Old Tracks Are Lost...

The last story in the *Ferozsha Baag* collection was set in Canada but with his first novel *Such a Long Journey*, Mistry returns to Bombay and the Parsi world. Even more than the short stories this novel is diasporic discourse. Here Mistry has very overtly attempted to deconstruct and repossess his past. He was born in 1952 and left India for Canada in 1975 -- so the India he has evoked is that of that period. More specifically, it is Bombay of that era that he has recreated in this novel. *Such a Long Journey* was the first novel by an Indian immigrant to Canada to win the Governor General's Award for fiction in the year of its publication -- 1991.

From the vantage point of the 1990s Mistry has reviewed the remembered past, the decades of the 1960s and 70s, when the ills that beset Bombay today, first began to manifest themselves. Recalling those decades when Bombay, before she became Mumbai, began to fall from grace, Mistry has pulled out all the stops and evoked all the real and apocryphal Bombay specials, which makes this novel a quintessential Bombay book.

Another significant aspect of this text is the leitmotif of 'journeying', which is also central to most diasporic writing. The three epigraphs which preface the novel set the tone. The first is from Firdausi's Iranian epic *Shah Nama*, and recalls both the glorious Iranian heritage of a mighty empire as well as hints at the downgraded condition of the present-day Parsis. The second is from T.S. Eliot's *Journey of the Magi* and reminds the readers of the ancient Zoroastrian religion and the belief that the magi who attended the birth of Christ were Zoroastrian priests. This epigraph also provides the title as well as the central metaphor of the novel: 'A cold coming we had of it,/Just the worse time of the year/For a journey, and such a long journey.' Finally, Tagore's lines from the *Gitanjali* sum up the way in which the Parsis have moved from one country to another and how they have had to adapt themselves to new realities.

In *Such a Long Journey* the Parsi world gradually moves out of its self-imposed isolation and interacts at the highest levels of finance and politics with the postcolonial Indian world. The catalyst is the 'factional' character of Major Jimmy Billimoria. This is a composite character fashioned out of the real-life State Bank of India cashier Sohrab Nagarwala and the Parsi agent from RAW (arm of the Indian secret service), who was close to Mrs. Indira Gandhi, the then Prime Minister of India. The story line however is more centrally concerned with the events that had overtaken Nagarwala. He was the man involved in the Rs. 60 lakh scam that had rocked the Indira Gandhi government in 1971. He claimed that he had received a phone call from the Prime Minister instructing him to hand over that large sum of money to a messenger. This was never accepted by the Prime Minister's office and Nagarwala was charged with embezzlement and arrested. He died in rather mysterious circumstances before he could be brought to trial. The missing sum of money was also connected with the 1971 war between India and Pakistan, which resulted in the creation of Bangladesh out of the ruins of East Pakistan.

It is against this backdrop that Gustad Noble and his family live out their lives in this book. Mistry has here provided an 'insider-outsider' view of the city at a time when it was witnessing the slow erosion of the idealism that had marked the beginning of the end of the Nehruvian dream of a secular India. The Chinese attack of 1962 was seen as a betrayal by Nehru of the Indo-Chinese friendship that he had fostered with that country since India's independence. He never recovered from that shock of seeing his vision of Asian socialism and regional cooperation crumble.

The end of the Nehruvian utopia also marked the beginning of sordid power-politicking, corruption at the highest level, nepotism and cynical manoeuvring of the electorate. In Bombay it marked the end of its famed religious tolerance. When large parts of Northern India were convulsed by Hindu-Muslim riots in the wake of the partitioning of India in 1947, Bombay had remained relatively trouble-free. This however changed in the 1960s with the rise of extreme right-wing political parties like the Shiv Sena in Bombay. The Sena raised the bogey of the other -- the religious other, the Muslims, the linguistic other, especially the Tamil speakers, and the regional other, all who came to Bombay from other parts of India and who according to the Sena snatched the bread out of the mouths of the sons of the soil.

Mistry, like many other political analysts and novelists (see Rushdie's *Midnight's Children*), places the blame for this at Indira Gandhi, the then Prime Minister of India's, door: 'how much blood-shed, how much rioting she caused. And today we have the bloody Shiv Sena, wanting to make the rest of us into second class citizens. Don't forget she started it all by supporting the racist buggers' (39). The language of this denunciation of Mrs. Gandhi's politics is indigenised in the tradition of postcolonial discourse. Mistry's texts are splendid celebrations of the Parsi idiom and faithfully capture its rhythms. Unlike earlier Indian English writers, notably Nissim Ezekiel, Mistry does not use Indian English to merely create a comic effect. He uses it consistently and naturally and thereby conveys its present status as one of the several Indian languages with its own distinctive phonetic and syntactic features -- a part of the phenomenon of global 'englishes'. This is a postcolonial mode of resistance offered by other contemporary writers too – like Salman Rushdie, Michael Ondaatje, Upamanyu Chatterjee and Bapsi Sidhwa among many others. They use the coloniser's language not to curse with but to subvert the privileging of colonial discourse and the hegemony of the Master Narratives of the West, thereby most effectively sabotaging the unequal Prospero-Caliban dichotomy.

The text begins at the beginning, the dawn of a typical day for its chief protagonist Gustad Noble, who turns Eastwards to the rising sun to 'offer his orisons to Ahura Mazda' (1). As he prays to the Supreme God, in other flats in Khodad Building, the milkman, known commonly to Bombaywallahs as the *Bhaiya* is busy dispensing milk to the women who queue up for this diluted commodity, it being his habit to adulterate it with water. This propensity is berated by the acerbic spinster Miss Kutpitia, whose name literally means 'the bickering one', recalling Mistry's own propensity for labeling, in the Dickensian tradition, rather than naming many of his characters.

The usual argument with the *Bhaiya* give way to the daily anxiety over the limited water supply as Mistry evokes yet another perennial Bombay problem -- limited water resources and an ever burgeoning population. The new day also brings to Gustad the glad news that his elder son Sohrab has been selected for admission at the prestigious Indian Institute of Technology. This is the news with which he wakes up his wife Dilnavaz. As they exult over this news he recalls how nine years back he had met with an accident saving Sohrab's life -- an accident that had left him with a limp. That was also the year, 1962, in which the Indo-China war had broken out and the unprepared Indian army had met with a humiliating defeat.

This is the first instance of many in the text when the personal and the political are interleaved. It was then that

Gustad had put up the blackout papers on his window panes and ventilators, that he had still not removed. The family had at first grumbled but then 'grew accustomed to living in less light' (11). The blackout papers thus become symbolic of the many hardships that families like Gustad's have to learn to live with.

Gustad's prudence was vindicated when Pakistan had subsequently attacked India in 1965 and the blackout papers had needed to go up again. Years later it was now the troubles in the then East Pakistan that caught Gustad's attention as he read out the headlines from the daily newspaper to Dilnavaz. The news item reminds him of his old neighbour Major Billimoria who had the year before suddenly disappeared from Khodad Building never to return again. It is Billimoria who provides the political context to the novel and through whom Gustad's Parsi world becomes involved with the wider Indian world.

Also introduced in this first chapter is the wall that surrounds the Khodad Building and is an important symbol that runs throughout the book. The Bombay Municipal Corporation wants to tear it down to widen the road. It is also under threat from passerbys who use it as an open-air urinal. The wall both includes and excludes. It is protective as well as reductive. It protects the Parsi minority from the ingress of the engulfing Indian world. However, it also makes this world isolationist.

In the second chapter, the reader is introduced to typical Bombay institutions, places and communities and things which make it Bombay. First, there is the Crawford Market, the wholesale and retail vegetables, fruits and meat market in South Bombay that dates back to the colonial period and has a fountain designed by the father of Rudyard Kipling, who was then the Principal of the Art School in Bombay. Gustad had been introduced to the market by his father who used to visit the market with a servant in tow and in taxis. This was in the days before bankruptcy had claimed his business – Noble and Sons, Makers of Fine Furniture – and much else, leaving his son with a few fine pieces of furniture. Thus Gustad's visits to the Crawford market 'with his meagre wallet and worn basket lined with newspapers...' (21), were of a different level from those made by his father. Gustad did not enjoy these visits where he had to negotiate 'floors...slippery with animal ooze and vegetable waste'. Neither did he relish bargaining with the butchers armed as they were with huge cleavers and knives. With the loss of his business, Gustad's father had lost interest in the weekly expeditions to the market, and it was instead Gustad's friend Michael who had taken over. It was under Michael's tutelage that Gustad had learnt more about chickens and cuts of meat.

Michael Saldhana, the 'tall and exceedingly fair-skinned' Goan, worked for the Bombay Municipal Corporation. The Goans and their exuberant culture and cuisine being yet another feature of the cosmopolitan fabric of Bombay. Malcolm's home was a haven for the music loving Gustad. Michael played the piano and his brother the oboe. It was there that he had been taught how to eat beef. In a subversive mode Michael would say: 'Lucky for us hat we are minorities in a nation of Hindus. Let them eat their pulses and grams and beans, spiced with their stinky asafoetida – what they call hing. Let them fart their lives away...we will get our protein from their sacred cow' (23).

Malcolm's family gives Mistry the opportunity to write about the introduction of Christianity to India: 'Christianity came to India over nineteen hundred years ago, when Apostle Thomas landed on the Malabar coast among the fishermen' (24). A longish piece on St.Thomas follows these introductory remarks, thereby maybe indicating a solidarity among the minorities of Bombay, in the face of the increasing hegemony of the dominant community.

This was the past though and in this chapter Gustad's trip to the market was occasioned by the need to buy a chicken for his daughter Roshan's birthday. These were the days before pre-packaged broilers hit the market and most people bought a live chicken, which was fattened for a few days and then slaughtered. In the Noble household, the soft-hearted women, Dilnawaz and Roshan and even the son Sohrab become attached to the chicken. However, on the appointed day the chicken had to be slaughtered and Gustad seeks the help of the butcher who visits his building with his wares, for this task. As they argue over payment, the chicken whizzes out of the flat, between their legs and this brings another important character -- Lame Tehmul, Tehmul Langra into the story.

The physically handicapped and mentally slow man could be symbolic of the fragile, endangered, in-bred Parsi race itself. Gustad was one of the few inhabitants of Khodad Building who had any time or patience with Tehmul. Tehmul was the victim of a hip fracture that had never mended properly. His fall from a tree had not only fractured his hip but 'although he had not landed on his head, something went wrong inside due to the jolt of the accident...' (30) and 'Tehmul was never the same' (30). So now in his mid-thirties he played with children and adored Gustad Noble who had immense patience with him. Most adults did not like him though, especially women, as he 'scratched perpetually like one possessed, mainly his groin and armpits' (31). Tehmul's manner of speaking also irritated most people as he ran his words together in breakneck speed.

There was also a rather sinister side to the child-like Tehmul. He was the unofficial rat-catcher in the building and most people got him to dispose off the rats they had caught in traps in their flats. Tehmul took the rats home and drowned them in a bucket or poured hot water over them. When this was discovered he stopped getting rats from most of his neighbours.

The following chapter brings in yet another eccentric and odd character – Dinshawji. He worked at the bank with Gustad and in him we have the kind of humorous Parsi character, we had first found in Mistry's short stories. It is Dinshawji who is also used as a mouthpiece to indict Mrs. Indira Gandhi for the corruption of Indian politics. In highly colourful and scatological language he critiques the newly powerful right wing parties and their attacks on the religious and ethnic minorities.

This happens at the dinner party for Roshan's birthday, where the contentious, runaway chicken is finally cooked and served up. Apart from politics, the party becomes an occasion where Gustad sings a song and then the chicken is served, 'with a vegetable stew' and 'fragrant basmati rice' (45). Just as they are about to start on the chicken the flat is plunged in darkness and then an argument begins between Gustad and his elder son Sohrab about the latter's future. Gustad wants him to join the prestigious IIT, Indian Institute of Technology, but Sohrab says 'IIT does not interest me...I told you I am going to change to the arts programme.' (48). Dinshawji plays the clown to save the situation and insists that somebody pull at the wishbone from the chicken with him. Finally, 'Gustad took hold of one end. They pulled and wrenched and fumbled with the greasy bone till it snapped Gustad's was the shorter piece' (49). This can be seen as an omen for the rather dangerous events that soon overtake Gustad's life.

As the story progresses the fissures between Gustad and his son Sohrab widen and the son becomes more and more rebellious. He again rejects the future his father had so lovingly and proudly mapped out for him – a degree from the Indian Institute of Technology and a successful career as a technocrat. Such a career graph would ultimately lead to immigration to a Western country and a prosperous life.

Major Billimoria is re-introduced in the text at this juncture through a rather mysterious letter he has written to Gustad.

The letter has requested Gustad to collect a parcel on his behalf. As he ruminates over the letter, Gustad wonders: 'What kind of life was Sohrab going to look forward to? No future for minorities, with all these fascist Shiv Sena politics...' (55). Worries over his son's future brings back past memories of the day when Gustad had saved Sohrab's life at the cost of a fractured hip and a lingering limp. Re-living the incident also reveals to the reader the more endearing side to life in Bombay. If it was a surly BEST bus conductor who was the cause of their jumping out of the bus in the middle of a lot of traffic, it was a kind-hearted taxi-driver who had come to Gustad's rescue and bundled out the passengers in his taxi, to take Gustad to a hospital. Gustad had preferred to go home and it had been Major Billimoria who had helped him out of the taxi and taken him to Madhiwalla Bonesetter. The traditional alternative medicine had healed Gustad -- apart from the slight limp -- while the western operation had maimed Tehmul for life. Here we have Mistry lauding the older ways of living and healing from his distant diasporic location. Is this an act of nostalgia?

Gustad writes back to the major agreeing to do help him but Dilnavaz is afraid this would lead them in some trouble. The letter being dispatched his life returns to its even tenor -- enlivened only by Miss Kutpitia's black magic. In an attempt to make Sohrab more amenable to his father's dream for him, Miss Kutpitia offers to help. She says to Dilnawaz: 'Your eldest, he reminds me so much of my Farad' (62). The death of Farad, who was her nephew, could have been the reason for Miss Kutpitia's subsequent retreat into isolation and eccentricity. Dilnavaz accepts her help in bringing about a reunion between her husband and her son, which involves at the beginning the rather innocuous lime and chillies and then a more dangerous magic potion. The potion has to be imbibed by someone, who would then take upon himself/herself Sohrab's ills. Poor Tehmul is the sacrificial victim selected by the desperate mother to cure her son.

Chapter three is also replete with the usual round of sexist and even racist jokes favoured by Dinshawji, that spice his days at the bank where Gustad and he worked. It is ironic that though Dinshawji deplored the fascist trends of right wing political parties, he himself cracked jokes at the expense of Madrasis and Gujaratis and mimicked their accents. Yet he is most concerned about the postcolonial tendency to rename roads and even cities. He chides Gustad when the latter thinks that this is an innocuous activity and should not be challenged. 'You are wrong. Names are so important.. My whole life I have come to work at Flora Fountain. And one fine day the name changes. So what happens to the life I have lived? Will I get a second chance to live it all again, with all these new names? Tell me what happens to my life. Rubbed out, just like that? Tell me' (74). As David Williams has put it, 'what Dinshawji laments in the loss of old names is the loss of the old logocentric security, that metaphysical reassurance via language' (217) of the meaning of the self.

In addition to his broad humour about the linguistic others, Dinshawji also cracked jokes in Gujarati at the expense of the Christian typist -- Laurie Coutinho -- in the office. This woman is the butt of Dinshawji's lewd jokes and as she does not understand Gujarati, she continues smiling at him as he insults her. Later however, in this as in much else, nemesis catches up with Dinshawji and she complains to Gustad that she now knows what was being said to her and is very hurt and offended by it. By then Gustadji is a dying man and he contritely gives up teasing Laurie and Gustad feels sorry for his much-reduced friend.

As for the wider world -- the problems within East Pakistan impinge once again on Gustad's family when his little daughter, Roshan, contributes a rupee to a raffle, proceeds of which would help the refugee children from there. Roshan wins the first prize in this raffle, a big doll, which becomes an important

Such a Long Journey: When Old Tracks Are Lost... 129

image in the text. The doll with its blue eyes and bridal finery becomes an obsession with Lame Tehmul who in his mid-thirties has a man's body, with a man's longings, but a child's mind. More politically the troubles in East Pakistan feature again when Major Billimoria once again writes to Gustad, this time asking him to go to a particular stall in Chor Bazar (the old thieves' market in Bombay), which would have displayed the *Complete Works of Shakespeare* and collect the parcel the stall owner would give him. He should then take it home and follow the instructions given in the note inside. The location from where the parcel had to be picked up enables Mistry to bring in yet another Bombay institution the Chor Bazar and also allows Gustad to dwell nostalgically on his earlier visits to that colourful market. The stall owner Ghulam Mohommed turns out to be the taxi driver who had intervened when Gustad had had the accident trying to save his son. He now hints that he is much more than a taxi-driver, in fact a sort of undercover agent who worked with Major Billimoria, who himself was part of RAW, an acronym for the Research and Analysis Wing of the Indian Secret Service. The contact address that Ghulam Mohommed gives Gustad is located in the notorious prostitutes' quarter of Bombay where women are displayed like so many cuts of choice meat, in tiny barred rooms which look like cages, thereby giving Mistry yet another opportunity to write about yet another aspect of Bombay -- its Red Light area. Gustad knew that area well as their family physician, Dr. Paymaster had his clinic there.

This reference to the doctor links the tale to the illness that now grips his daughter Roshan. It starts innocuously enough with diarrhoea, but then turns serious. Concurrently, with the illness come more parcels from Major Billimoria, which he wants his friend to keep for him. They come accompanied by books -- the first was Shakespeare and the second was Plato. The second parcel had also contained a huge number of currency notes wrapped in brown paper. Gustad was shocked by such a large sum of money and even more worried that Tehmul had been the unwitting witness to the unwrapping of this money and '..with a roar, he slammed shut the window, cutting off from Tehmul's vision the sight that had made his eyes shine as they had on the day he saw the naked doll' (117). A letter from Billimoria reassures Gustad that this was not black market money but government money and he was to open an account in his bank and deposit it there in the name of Mira Obili (an anagram for Billimoria as pointed out by Sohrab) and the address was to be either Gustad's own or his post office box number in Delhi. Gustad and Dilnavaz decide that when he had agreed to help Billimoria he hadn't known what a risk he would have to take and that he would have to deal with such large sums of money. It would be too dangerous for Gustad to deposit this huge amount of money in his own account or in any other. So they decide to hide the money in the house till such a time when Gustad could hand it back to Billimoria's contact in Bombay, Ghulam Mohammed. The latter however, is out of the city and cannot be contacted -- so the money remains with the Nobles. In the meantime refugees from the troubled East Pakistan continue to pour into India and some even find their way to Bombay. Gustad wonders how long a poor country like India could afford to feed millions of more people.

Gustad's work for his old friend takes place against the ominous backdrop of the breaking of the Bombay monsoon, yet another Bombay familiar that Mistry would definitely have recalled with nostalgia or irritation (for the inconveniences it causes in flooded roads) in Canada. For Gustad the rains also bring back the old pain in his broken hip, the result of the old accident. This provides Mistry with the opportunity of evoking yet another old Bombay institution, the traditional bone setter Dr. Madhiwala. The skills of Madhiwala and now his descendants are fervently sworn to by generations of Bombayites, Parsi and non-Parsi. In his invocation of all things

Bombay Mistry does not spare even the ubiquitous crows, who are pictured wet and half-scuttling and half-flapping across his pages (133). The occasion for this flapping being the discovery of a dead bandicoot in Gustad's medicinal plant the vinca – *subjo* in Gujarati. The building Gurkha is summoned to deal with this nuisance and apprehend the culprit. The Gurkha of course is/was yet another Bombay speciality – the tough Nepali ex-serviceman who would eke out his army pension by working as a watch man for residential complexes in Bombay. The bravery of the Gurkha soldier in war and his legendary loyalty made him an ideal watchdog in an increasingly crime ridden city. However, this once the Gurkha was not of much use to Khodad Building: The decapitated rat is followed by a similarly treated cat and Inspector Bamji the police officer who also lived in the building looked at the cat and said to Gustad, 'somebody's knife is very sharp. A very skilful knife. Anybody has a grudge against you, wants to harass you?' (138).

Soon it becomes clear that the dead animals are a warning and are connected with the huge amounts of money collected on behalf of Billimoria and not yet deposited into the bank as instructed by him. It is now clear that the note that followed the dead animals into the vinca bush meant that they had to get rid of the money. So Gustad decides to deposit it little by little so that nobody would get suspicious. However, this threat to him and his family leaves him feeling very betrayed and bitter. He feels let down by his friend for exposing him to such danger, '...like a brother I looked upon him. What a world of wickedness it has become' (142).

In the wider world outside the Khodad Building compound too the clouds of war and danger gather as India begins to prepare itself for defence against a possible attack from Pakistan. It is then that Gustad on his way to his bank, comes across the pavement artist who draws pictures of gods and saints. In a world in which corruption and it stench was widespread there was the artist whose pictures momentarily arrested the world and made it pay obeisance to the portraits.

In his moment of trouble Gustad turns to Dinshawji for help and confides in him the story of Billimoiria, his letters and the money. Gustad emphasises how helping Billimoria would contribute to helping the national effort against Pakistan. With Dinshawji's help the money in the alcove at Gustad's home slowly depletes and finds its way bit by bit into the bank account. By that time Dinshawji's health is in a rather precarious condition and Gustad feels guilty about compromising his sick friend 'who was now willing to break banking laws and jeopardize (ing) his job and pension this close to retirement' (144). This slow process is accompanied by other family problems. As noted earlier, with the help of Miss Kutpitia's little spells Dilnavaz was trying to effect a reconciliation between her husband and son Sohrab. However, this meant transferring the onus of that trouble onto the unsuspecting Lame Tehmul who had been selected to drink the glass of lime juice over which the spell had been laid. So while Gustad in a sense duped Dinshawji, Dilnavaz was doing something even worse to Tehmul -- who fortunately for him seemed resistant to spells and drank the daily glass with 'a burp and a grin' (147) and returned it with the usual thanks murmured in his superfast style. To add to Dilnavaz's troubles her little daughter Roshan now becomes really ill and once again Miss Kutpitia intones that it was the evil eye and that 'doctor's medicine is no prevention or cure for that' (149). So Dilnavaz takes recourse to some more spells to help her daughter. This time though they merely involved the hanging of a bunch of dried chillies and lime over her door and did not include making anyone swallow glasses of spell ridden liquids.

The domestic world of Dilnavaz and Miss Kutpitia is far removed from the world of Gustad Noble. Gustad's world was interlinked through the Major with the world of big-time finance and murky military-industrial-capitalism. *Such a Long Journey* is obviously a novel written from a male point of view. The female characters are the passive recipients of the actions undertaken by their male counterparts. Dilnavaz, her daughter Roshan and Miss Kutpitia are female stereotypes. Dilnawaz is the perfect foil to Gustad. She is soft and pretty, while he is big and muscular. As a couple they exhibit the typical features of male aggressiveness and female passivity. As Kate Millet has noted: 'If aggressiveness is the trait of the master class, docility must be the corresponding trait of a subject group'.

The child Roshan too is a doll-like creature, sickly and fragile. She is in direct contrast to the sons Sohrab and Darius. As is the wont of such female children, she cries, gets scared and is petted and cosseted by Daddy.

Miss Kutpitia, is the archetypal spinster, much reviled in the neighbourhood. She is the 'ubiquitous witch of fairy stories come to life', Mistry informs us. Miss Kutpia could have been a strong character, privy to ancient wisdom of women, living a life of independence. However, all we get is a caricature of a silly, superstitious woman. Miss Kutpitia's spells and magic, her being a 'witch' is not at all in a positive feminist sense.

Instead her magic spells are reduced to being a mere manifestation of women's irrational nature. Mistry appears to be poking fun at this female behaviour. Miss Kutpitia, being a spinster and a little batty is to be allowed her superstitions. However, Dilnavaz, the happily-married woman, and 'fulfilled' mother is critiqued for her belief in the spinster's spells. This critique is not too serious as the reader is told that it is only because Dilnavaz is so concerned for her husband and children that she succumbs to Miss Kutpitia's '*jadu-mantar*' nonsense. Whenever Dilnavaz is not busy cooking or filling water, she is seen conspiring with Miss Kutpitia in creating spells for her family's well-being. Sohrab's intractability is sought to be removed by a spell involving a lizard's tail. Limes and chillies as noted earlier and even poor Tehmul are pressed into service to cure Roshan's illness.

Gustad the rational male is never party to this and his mind is occupied with important matters of national importance. Dilnavaz's universe is restricted to the world of her home. Mistry does not probe beneath the surface of the reductive lives of Dilnavaz and Miss Kutpitia. He does not seek the reasons for their beliefs in spells and instead has exploited them for comic relief. The pathos underlying the lonely life of Miss Kutpitia, or Dilnavaz's never-ending household drudgery are not explored. Indeed all the pathos and sympathy in the book are reserved for the eponymously named Gustad as he nobly strives for the welfare of his family. There is sympathy even for the retarded Tehmul as he tries to copulate with Roshan's doll but none for Miss Kutpitia. Her stridency and apparently unbalanced behaviour could have been the result of repressed sexuality too. Mistry does not appear to be interested in female sexuality. Dilnavaz interacts with her husband in a romantic manner rather than in a sensual way. Miss Kutpitia is celibate in the cause of her departed nephew, like Miss Havisham in Dicken's *Great Expectations*, was in the bitter memory of having been abandoned on her wedding day. Little Roshan too is amazingly innocent and is not the least curious about her body.

In a novel entitled *Such a Long Journey*, the female characters in it do not journey at all. They remain stationary while the world around them moves and changes. Theirs is a static universe where they are denied knowledge of even their own stultification and repression by their creator. This text which is a fictional account of recent Indian history is in the genre of what Greene and Kahn have called history as 'written by men, from a male perspective. What has been designated historically significant has been deemed according to a valuation of power and activity in the public world'.

It is to this deemed important world of history and rationality that the text returns when Miss Kutpitia's spells fail and Roshan does not get any better. Gustad has to then take her to Dr. Paymaster, the family physician, who has his clinic in the Prostitute's quarter, giving Mistry yet another opportunity to walk down nostalgia lane and even bring in a bit of squalid erotica in the form of the *Panwalla* – the betelnut seller – there who specialised in selling aphrodisiac *paans* to the men who went to the prostitutes. The doctor's medicines do not help Roshan who continues being very ill and to add to Gustad's troubles the female stenographer with whom Dinshawji flirted and made lewd jokes in Gujarati, finally realises what he was saying and complains to Gustad. When Gustad tells Dinshawji to lay off her he 'changed utterly....suddenly fragile and spent..' (180). The only bright spot in all these dark event is the commissioning of the pavement artist by Gustad to cover his building wall with religious portraits, so that it would stop people from using it as an open air urinal.

So, the Wall of all Religions comes into existence and re-affirms Bombay's famed tolerance in the face of increased fundamentalism and violence: 'Over the next few days, the wall filled up with gods, prophets and saints. When Gustad checked the air each morning and evening, he found it free of malodour' (183). Here however recurs the metaphor of journeying and the artist begins to have misgivings about the wall and becomes restless: For him the wall becomes a bind, and he longs to get away, 'the journey – chanced, unplanned and solitary – was the thing to relish' (184). As he ponders his next move his creations, 'Swami Dayananda, Swami Vivekananda, Our Lady of Fatima, Zarathustra and numerous others..' (184) awaited their uncertain futures – uncertain being the key word for Bombay's minorities, religious and linguistic in a city in the clutches of a political and criminal mafia.

Now the political and personal both start coming to a head in Gustad's life as Roshan's illness becomes graver and Dinshawji brings the news of Major Billimoria's dismissal from RAW on charges of corruption. Here in a postmodernist mode Mistry juxtaposes facts with fiction and the newspaper report on Billimoria's dismissal is lifted almost verbatim, with just a change of names, from the reports in the press about the dismissal of the real life State Bank Cashier, Nagarwalla (194--195). Both Gustad and Dinshawji are now frightened about the money they have been depositing in their bank on Billimoria's behalf. Gustad begins looking for Ghulam Mohammed once more and finds him ultimately in a hideout in the Prostitute's Quarter. Mohammed tells him that the Major's life is in danger and wants Gustad to withdraw all the money he has deposited and send it back to Billimoria. Gustad has thirty days to withdraw the money and return the package to Mohammed. The visit also yields a surprise in the form of Lame Themul who is heard beseeching a prostitute to pleasure him, even as she moves away repelled by his physical and mental disabilities. Gustad leaves with the warning, 'If the money is not delivered on time, things will go badly for all of us' (205) ringing in his ears.

So, the dangerous withdrawals begin and halfway through the deadline Mohammed leaves a reminder for Gustad in the form of the uprooted Vinca plant. The tension proves too much for Dinshawji whose illness now necessitates a removal to hospital. The Wall of all Religions however seems to flourish amidst all these problems and the artist having overcome his wanderlust and uncertainties finally settles down to re-painting his gods and goddesses in oils and enamels instead of the usual ephemeral crayons.

The entire sum of money is finally returned to Mohammed who then entreats Gustad to go to Delhi to see Billimoria who is being victimised by the authorities. A letter from Billimoria carries a similar request and Gustad leaves with a promise to think it over. In the meantime the Goan friend Malcolm is once again introduced into the narrative, this time to facilitate Mistry's description of the holy shrine of Mount Mary's, which Gustad visits in his company. So one by one, all the Bombay landmarks are covered by the narrative, even as Dinshawji finally dies in the hospital and Roshan's health shows no signs of improvement. Dinshawji's death brings in the unique death rites practiced by the Parsis – the consigning of the corpse to the Towers of Silence where it is devoured by scavenging birds such as the vultures. Mistry expends several pages over these death rites in his 'Last Witness' manner.

News from Mohammed once again indicates that Billimoria has been sentenced and is very anxious to see Gustad. So Gustad finally makes the trip to Delhi. Mistry now has the chance to describe the fabled Indian train journey – the fight over seats, the food packets, the toilets. The journey also enables Gustad to ponder over whether, 'would this long journey be worth it? Was any journey worth the trouble?' (259). This question being more rhetorical than demanding of an answer as the entire narrative hinges on the importance of journeying, real and metaphorical.

Gustad's meeting with Billimoria reveals Mrs. Gandhi's sordid involvement in corruption at the highest levels in the Indian government and the manner in which she used men like Billimoria to further her own political ends (270–72). Even as Gustad leaves his troubled friend the war with Pakistan finally breaks out and he returns to Bombay. Here before going home he has an encounter with the pavement artist but the discussion is cut short when Gustad realises that a fire engine has turned into the Khodad Building compound. In quest of better health for little Roshan, Dilnavaz and Miss Kutpitia have continued to invoke spells and the burning of things has finally resulted in a little fire that is fortunately put out easily. Greater fires however rage as the war with Pakistan continue and blackout papers go up all over Bombay and Gustad and his younger son Darius repair their old blackout papers -- Sohrab by this time having left home after an altercation with his father -- so that not a chink of light escapes them. On one such blacked out night Gustad catches Tehmul masturbating in his flat with Roshan's doll, who had continued to fascinate him. This solves the puzzle of the missing doll for Gustad who is repulsed and at the same time sorry for Tehmul. Gustad lets him keep the doll, 'Somehow the loss to Roshan would not be as great as it would be to Tehmul' (309).

The war finally ends in victory for India and wipes out the 'rankling memories of ignominious defeat at Chinese hands nine year's ago, and 1965's embarrassing stalemate with the death in Tashkent of Shastri...' (310). In the midst of all this euphoria the small newspaper item regarding Billimoria's death in Delhi catches Gustad's eye and he tears out the page and 'folds it small to fit his pocket' (311). In a mysterious manner Billimoria's body is brought to Bombay for a funeral at the Towers of Silence and Gustad decides to attend the funeral to find out who had organised it. He fails in this mission but Mistry uses this second funeral to write with black humour on the vultures who eat Parsi corpses and the debate in the community between what he calls 'the vulturists' and the opposing group who objected to such disposal methods of the dead. 'The orthodox defence was the age-old wisdom that it was a pure method, defiling none of God's good creations: earth, water, air and fire...But the reformists, who favoured cremation, insisted that the way of the ancients was unsuitable for the twentieth century. Such a ghoulish system, they said, ill became a community with a progressive reputation and a forward-thinking attitude' (317).

The novel now draws to an end with the ironical touch of Gustad's friend Malcolm in his official capacity as a Municipal Corporation employee entrusted with the task of demolishing

Gustad's wall of all religions, in order to widen the road outside. The name of the building around which the wall stands fails to immediately strike Malcolm as the one in which Gustad lives. Instead he muses on the slow erosion of beautiful music from Bombay. As a Goan – usually rather westernised – and one who is steeped in Western music, he mourns the near death of such music in Bombay and is thankful that Western cultural institutions such as the British Council and the Max Mueller Bhavan and the home-grown Time and Talents Club still keep it going. This section reveals Mistry's own limitations vis-à-vis music of the Indian type which is well and alive in the city of Bombay. Such a definition of 'culture' could also be called an instance of a colonial mind set that has survived the end of empire.

As Malcolm and his demolition crew drive towards Khodad Building, Gustad's estranged son Sohrab pays his customary visit to his mother in his father's absence. Gustad on the way back home from Billimoria's funeral realises that it was Ghulam Mohammed who had organised the funeral. Mohommed had reverted to being a taxi driver his old cover as a RAW agent. In spite of the way in which Billimoria had been treated, Mohommed carries on in RAW as it was 'Still, much safer for me to be inside RAW than outside' (322) also he felt that would provide him with an opportunity to get even with those who had destroyed Billimoria, whom he called 'Bili Boy'.

Malcolm having reached Khodad Building at last realises that it was where Gustad lived. The first person to know what was to happen to the wall is the pavement artist, who crumples and is unable to even summon 'a trace of the resources that had fuelled his wanderings in the old days' (324). In the meantime a procession protesting against the highhanded behaviour of the Municipal Corporation enters the street. Mistry can now conclude on the high note of yet another Bombay special – the ubiquitous *morcha*. Reaching the wall of all religions the *morcha* halts briefly to pay its obeisance to the multitude of gods and when they are told that the wall was about to be demolished to widen the road the *morcha's* mood becomes ugly and 'it howled, the tempest raged and threatened' (327). Gustad's return coincides with this moment and his friend Malcolm appeals to him for help but it is some time before Gustad realises what is happening and finds that the morcha consists of old friends like Dr. Paymaster, the Panwallah outside his clinic -- he of the aphrodisiac paan fame and even prostitutes. The *morcha* was on its way to the Municipal office to protest against what it considered unfair practices in the prostitute's locality, when it halts before the wall of all religions.

The small contingent of policemen accompanying the *morcha* led by Inspector Bamji, wait to see what would happen and soon big stones begin to fly and one lands on the head of Tehmul who has been an avid spectator so far. Dr. Paymaster now abandons his role in the *morcha* and becomes a doctor again. An ambulance is summoned to take Tehmul to the hospital as he has suffered severe blood loss. But before this could happen Tehmul dies and a disheartened Dr. Paymaster is helped to his feet by the visiting Sohrab. The hearse is now called to take Tehmul to the Towers of Silence instead, but since this would take some time and as Miss Kutpitia says it 'does not look right, the *ruvaan* lying like this near the gate' (334), Inspector Bamji suggests that since Tehmul was too heavy to be carried up to his own flat, he should be shifted under the shade of a tree at least. Gustad overcome with grief for the poor dead man, hefts him up in his arms and 'without a trace of a limp, without a fumble' (335) carries Tehmul up the stairs to his flat and kicks the door shut behind him. In the few moments of privacy he has, he lays him on the bed, covers up the naked doll lying there and puts a cap on Tehmul's head and softly intones the Zoroastrian prayers as tears run down his face. When Sohrab comes looking for him he hugs his son tightly – having lost poor Tehmul, Sohrab becomes too precious to be ignored any more.

The *ruvaan* now being decently laid in its own bed and the *morcha* having prudently melted away, Malcolm instructs his men to begin the demolition of the wall. The artist too is resigned to the destruction of his work of art and decides that it is time to journey once again. In reply to Gustad's question as to where he would go, he says: 'In a world where roadsides become temples and shrines and temples and shrines become dust and ruin, does it matter where?' (338).

The artist begins his journey once again, accompanied only by his satchel in which he has his box of crayons -- the fancy oils and enamels being abandoned -- and Gustad turns back to his own flat. Once inside he stands upon a chair and pulls off the blackout papers covering his ventilators.

The novel thus ends on the dual note of journeying and staying rooted -- Gustad having chosen to stay. However, even this staying back has changed as it now is in the context of Gustad having pulled down the blackout papers and letting in light, allowing the moths of the past to fly out of his life. At another level this could also signal the letting in of the wider Indian reality into the enclosed Parsi space. It could mean that the wall having gone and the old tracks thus being lost, as the epitaph to the novel from Tagore's *Gitanjali* had said, 'a new country is revealed with its wonders'. In Mistry's own words: 'Life itself is... a journey without destination. Sort of like a wall that goes on and on with pictures' (Interview with Ali Lakhani).

5

A Fine Balance:
Making the Subaltern Speak

A Fine Balance is Rohinton Mistry's third book and second novel after the collection of short stories *Tales from Ferozsha Baag* and his first novel *Such a Long Journey*. The short-stories were ethnocentric and focussed on the fads and foibles of the minuscule minority Parsi Zoroastrian community in Bombay. In *Such a Long Journey*, Mistry had returned to Bombay and the Parsis, but this time his canvas was extended to take in the Postcolonial order in India and the backdrop of this text was the war which India had fought with Pakistan in 1971, leading to the creation of Bangladesh out of the eastern wing of Pakistan. The text engages with the increasing criminalisation of politics in India and the rise of Mrs. Gandhi's brand of real politik, that effectively spelt the end of her father, Jawaharlal Nehru's value-based practices in public life. In *A Fine Balance*, this theme has been extended to take in the internal emergency imposed by Mrs. Gandhi in 1975 to save her tottering government from increasingly strong attacks by the opposition parties. The Emergency saw the suspension of the basic fundamental rights guaranteed to every Indian citizen by the Constitution of India. These draconian measures were supposed to safeguard the country from what Mrs. Gandhi and her cohorts referred to as 'threats from outside'. By 'outside' was meant Pakistan and her supporter, the United States of America. These 'threats', although they did exist to some extent, were really a pretext to crush the opposition to Mrs. Gandhi's rule. Opposition and criticism is what all democratic governments have to contend with and if you suppress them, you are jeopardising the very foundations of democracy. This is exactly what happened during the Emergency and for the very first time since India had been decolonised in 1947, democratic institutions were suspended. What followed was one of the most inglorious chapters in independent India's history.

Mistry's *A Fine Balance* records this dark and shameful episode with unrelenting honesty. In an interview soon after the publication of this novel, Mistry has said that after he finished writing *Such a Long Journey*, which he had placed in 1971: 'It seemed to me that 1975, the year of the Emergency would be the next important year, if one was preparing a list of important dates in Indian History. And so it was 1975' (Gokhale, October 27, 1996).

A Fine Balance is also a text in which Mistry has made a conscious effort to 'embrace more of the social reality of India' (ibid.), so although the novel opens with a Parsi woman Dina Dalal's story in Bombay, it soon enlarges its scope to include her lodger Maneck Kholah from a hill station in North India and her tailors, Ishvar and Omprakash, who come to her from a village. The narrative also encompasses what Walter Benjamin has called the city poet's special concern with ragpickers, beggars and suicide victims/heroes. As their tragic tales unfold, one gets the impression that Mistry's text is attempting to articulate the silences of centuries of exploitation, domination and oppression of the poorest of the poor of India.

However, this is not to imply that Mistry's characters are in any way able to change the power balance which in the first place made their marginalisation and silencing possible. In fact they appear to maintain the titular 'fine balance' between the exploiter and the exploited. The two characters who are unable to maintain this balance -- Maneek Kholah and his friend

Avinash -- either commit suicide or else are 'murdered'. The victory of the rest against the forces who try to destroy them is that they survive, even if in much reduced forms. So, Mistry's book fits in more with those of Charles Dickens, George Eliot, Honore de Balzac and Victor Hugo than it does with the work of a Bertolt Brecht or a Mahashweta Devi, whose marginals are linked to workers' struggles and a desire for change and if required, a blowing up of existing power matrices. As Guy Lawson has put it in his review of *A Fine Balance*: 'Mistry and Dickens are interested in those to whom history happens, those with little control over their circumstances.' According to Gayatri Spivak, this is an 'unrecognised contradiction within a position that valorises the concrete experience of the oppressed, while being so uncritical about the historical role of the intellectual, is maintained by a verbal slippage' (Can the Subaltern Speak?). So Mistry's subalterns do not really speak but their silences are represented through the mediation of Mistry's narrative. Spivak and other ideologically committed theorists find this unacceptable and Spivak dubs this the intellectual's attempt to constitute the subalterns and marginalised as the 'Other of the Self's Shadow'. Yet is it *really* possible for the subaltern to speak? Can men and women of the lowest socio-economic, caste strata articulate their own conditions? Or are they forever to be represented through what Ranjit Guha has called 'bourgeois elitism' (1). Which in turn raises what Edward Said terms the problem of 'the permission to narrate' ('Permission to Narrate').

Does this, in Spivak's words, make Mistry a member of 'certain varieties of Indian elite [who] are at best native informants for first-world intellectuals interested in the voice of the Other'? Foucault suggests that even if there is 'bourgeois elitist' mediation and 'representation' in articulating the voice of the subalterns to the readers, in the ultimate analysis, 'to make visible the unseen can also mean a change of level, addressing oneself to a layer of material which had hitherto had no pertinence for history, and which had not been recognised as having any moral, aesthetic or historical value' (*Power/Knowledge* 49–50) and is also of vital importance.

However, even if one grants Mistry the right to speak/represent/articulate the silences of the subalterns and the marginalised of India in 1975 (the locale and time being as important as the actual 'subject/signifier'), there is the problem of the hegemonic – all inclusive nature of what Mistry categorises as the Marginals. The 'upwardly mobile' tailors, Ishwar and Omprakash, who have thanks to their forebear Dukhi, moved out of one of the lowest of Hindu castes – the *Chamar* caste, are lumped together with the Monkeyman, of the *Madari* caste, the Muslim Ashraf *Chacha*, a religious minority and the urban Beggar Master – an Indian version of the extortionist, protectionist Western Mafia Man. To compound the heterogeneous mix even further is the fact that to this group of Marginals belongs Dina Dalal, a Parsi woman, whose marginalisation is due to her gender rather than her socio-economic/caste grouping. Clinging to this rag-tag group are Maneck Dalal and his erstwhile hostel friend and mentor Avinash. The unspeakable silence that these two young men, belonging to middle-class Parsi and Maharashtrian groups respectively, are unable to articulate, concerns the covertly homosexual ragging they had been subjected to in their hostel.

A classic Marxist would hardly accept a Dina Dalal, a Maneck Kholah and an Avinash as subalterns/marginals/the people. For him/her they would be the bourgeois. As for the Beggar Master, he would be an agent of an exploitative capitalist order. So how does one even begin to untangle these ideological skeins in Mistry's *A Fine Balance*? Or does one put these issues on the backburner and decode the book as a humanist construct? After all Mistry does not claim to be ideologically motivated and has said that 'Fashions and trends are things for which I have no talent and it would be hard work for me to try and follow them.... Faithfulness to the story and the characters is what concerns me most' ('Interview with Gokhale').

How faithful then is *A Fine Balance* to its story and characters? How has Mistry constructed this story? Who are his characters? What are the central motifs and metaphors he has utilised to narrate their stories?

The text is prefaced by a warning 'Holding this book in your hand, sinking back in your soft armchair, you will say to yourself: perhaps it will amuse me. And after you have read this story of great misfortunes, you will no doubt dine well, blaming the author for your own insensitivity, accusing him of wild exaggeration and flights of fancy. But rest assured: this tragedy is not a fiction. All is true' -- Honore de Balzac, *Le Pere Goriot*. Having thus put the onus squarely on the reader, the author proceeds to tell us his 'true' tale which is organised into sixteen evocatively named chapters, preceded by a Prologue dated 1975 and ending with an Epilogue dated 1984. Thus, the time-frame begins with the year of the declaration of the Emergency and ends with Mrs. Indira Gandhi's assassination. Mistry obviously sees the latter as being contingent with the former. Between these two cataclysmic political events are the stories of Dina, her tailors, her lodger and their motely friends and acquaintances. The chapters deliberately do not identify the locales of action and are titled 'City by the Sea' and 'Mountains', rather than Bombay/Mumbai or Himachal Pradesh. This gives a nice touch of the abstract and even universal to an otherwise localised set of events. Thereby strengthening the aura of a universalist-humanist story rather than one narrated in ideologically defined terms.

The central motif in the text is once again that of journeys as it was in *Such a Long Journey*. However, in that novel, the journeying had begun with the Parsi Zoroastrians' journey from their homeland Iran to their land of refuge India. This was followed by their metaphorical journeying into the ambit of

Colonial dominant community status and then showcased their movement into mainstream postcolonial India. In *A Fine Balance* the journeys are not restricted to the Parsis' diasporic peregrinations. Here the novel opens with Maneck Khohlah's journey from the mountain village to the city by the sea. In an interview with Indu Saraiya, Mistry had said that he used to visit Dharamshala to meet his uncle who lived there, 'They have got a business there for the last five generations – general stores selling everything from blankets to knick-knacks' (Saraiya 14). Maneck's father's store could have been modeled upon this family tie with mountains. In a cris-cross trajectory his journey leads him back to his village before taking him to a job in one of the Gulf countries. It is a journey that ultimately ends in his inability to face ghastly personal, social and political realities. So Maneck takes that terrible step from the crowded railway platform that hurls him under the wheels of the express train. In her review, Rukmini Bhaya Nayar has seen this not as a suicide but as what she calls 'a senseless train accident of the sort we know only too well'. Bhaya Nayar has further seen Maneck as an 'unblemished' youth in a Greek tragedy, who has to be sacrificed to underline the 'bleak vision' of Greek tragedy. However, I prefer to see Maneck's death as a suicide, a suicide which is a result of his having lost that 'fine balance' which enabled the other protagonists to survive even more traumatic events and upheavels in their lives. Compared to them, Maneck's problems are of little relevance. There is the usual problems adolescent boys have with their fathers and their obsessions with their mothers. Even though the father's business of bottling his own cola suffers from multinational competition he still has the cushion of his middle class background to fall back upon. Even within the blood-letting of Sikhs in the riots that followed Mrs. Gandhi's murder by her own Sikh bodyguards, Maneck's Parsi Zoroastrian ethnoreligious status is a safeguard. The unarticulated trauma of having been ragged in a covertly sexual mode in the college hostel, pales into insignificance when placed before the castration and amputation of the tailors.

Dina Dalal, nee Shroff, also has her own share of journeying to accomplish in the text. She moves from protected girlhood under the indulgent care of her doctor father, to the harsh reality of reductive femaleness under the 'protection' of her brother Nusswan. Her awareness of her autonomous existence does not allow her to bow down to the patriarchy that Nusswan seeks to impose on her. She moves away from the economic well-being and social security that a marriage to one of Nusswan's friends would have offered her. She chooses to marry an economically unsuccessful Rustom Shroff, whom she had met at a music concert organised by a local music society. Dina's happiness is short-lived as Rustom is killed in an accident. The shock numbs Dina and lets her accept Nusswan's offer to go back to live with him and his family. Dina does so, but with the wisdom of the Bombay-born, where real-estate prices are one of the highest in the world, retains Rustom's flat. Very soon, her numbness and Nusswan's sympathy wear off and the brother and sister indulge in a typical Parsi exchange of invectives and insults. To Nusswan's 'Do you know how fortunate you are in our community? Among the unenlightened, widows are thrown away like garbage. If you were a Hindu, in the old days you would have had to be a good little sati and leap into your husband's funeral pyre, be roasted with him.' 'I can always go to the Towers of Silence and let the vultures eat me up, if that will make you happy' (52).

Nusswan's words reflect the deep-rooted Parsi feeling of the superiority of their 'enlightened' religion versus what they consider the superstitious, exploitative nature of the Hindu religion and its treatment of its widows. However, his words are ironical since Dina considers Nusswan to be the oppressor and the 'unenlightened' one and offers to take herself off to the

Towers of Silence. This being a reference to the Zoroastrian mode of disposal of dead bodies in Iran – a mode which has been retained by Indian Parsi Zoroastrians in India. Such a mode of disposal of the dead was also called a 'sky burial' and enabled the social and eco-conscious Parsis to make their final charitable offering (their bodies to birds) and do so without polluting the earth, water or fire.

However, before Dina could be eaten up by the vultures she has to journey back to her late husband's flat, set up her own business, experience the self-centred entrepreneurial practices of the Fashion Export House manager Mrs. Gupta, share the joys and sorrows of her tailors, Ishvar and Omprakash and get to know Maneck Kholah. With their help she has to also sew the Quilt -- each square of which tells its own story. The quilt however, forms yet another important motif in the novel and will be focussed upon later in this chapter. Dina's journey back to her husband's flat and her work for the Au Revoir fashion house brings Ishvar and Omprakash Darji into her life. After initial suspicions the tailors become part of her family and along with Maneck Kholah, who she takes in as a lodger, succeed in bringing some joy to her. This soon comes to an end when Maneck leaves for a job in the Gulf and the tailors on a visit to their village are mutilated by their old high-caste enemy the Thakur. Bereft of her tailors and without the rent that Maneck paid her, Dina is forced to go back to Nusswan's home and her circle of journeys is thus completed.

Ishvar and Omprakash Darji also journey in this novel. Their journey from their village by the river to the city by the sea, is foreshadowed by the journey Ishvar's father Dukhi Mochi makes his sons Narayan (Om Prakash's father) and Ishvar undertake from the *Chamar* caste to being *darjis*. Thereby changing their profession-defining surname from Mochi -- shoemaker -- to Darji – tailor. This is the most daring journey in the entire text as it involves moving away from being the lowest of the low, the most despised caste, which flayed dead cattle for the upper castes, tanned its hide and fashioned it into footwear.

Dukhi mochi journeys from his village to the nearby town where he is befriended by the Muslim tailor Ashraf, who by virtue of his religion is outside the caste system. Dukhi, however, moves back to his village, but when his sons are beaten for 'polluting' the village school by their presence, he sends them off to Ashraf to be apprenticed to him as tailors. This daring gesture is noted by the village upper castes -- the thakurs -- and punished twice over at intervals of several years. Thereby suggesting that caste memories are very long indeed.

The novel opens with the prologue set in 1975 which marks the coming together of the chamar turned tailors, Om and Ishvar with Maneck Kolah in a commuter train in Bombay, the city by the sea. All three are then at different stages of their respective journeyings and are in a common quest of Dina Dalal, who they seek as a refuge in different ways. For the tailors she symbolises employment -- an opportunity to earn a living in the indifference and hugeness of Bombay. For Maneck she promises shelter from the horrors of the college hostel. This refuge motif however becomes ironical as the narrative progresses and Dina is revealed to be in as much need of succour as the three men who seek her.

When the three seekers find Dina she is already well into her middle-age, although still attractive. Because of her failing eyesight she is unable to cope with the sewing orders from the export house and desperately needs the tailors and also the little more money that Mancek's rent would bring in. Thus in Dina and her modest flat the diverse trajectories that had brought the tailors in from their village and Maneck from his mountain home finally converge and the stage is set for the events in the novel.

The first chapter of the novel -- The City by the Sea -- details the early years of Dina's life as the pampered and intelligent daughter of Dr. Shroff. However with the death of her father, the power in the family passes into the hands of her despotic brother Nusswan and Dina's dream of studying to be a doctor like her father have to be laid to rest. Patriarchy in the form of Nusswan tries to crush all that is bright and fine in young Dina. He and his wife Ruby withdraw Dina from school and turn her into a household drudge. Dina however shows spunk and as she grows older tries to educate herself by visiting public libraries where she reads voraciously even if without direction. She also listens to classical music, in the music section of these libraries and sneaks away to attend free music concerts in the city. It is here that she meets her future husband Rustom. In an interview with Angela Lambert, Mistry has said that he had met his wife Freny Elavia at a music school 'where she was taking voice and piano lessons and I was doing classes in music theory and composition'. This real-life memory could have been the basis of the genesis of Dina and Rustom's romance. Their marriage is happy but ends in an abrupt tragedy when Rustom dies in a road accident on their third wedding anniversary. As noted earlier the return to the brother's home is not very successful and Dina goes back to her old marital home and begins her existence as a seamstress. Her widowhood progresses into its twelfth year against the backdrop of the wider world of politics. These are the years of the agitation for the bifurcation of the old colonial Bombay state into the language based states of Maharashtra and Gujarat. Dina's life moves gradually into its middle years and her eyes abused by years of sewing and close work begin to fail, necessitating the hiring of tailors for the sewing orders she undertakes. It is thus that the tailors Om and Ishvar enter the life of Dina Dalal in the company of the young Maneck. Their trajectories having now converged, enables the novelist to move away from the city by the sea to the village by the river from where the tailors have come to the city where dreams grow but also sour and die.

In the village by the river chapter, Mistry has taken a quantum leap from bearing witness to the idiosyncratic last flamings of the demographically endangered Parsis community into the badlands of the Indian countryside, where age-old caste oppressions continue to flourish. The Indian constitution adopted in 1950 had declared that all Indians would be equal under the law and no discrimination be made on grounds of caste, creed or gender. A constitution that was drafted under the leadership of an untouchable, Dr. Ambedkar, who was a Mahar and thus belonged to an even lower caste than the chamars-tailors in Mistry's narrative. Here Mistry through good-intentioned appears to be striving after effect as he leaves his familiar Parsi spaces and ventures into hitherto unexplored territories. It is not given to all writers to expound with authority on the underbelly of society, especially if they do not have first-hand experience of it. This section of the text therefore sadly lacks in authority and authenticity that is immediately evident to Indian readers who are able to see this, though ironically it is these parts of the text that most impressed several Western reviewers and general readers.

Parsis today are a very urbanised group even though they began their Indian sojourn as agriculturists in Gujarat. As such Mistry's experience of rural India and especially of its lower castes would have been limited and at the most extend to those among its members who through centuries of interaction with Parsis in Gujarat, had come to be known to them. This though would have been in subordinate capacities as farm-hands or domestic servants. So while describing the village of Om and Ishvar, Mistry is in an uneasy position. The knowledge, the experience here is second-hand and derived from textual material or family hearsay. Mistry soldiers on bravely though as he defines the caste boundaries of Isvar's father Dukhi Mochi's existence. The upper caste Thakurs and the Pandits in the village oppress his family and caste associates and as noted earlier, Dukhi finally leaves the village to ply his trade as a cobbler in the nearby town. Here he is befriended by Ashraf, a Muslim and is exposed for the first time to the message of Mahatma Gandhi who was fighting a dual battle against colonialism and casteism -- the external and internal enemies of India. His Muslim friend offers to teach his sons his own trade, tailoring. This would enable them to get away from the caste equated professions in the village. Dukhi refuses this offer and returns to his village thinking it best to remain where one has been born. His boys Ishwar and Narayan drawn by the lure of learning, infiltrate their little untouchable selves into the village classroom and the entire family has to bear the burden of this unknowing subversion. The village Pundit recites the age-old shlokas to justify the caste system and disgusted at such sophistry, Dukhi finally apprentices his boys to the Muslim Ashraf to be trained as tailors. The boys flourish under the care of the Muslim family and for a time it seems that Dukhi's family fortunes have taken a turn for the better.

The idyll is threatened by the anti-Muslim rhetoric spouted by the Hindu nationalist party members -- the one which is in power in India today -- men in 'white shirts and khaki pants' (123), whose hate campaign against the religious other was dissipated at least partly by the moral force of the Mahatma. The reprieve however is temporary and as Lord Mountbatten's schedule for India's simultaneous independence and partitioning gathers momentum, Ashraf's family feels increasingly threatened. Against this tumultuous backdrop the resentment against Dukhi Mochi for trying to distance his sons from the caste system also gathers pace in the village. The time is therefore ripe for tragedy for both Ashraf and Dukhi. However, before this happens the lower caste boys avert it from happening to their adopted Muslim family by claiming that they are their own family and are Hindus. In such troubled times the wider religious belonging gains ascendancy over narrower caste divides -- thus independence arrives. Even in Dukhi's village news of the parliamentary elections and social reforms seeps through. However, the promises of equality and justice offered by the new system is subverted by casteist politics and things carry on much as before. Narayan however rebels against the elision of his vote at the elections and this puts him in direct conflict with the village thakurs. Retribution is swift and a fiery death claims all the family except Ishvar and Narayan's young son Om, who were in town with Ashraf.

After initial ruminations on vengence the two retreat to Ashraf's shop in the town, from where the changing economic situation that favours ready-made clothes to those made to order by the tailors, ultimately takes the two men to Dina Dalal's home where the trajectories of gender injustice and caste oppressions meet and meld.

Life in the city by the sea although not riddled by casteist oppressions like in the village, has its own savage price to exact from those who do not have the cushionings of either economic or class privileges and neither the tailors nor their female mentor have access to either.

The tailors' search for shelter in the big city leads them inevitably to the slums as it does millions of others who flock to it in search of its fabled but to them unavailable wealth. In the slum their neighbour Rajaram, the Hair Collector, guides them through the intricacies of filling up the day's quota of water from the communal tap, to the best places where they could squat on the railway line which ran past the slum for their morning evacuations. They become part of the eclectic fraternity that includes apart from the Hair-collector, the sorcerer Dayaram, the Harmonium-player and the Monkey-man who also in-dwell that space. In passages redoent of an almost socialist nostalgia perhaps engendered by the memories of boyhood viewings of the 1950s film *Shri 420*, Raj Kapoor's socialist epic, Mistry has the tailors sitting outside their hut in the evening listening to the harmonium player as he plays his instrument and sings old Hindi film songs, in a rather idealised poor man's camaraderie.

This however is an uneasy calm as the tailor's residence in the slum is illegal without the all-important validation of the ration card, which naturally eludes them as they have no way of proving uninterrupted stay in their current home. This results in the precarious nature of their existence in the city, where they like their comrades in poverty remain unacknowledged and invisible but perform services without which the city would grind to a standstill. The quest for a ration card and a viable existence, even though on the margins of the city, introduces the tailors to the current politically motivated supposed solution for India's overpopulation – vasectomy. The Ration Officer advises them to undergo vasectomy, the reward for this sacrifice of their fertility would be not only a ration card but also a transistor radio. Rather cynically, they are told that some men underwent the operation twice to reap double benefits. The tailors spurn this offer and reject the validity that demands such a high price from them.

This is first time that the text brings in the problem of overpopulation and Mrs. Gandhi's son Sanjay's ingenious solution to it – vasectomise all the men in the crucial age-group and all will be fine. Mistry's text goes on to show how this vasectomy drive intensified during the Emergency imposed by Mrs. Gandhi between 1975 and 1976 and proved to be the undoing of the tailors. The vasectomy programme coupled with the 'Beautification' campaign undertaken by Sanjay's acolytes in the Youth Congress, which attempted to sanitise the Indian urban spaces of its 'unsightly' poor, drive Ishvar and Om to their ultimate tragedy.

However, before this happens, Mistry wafts us off to the mountain home of Maneck Kolah, thereby moving in geographical spaces from the city by the sea, to the village by the river, to the mountains. If the cityscape is a contrast of riches and poverty and the village riddled with caste factions, the mountains loom pristine and pure above both. However, even here the familial politics of the Kolahs and the troubled relationship between Maneck and his father provide the canker in the Eden and is reminiscent of the problematic relationship of Gustad Noble and his son in *Such a Long Journey*. Also lurking in this Eden is the shadow of history, India's colonial past that continues to haunt the postcolonial present, in the form of the bitter legacy of the partition what Mistry has described in relation to Maneck's own birth as 'but long before that eagerly awaited birth, there was another, gorier parturition, when two nations incarnated out of one. A foreigner drew a magic line on a map and called it the new border; it became a river of blood upon the earth..' (203). This bloody birthing had impacted negatively upon the fortunes of the Kolah family who were economically impoverished by the new borders, though not physically threatened by it as their Parsi identity, neither Hindu nor Muslim, provided them with an immunity that left them untouched by the carnage of the partition. However, they were economically ruined as their assets were now on the other side of the new border.

Moreover, the new capital class in post-Nehurvian India of the 1970s, ensured the further deterioration of the Kolahs' limited wealth, by ushering in the multinational consumer goods against which Maneck's father's cola was no competition. This is a reference to the cola giants who were later in the same decade, banished from Indian markets, by the government that succeeded Mrs. Gandhi's. The cola companies only re-entered the liberated Indian market in the mid-1990s. However, for Maneck, this seals his exile from his beloved mountains as his father sees no future for him there. He is first sent to a boarding school, where Mistry makes him undergo the almost mandatory rites of passage brush with homosexual advances and then to a college in the city by the sea, where in the college hostel he is once again traumatised. It is in the hostel that he is befriended by the politically conscious and socially proactive Avinash. Avinash however disappears mysteriously in the aftermath of the declaration of the Emergency and Maneck is once again cruelly ragged in the hostel. His desperate letter home elicits the offer of alternative accommodation with his mother's old school friend Dina Dalal. Thus the boy from the mountains, meets the men from the village by the river and their lives become interdependent with that of the woman who lives in the city by the sea.

In the chapters that follow this mountain idyll, the tailors' already precarious existence in the slum becomes further endangered when the bureaucratic hordes of Mrs. Gandhi's government descend on them to 'persuade' the male population there to vasectomies themselves. The incentive being offered a measly rupees five and free tea and snacks -- a sad reflection of the poverty that co-existed with wealth in the city. In addition to showing the people that in the Emergency, the family planning statistics had received a positive boost, the Prime Minister also had to appear in the public eye at rallies and like a goddess give *darshan* to her 'devotees'. During the Emergency, the Indian politicians had tried to surpass one another to meet with Mrs. Indira Gandhi's approval and some had declared that 'India was Indira and Indira was India' and even some 'intellectuals' were not laggards in this game. India's famous modern painter, M.F. Hussain had painted a series of pictures where he had imaged Mrs. Gandhi as the Hindu goddess, Durga, riding her mount, a tiger. The tailors and their friends in the slum are rounded up and herded into a bus to attend one such rally where they see the obsequious manner in which the local politicians and dignitaries receive Mrs. Gandhi. For these poor men the spectacle provides much amusement and like the citizens of ancient Rome who were likewise beguiled by circuses, these people feel entertained but see through the charade: 'See? Said Rajaram, 'I told you its going to be a day at the circus -- we have clowns, monkeys, acrobats, everything' (261).

In this section of the text, 'Day at the Circus, Night in the Slum', which of course has its tongue-in-cheek intertextuality in the reference to Angela Carter's *Nights at the Circus*, focuses mockingly on Mrs. Gandhi's Emergency agenda, the Twenty Point Programme, which included the removal of poverty – *Garibi Hatao*, population control and the beautification of cities. All three points rebound adversely on India's poor as the *Garibi Hatao* slogan covertly became the *Garib ko Hatao* – remove the poor. Such a move would automatically make the cities more 'beautiful', so the 'ugly' poor were forcibly removed from the urban spaces. In an augury of the tragic times to come the disillusioned tailors and their friends return to find that the Monkey Man's dog had killed his performing monkeys in their absence.

Maneck's apparently safer bourgeoisie existence in Dina's flat is enlivened by the gossip of the tailors and he learns of their encounter with Mrs. Gandhi's Twenty Point Programme and its little personal tragedy in the form of the destruction of Rajaram's monkeys. The growing closeness of the boys Om and Maneck, upsets Dina's notions of class boundaries but the friendship continues and Maneck much to the horror of Dina is invited for dinner to the tailors' hut. However, before this dinner party could happen, the slum is torn down by Mrs. Gandhi's minions in their beautification drive. The tailors and their friends salvage what they could from the debris. Dispossessed and unhoused they desperately look for shelter but are rebuffed everywhere.

Here we have Mistry detailing the trauma of the millions of Mumbai's unhomed and homeless citizens, whose plight has not changed dramatically for the better since the dark days of the Emergency. The tailors have to sleep rough on the streets, carrying their belongings in a trunk, until Dina finally relents and lets them keep it in her flat. She however, refuses to let the tailors live in her flat for fear of her landlord and her own class and ethnic prejudices.

As a result the tailors are rounded up with other homeless people and dragged off to the beggar's camp where Mistry unleashes one horror after another not only on Om and Ishvar but also on the readers, making them realise how serious he was when he had prefaced his story with the epitaph from Balzac, about it being a 'story of great misfortunes'. This expedition to the Beggar's Camp, enables Mistry to introduce the character of the Beggar Master into the narrative – the man who plays an important role in the denouement of the action. With the Beggar Master and his hapless wards, the reader is transported into the world of children whose limbs have been deliberately maimed to make them better objects of pity and hence more successful beggars.

At this point, the reader might well retreat crying 'Horror! Horror!' but the greatest pity of it all in Aristotelian terms is to be resolved in a cathartic action and this is still many, many pages away in the narrative. Drawing a parallel with Dickens is once more instructive here. With Dickens at the crucial moment when the load of horror becomes too much to take, the discourse is leavened with the inimitable wit and humour for which Dickens was justly famed. In *A Fine Balance*, however, Mistry has unfortunately divested the book of the wit and irony that had shone through so brightly in his earlier books. The sly fun that is had by Dina and Maneck when they visit her brother's office is too slight to count as comic relief. It is not for nothing that Shakespeare's greatest tragedies were speckled with clowns and fools and Greek tragedies relieved by choral intervention. As T.S. Eliot has put it so aptly in *The Four Quartets*, 'Human kind cannot bear very much reality' (Burnt Norton).

'The sailing under one flag' chapter reveals Mistry at his postmodern, word-conscious, writerly best. The opening paragraph has him revelling in words and phrases that describe the city as seen through the eyes of the traumatised tailors returning from the Beggar's Camp – the 'sleeping shanty towns pullulated on both sides of the highway, ready to spread onto the asphalt artery...' (373). This chapter also includes the most bizarre episodes concerning the character of the Beggar Master. The Beggar Master is like Dickens' Fagin but only darker and his wards maybe a shade more maimed and hapless. This postmodernist intertextuality is followed by the tailors calling the city 'a story factory' (377). However, the 'reality' of the tailors' suffering makes these stories almost too difficult to read. Now trouble upon trouble are heaped upon them and their Dinabai -- 'bai' being a suffix of respect in Marathi speaking parts of Western India.

In this chapter too, Dina ultimately gives in to Maneck's insistent pleadings on the tailors' behalf and allows her own compassion for their plight to have its way by letting them stay in her flat. There is also the practical reason of not being deprived of their labour if on account of not having any accommodation they were to return to their village. This results in an uneasy co-existence that ultimately ends in true friendship and understanding that crosses gender, class, religious and ethnic boundaries -- hence the sailing under one flag.

Binding their stories of sorrows, troubled times and little joys such as the joint cooking sessions of the tailors with Maneck in Dina's kitchen, is the motif of the quilt that Dina makes most evenings. The quilt is a mnemonic device that enables Dina, her tailors and Maneck to recall their lives together. Each remnant, salvaged from the fabric used to make up the Au Revoir orders, has its own particular memory attached to it. Each diverse square, triangle and polygon when sewn together makes a connection with the other pieces to provide a new meaning of its own -- 'Just keep connecting patiently, Dinabai -- that's the secret. Ji-hahn, it all seems meaningless bits and rags, till you piece it together' (p.197). The 'connecting' can lead the vigilant reader to E.M. Forster's *A Passage to India* with its exhortation, 'connect, just connect'. Later in the narrative, when she has to return to her brother's flat, Dina lies under that quilt at night and each piece helps her remember the one year in which Ishvar, Om and Maneck had been a part of her life. Like the 'bits and rags' in Dina's quilt, Mistry's stories are also separate but when 'connected' hang together -- distinct but united by the pen of the 'Story-Master'.

The 'connections' stretch from Om to Maneck, from Om and Ishvar to Dina, from Om and Ishvar to the professional beggar Shanker and as the quilt grows larger and larger it expands to also include the tailors' friend Jeevan, who is also a tailor.

Jeevan seems to have been introduced to allow leeway for the expression of the raging hormones in the young Om and Maneck. Through Jeevan they have the opportunity to be Peeping Toms when his female customers try on their saree blouses tailored by Jeevan. The boys' fun and games however take on even more unsavoury aspects when they horse around with Dina's home-made sanitary napkins.

All this however comes to an end when Dina's landlord employs strong-arm tactics to get her to vacate her flat. It is then that the Beggar Master comes to the rescue and as the tailors are his clients (they have been paying him a monthly sum ever since he rescued them from the Beggar Camp), he has his own interests to protect. The Beggar Master's threats to the landlord work and Dina and her tailors get a reprieve as does Maneck.

Mistry's 'story-factory' now moves into top gear for the final four sections of the book, the ones that detail how the horrors of the Emergency once more take hold of the tailors and ruins their lives completely, turning one into a Eunuch and both into beggars. Without her tailors Dina is reduced to again becoming dependent on her brother and nemesis catches up with Maneck too, when he is brought face to face finally with what had actually happened to his hostel friend Avinash. Interlocking diagonally with this story, is the unexpected end of the beggar Shanker, who spoilt by the attentions of the Beggar Master, ever since the latter had discovered that Shankar was his half-brother, throws a tantrum that leads to his death.

While Shanker is being killed, Maneck discovers that Avinash had died in the hostel and his body had been dumped on the railway tracks to make it look like a suicide. From there it had ended in the morgue. His parents had ultimately been able to trace his body there and had just cremated him quietly. However, they had been unconvinced that it had been an accident as his nails had been ripped off. Shocked by these revelations, Maneck returns to Dina's flat to be told of Shanker's death and all of them go to his funeral – even Dina, which earns her the gratitude and respect of the Beggar Master.

Events now gather momentum and the tailors leave for their village for Om's marriage. There however they come across their old enemy, Thakur Dharamsi and the happy occasion is turned into a ghastly tragedy. Under the instigation of the Thakur the tailors are rounded up and forcibly sent to the sterilisation camp for a vasectomy. There while Ishvar is only sterilised, Om's testicles are cut off and he is turned into a Eunuch. Now miseries pile upon miseries again in an almost unreal fashion and even Ishvar's condition worsens as the operation had been performed in less than sterile conditions. His wounds turn septic and eventually both his legs have to be amputated. Five months after they had set out from the city by the sea, the tailors return, Om an eunuch and Ishvar a man without legs, who has to be pulled on a little trolley by his nephew, in the manner of the beggar boy Shankar.

The circle which is yet another motif in the text, as Mistry has said, is now complete. Dina is bereft of her tailors and without the protection of the Beggar Master who is killed, and also without Maneck who goes off to a job in a Gulf country. She is now forced out of her home and though she goes to court, she is not successful. This gives Mistry an opportunity though to expound on the corruption of the judiciary during the Emergency. The lawyer, Mr. Vasantrao Valmik, B.A., LL.B., whom she retains to plead her case becomes a mouthpiece for Mistry as he puts his final philosophical justification for his long saga into the mouth of this lawyer. To Dina's question about whether there was any hope for her case, he replies: 'There is always hope – hope enough to balance our despair. Or we would be lost' (553). Other words of philosophical import are, 'our lives are but a sequence of accidents...A string of choices, casual or deliberate, which add up to that one big calamity we call life' (554). Also, 'loss is essential. Loss is part and parcel of that necessary calamity called life' (555). More comes forth in the form of 'thanks to some inexplicable universal guiding force, it is always the worthless things we lose – slough off, like a moulting snake. Losing and losing again, is the very basis of the life process, till we are left with the bare essence of human existence' (555).

However, even before her case could be heard, Dina is evicted by the landlord's goons, the same ones who had had their hands broken by the Beggar Master. This time there is no Beggar Master to rush to Dina's rescue and the landlord has enlisted the help of the police. The police inspector pleads helplessness and advises Dina to call her relatives for help. She calls up Nusswan to send a truck for her furniture. At her brother's home she is deprived of her private effects and everything that makes up her memories – her life. Nusswan decides that her furniture is too old and rickety and sells it all off. Finally Dina is reduced to possessing just the mnemonic quilt which she drapes over her bed in the day time and snuggles under at night. 'At night in bed, she covered herself with the quilt and took to recounting the abundance of events in the tightly knit family of patches, the fragments that she had fashioned with needle, thread and affection' (563).

Mistry now rounds off the narrative with an epilogue, set in 1984, eight years after the events narrated in the novel. Maneck who has spent all of that time in Dubai, in the Gulf, returns to India to be confronted by the riots that have broken out after the assassination of Mrs. Gandhi, killed by her own Sikh security guards over the issue of the storming of the golden temple, their holy shrine in Amritsar by the Indian army under the orders of Mrs. Gandhi who wanted the Sikh separatists hiding there to be flushed out. So although she does not actually pay for the crimes committed during the Emergency, she is still penalised for other high-handedness and political excesses.

The reason for Maneck's return is also a death -- that of his father -- whose funeral he had come to attend. After the funeral Maneck decides to tidy up their home for his mother and descends into the cellar. There he comes across a pile of musty old newspapers and here Maneck becomes Mistry, the diasporic writer, who like his creation also dusts off old cobwebs and catches up with the happenings in India during his absence from it -- in his case in Canada. The litany of past events that catch Maneck/Mistry's eye includes exciting cricket matches, floods, man-made disasters and even the sad story of the three young sisters who had killed themselves by hanging from a ceiling fan as their parents could not find the money to provide all of them with dowries for their marriages. What also catches Maneck's eye as he flips through the old papers is a report on his old friend Avinash's death.

This sets off a morbid reaction in Maneck who returns to the city by the sea in search of Dina and the tailors but is accidentally led to the old Hair Collector who is now a Holy

Man -- Bal Baba. The word 'Bal' in Hindi meaning both a young lad and hair. He also meets his lawyer, Mr. Valmik, once Dina's legal advisor. Once again it is Valmik who reminds Maneck and the reader how one must recall the past, re-tell one's stories as 'it helps to remind yourself of who you are. Then you can go forward, without fear of losing yourself in this ever-changing world' (594). It is instructive here to also remember that in the Indian epic the *Ramanaya*, the narrator was the bandit turned sage, Valmiki. Here though the character of Valmiki is split into two -- that of the murder-turned-saint Bal Baba and the wise lawyer, Valmik.

To round off his re-possession of the past, Maneck goes to meet Dina, who he locates at her brother's home. He finds her nearly blind but still with some flashes of her old fire. She tells her old lodger about what had happened to the tailors and returns him Avinash's old chess-board which he had left behind when he had left for Dubai and which she had saved from the debris of her old life. As he leaves her he sees his old friends reduced to being beggars, making their way to seeing her. The cart on which Ishvar sits is padded with Dina's old quilt -- an ultimate stroke of irony. In an attempt to find some trace at least of his past unaltered, Maneck goes to the restaurant where he and the tailors used to go in the old days. This too has changed and as Maneck stumbles out everything becomes a blur. He reaches the railway station where he stares 'at the rails. How they glinted, like the promise of life itself, stretching endlessly in both directions...' (601) but as the train enters the station Maneck choses death over life – 'when the first compartment entered the station he stepped off the platform and onto the gleaming silver tracks' (601). *A Fine Balance* begins and ends with a death -- Avinash's at the beginning and Mancek's at the end. The circle thus comes full as Maneck dies with Avinash's chess-board clutched to his chest as he jumps in front of the train. Dina's life too begins at her patriarchal home and the end of the novel finds her back with her brother. Ishvar and Om also try to break out of the cycle of poverty and exploitation but are drawn back into the circle of misery.

Apart from the motifs of the journey, the quilt and the circle, there is also the motif of 'balance' – a 'fine' balance. It is this fine balance which if the persons concerned learn to master, helps them to lead a relatively peaceful, happy life; if they fail, it tips them over into the abyss. Dina as a young girl, a married woman and a dependent widow, constantly upsets the balance of patriarchy and has to pay for it in her truncated education, her husband's death, the loss of her tailors, her home and ultimately her much-prized independence. Dina however is a fighter and after every loss of balance, she clambers onto the knife-edge again to once more achieve that ever-elusive fine balance. Maneck too has to learn how to 'balance' between the love of his parents, their mountain home and his need for independence. His sensitive nature fails to achieve a balance between a serene inner life and the outward turmoil of life in the city and has to pay for it with his life. Ishvar and Om have to balance between their low-caste origins and their new *darji* status. Their origins ultimately destroy this delicate balance and hurl them down into an abyss of abject bodily and spiritual horrors. There is also a fine balance in the life of nations and the Indian nation had lost that fine balance during the Emergency. India however had hauled itself out of that dark abyss and Indian democracy had compelled Mrs. Gandhi to call for fresh elections in which she and her party had been thrown out of office. The fine balance had been restored -- no matter how temporarily.

So what do we make of this gallery of characters and cluster of motifs? That the narrative is unrelentingly dark is indisputable. Mistry provides us with a horrorscape of poverty and misery and even if we do not penalise him for this, the question is how well do all the pieces in his 'story-quilt' fit together. How much justice has he done to all those silenced constituencies he has chosen to 'represent'?

Mistry's Dina Dalal and Maneck Kholah ring true – as did his other Parsi characters in his earlier novels. While Mistry has to be appreciated for trying to magnify the scope of his narratives and making them take in a wider Indian reality, there is a heavy prices he has paid for moving away from his ethnocentric discourse. His rural, lower-caste characters and his urban beggars and conmen come across as cardboard figures – an urban, westernised Indian's construct of the Dalit classes. Moreover, as already said, the novel itself often appears to have been pieced together from fragments of newspaper reports, with the author rifling through pages of old newspapers from 1977 to 1986. In fact, Mistry himself has said that 'My novels are not "researched" in the formal sense of the word. Newspapers, magazines, chats with visitors from India-these are things I rely on. Having said that, I will add that all these would be worthless without the two main ingredients: memory and imagination' ('Interview with Gokhale'). While the newspaper mode of research is amply evident in the text, memory and imagination have not always sufficiently salvaged it. This is a great pity for the wider canvas on which Mistry has worked in this book and the importance of 'remembering' in a nation's life, could have made *A Fine Balance* a very significant text – not just in Mistry's *oeuvre* but also in the newly emerging canon of Indian Literature in English.

6

Family Matters:
About Happiness and Unhappiness

In *Family Matters* published in 2002, Mistry returns to Bombay and the Parsi world with a vengeance. Left behind are the villages by the river, the mountains and the absolute dregs of society. The focus once again is firmly on the Parsi community and the canvas has thus shrunk considerably but this is not a reductive book. It is a book which is very 'big' in compassion -- it is indeed Mistry's most compassionate book to date. At the age of 50, from his Canadian point of vantage, Mistry has viewed the life of a middle-class Parsi family in Bombay in the mid-1990s. The old *bete-noir*, the Shiv Sena, is still around but this is the post-Babri Masjid Bombay where the religious chauvinism of Shiv Sena has been augmented by the pan-Indian militant Hindutva of the BJP. The focus has thus shifted from the 1970s and the years of the Emergency under Mrs. Indira Gandhi, to more recent times. Hence the diasporic time-warp has been minimised here to a considerable extent. However, the 'reality' captured here of Bombay, re-named Mumbai in 1995 by the Shiv Sena that had won the state-level elections, is still largely based on heresay and there is still a heavy dependence on newspaper reports of these years, as noted earlier in the case of *A Fine Balance*. Also, a little disturbing for someone who has lived through the tumultuous period from 12 December 1992 to 12 March 1993, is that there is only a passing reference to the series of bomb blasts that rocked Bombay on the latter date.

Mistry's political consciousness and acumen thus begs comparison with another diasporic book on that same troubled and shameful time that Bombay went through – Salman Rushdie's *The Moor's Last Sigh*. Rushdie's in-the-face tackling of the complicity of the Shiv Sena in the Hindu-Muslim riots that rocked Bombay in the wake of the demolition of the Babri Masjid, in Ayodhya in Northern India, by militant Hindu mobs, while the state administration stood by as mute witnesses, is papered over in Mistry's book. Also missing is any elaboration on the suspicion of the involvement of Islamic fundamentalists, in nexus with the Underworld, in the Bombay blasts. One could of course say that this is because the focus in on the personal rather than the political, but the political is allowed to intrude in a major way into the text in the manner in which it impacts on the professional life of one of the central characters – that of Yezad Chinoy. It is through Yezad that the reader comes in contact with his office attendant, Husain, the victim of the Post-Babri Bombay riots and Mr. Kapur, his boss, a victim of the 1947 (partitioning of India) Hindu-Muslim clashes.

Family Matters is in many ways a rites of passage book in which the child is the witness – a kind of 'the child is the father of man' text. The child in question is the nine year old Jehangir Chinoy, the younger son of Roxana and Yezad. The father/patriach figure is that of the seventy-nine year old Nariman Vakeel, his paternal grandfather. It is through Jehangir/Jhangla's eyes that the reader is made privy to much of the family politics that pervades the book. The central motif of *Family Matters* is the jigsaw puzzle that the boy tries to fit together, much like he tries to puzzle out the quarrels and power politics that rock his family and which he wishes hard would cohere together in happiness and harmony, like the pieces in his jigsaw puzzles. This however is a vain hope as his elders keep falling apart and happiness eludes the family.

Another recurrent motif is that of the books of the children's writer Enid Blyton. Blyton's books provide not just intertextuality but also opportunities to Mistry to bring in discussions on the alleged racism and sexism supposedly rife in them.

Yet another motif that surfaces at different points in the text, is that of immigration. Yezad had once dreamt of immigrating to Canada, but his dream had been thwarted by unfair interview practices at the Canadian High Commission.

Apart from these leit motifs and intertextuality there is the narrative technique of the flashbacks, marked by italics, that re-construct Nariman Vakil's guilt-laden past. These passages are also psychoanalytical in nature as they form part of Nariman's subconscious and usually occur in a dream-like state between sleep and waking, in which there is also sub-vocalisation.

Family Matters has a wonderfully quiet opening in which the age of the central protagonist Nariman Vakeel is stressed as much as is the author's own love of words, which had first manifested itself in *Tales from Firozsha Baag*, and is here marked by one magnificently crafted sentence after another: 'A splash of light from the late-afternoon sun lingered at the foot of Nariman's bed as he ended his nap and looked towards the clock. It was almost six. He glanced down where the warm patch had lured his toes. Knurled and twisted, rendered birdlike by age, they luxuriated in the sun's comfort. His eyes fell shut again' (1). If Nariman luxuriates in the warmth of the sun, Mistry does his own basking in the luxuriance of language – an indulgence he is able to allow himself, almost throughout the book, through the agency of Nariman, who by virtue of having been a professor of English, not only speaks in beautifully wrought sentences but also delights his little grandson, Jehangir, with yet newer and more mellifluous words.

The calm of the opening paragraph is frazzled to shreds by the shrill importunings of his step-children, Jal and Coomy Contractor, who beseech him not to go out of the apartment. They are afraid that due to the Parkinson's disease from which he suffers, he would lose his balance and fall down. The fears of these two middle-aged siblings has to be seen in the context of the geriatric Parsi community in which there are today too few young and able members to care for the old and disabled. Even in a wider context, in India where health care and state support for the care of the elderly and sick is almost non-existent, this responsibility falls squarely on the younger generation within families. As noted earlier, late marriages and/or a rampant individualism that does not brook the adjustments required within marriage, have led to most Parsis not marrying at all, or if married, either opting not to have children or being forced into a childless state by infertility caused by the advanced age of one or both spouses at the time of the marriage.

There is also the fact that in the Parsi community thanks to economic pressures (high property prices in Bombay, where most of the Parsis live) and general societal norms (which are common with other communities in India), unmarried adult children, continue to live with their parents. Those who do get married generally opt to move away and lead independent lives. Hence the burden of caring for ageing, ill and often cantankerous parents falls on the unmarried offspring. This often results in feelings of resentment towards the married siblings who it appears have shrugged off their responsibilities towards ageing parents. This is clearly evident in *Family Matters*, where Coomy resents her half-sister Roxana for having 'escaped' parent-care duties and goes to inordinate lengths to force her sister into taking care of Nariman, when he falls down and breaks his ankle.

That however is still in the future, when Nariman uncurls his ageing and frail limbs, and in blithe disregard of the injunctions laid on his movements, leaves the apartment for his usual evening walk. When his step-daughter Coomy asks, 'How many people with Parkinson's do what you do?' (3), he shrugs off her fears by saying, 'I'm not going trekking in Nepal. A little stroll down the lane, that's all' (3). He counters Coomy further by pointing out that dangers lurk indoors as well as outdoors. This brings into the text, the first mention of the Babri Masjid riots. The reference here is to the burning down of an old Parsi couple by rioting Hindu mobs, under the mistaken impression that fleeing Muslims had been given shelter in that building. However as Coomy points out even in spite of the fact that Bombay burnt for months after the razing of the mosque in Ayodhya, 'How often does a mosque in Ayodhya turn people into savages in Bombay? Once in a blue moon' (5). What is a more real danger, are the increasing attacks on aged Parsis, who live by themselves and who are killed for monetary gains, usually by their domestic help. This is a danger experienced by other senior citizens in Bombay too, not just the elderly Parsis, as Mistry's meticulous reading of Indian newspapers would have revealed to him, on this however he is silent. Such silence might imply a particular targeting of Parsis, which in this case is untrue.

While Jal and Coomy bicker among themselves as to what really constitutes a danger to Parsis in Bombay, Nariman Vakeel slips out of their building, Chateau Felicity, and the 'stale emptiness of the flat' (5) into the bustling life of the city. Nariman's longing for fresh air and life outside the ambit of his step-children, is symbolised by the picture on the cover of the text, that of an old Paris, in a trade-mark Sola Topee, that harks back to the colonial times, standing with his back to the camera, gazing out at the sea that girdles the island of Bombay and twice a day with its life-giving breezes flushes out the stale odours from the city. Nariman's bravado is a bit dented though when on the eve of his seventy-ninth birthday, he returns home 'with abrasions on his elbow and forearm, and a limp. He had fallen while crossing the lane outside Chateau Felicity' (6). This fall results in a tirade from Coomy and also brings up old resentments and unhappy memories. This is the beginning of the unraveling of the causes of the unhappiness of the Vakeel/Contractor families. Irritated by Coomy's scolding Nariman lets slip that thanks to his parental pressure he had ruined his life by marrying Yasmin Contractor, the mother of Jal and Coomy and that he would now not let them 'torment my old age. I won't allow it' (7). In retaliation Coomy flares up with 'you ruined Mamma's life, and mine and Jal's. I will not tolerate a word against her'. The quarrel now gathers pace and contemporary resentments are added to old insults – 'will he go out and break his bones and put the burden of his fractures on my head?' (7). While Coomy is here presented as a termagant, as have been female characters like Miss Kutpitia, in *Such a Long Journey*, her brother Jal is the compassionate voice of reason. Notwithstanding these gender stereotypes, what does emerge very clearly is how aged parents are seen as a burden. In the case of Coomy the resentment is heightened by the fact that it is the 'second class' children who are landed with this responsibility while the 'flesh and blood' daughter Roxana, has slipped away by virtue of her married status. However, Mistry does give Coomy her due and lets the reader know that she loves her 'little Roxana' and it is she who pulls them out from 'their swamp of rancour; unhappiness was thwarted from the time being' (9). This again has echoes of *Such a Long Journey*, this time the related character is the girl child Roshan, like Roshan, Roxana too is the one who heals rancours within the family circle.

At this point in the text we have the first of the many flashbacks, marked by an italic font. This first flashback provides the initial piece of the jigsaw puzzle that when finally completed would reveal the entire story of Nariman's unhappiness. The first piece is about how one evening thirty-six years ago, Nariman had finally capitulated to his parents' insistent demand that he 'end his liaison with that Goan woman...and agreed to settle down' (11). That evening had been preceded by the evening at the Breach Candy beach when he had told Lucy Braganza that he was ending their long relationship -- 'they had been ground down by their families' (13). Lucy's family too was against her marrying a non-Catholic and she had had to leave home. This could have been the point in the narrative for a mention of most Indian communities being averse to inter-religious marriages and not just the Parsis. A parallel in the USA could be Black/White marriages or in Britain White/Asian marriages. This is not a defence of Parsi orthodoxy but merely an attempt to set the record straight that Parsis are not unique in being allergic to their offspring marrying outside their community.

With Lucy out of the way, a more suitable replacement had been found for Nariman in the form of 'a widow, Yasmin Contractor, a widow with two children, they told him. 'And that's the best you can expect, mister, with your history' (15). That was how Nariman had found himself the husband of Yasmin Contractor and the father of Jal and Coomy. Although he had adopted them, it was decided they would keep their biological father's surname, as otherwise Yasmin felt it would 'be like rewriting history...the simile appealed to his academic soul: he acquiesced' (16).

The flashback over the text moves into contemporary times again as the family gets together to celebrate Nariman's seventy ninth birthday. In the light of the events that follow, this party has a poignant appeal as it's the last time that Nariman and his family are more or less happy. The son-in-law Yezad and the grandsons Murad and Jehangir's love for the old man is palpable and even Coomy ultimately yields to the general atmosphere of good will, as her brother Jal keeps fiddling with his recalcitrant hearing aid to catch all the family chatter. Political gossip also forms part of this chatter and the family fulminates against the corrupt politics of the Shiv Sena and their double standards vis-à-vis the insistence of adherence to Indian culture and at the same time organising a concert by Michael Jackson, the Western pop idol. This notwithstanding their general branding of Western culture as degenerate irritates the family. So politics intrudes into the closed family circle as do other events that had marked the public arena of the 1990s, including the charged atmosphere at Indo-Pakistan cricket matches and the cricketers' coloured uniforms splashed with the logos of commercial sponsors that had replaced the white flannels in the one-day matches.

The unhappiness that was lurking in the near future though is presaged at this party in the form of Coomy's apprehensions about a possible serious fall for Nariman if he continued ignoring her injunctions on going out. In a half-serious manner she warns her half-sibling that if that were to happen 'she and Jal would deliver him straight-away to the Chinoy residence' (13). This is countered by Yezad's 'The chief is welcome, just make sure you bring one of your extra rooms. We live in a two-room flat, not a seven room palace like this one' (13). So the party ends but not without a reference to Lucy by Coomy, when her step-father had irritated her by asking her to bring out the best china and then upset her further by switching on the usually unused and hence dust-laden ceiling fan. The elders had immediately changed the subject, but the young boys had caught the reference and brought it up at the bus stop on their way home. As Yezad and Roxana try to explain the problem Nariman's parents had with inter-religious marriages, Mistry is able to bring in the dilemma facing contemporary Parsis about inter-communal marriages. This confuses young Jehangir. 'He asked if there was a law against marrying someone who wasn't a Parsi. His father said yes, the law of bigotry' (40). There is considerable dramatic irony in Yezad's response as towards the end of the text, he turns into a bigot himself and opposes his elder son Murad's relationship with a non-Parsi girl.

In yet another textual echo, the Chinoy family is hassled at the bus stop by drunken rowdies, much as had happened in

"Auspicious Occasion", to Rustomji in *Tales from Firozsha Baag*. This once again brings in the fear of the Shiv Sena and its anti-minority policies. Also brought are in Yezad's one time dream of immigrating to Canada. This runs like a thread though the rest of the text, and provides Mistry with a chance to talk about Canada and its official policy of multiculturalism which does not really mitigate racism in that society. This also gives Mistry the opportunity to make snide references to what governments consider useful skills and qualifications for people who wish to immigrate to their countries. So Yezad counsels his son Jehangir, 'Study useful things – computers, MBA, and they'll welcome you. Not useless things like me, history and literature and philosophy' (43). There is a personal irony involved here too as Mistry himself when he had immigrated to Canada in the mid-1970s had had 'useful' educational qualifications in the form of a Science degree and only later, once settled in Canada, had acquired a 'useless' second degree in English Literature.

Fulfilling Coomy's Cassandra-like prophecies, Nariman does fall down again soon after his Birthday party. This second fall does more serious damage and he has to be carried home. Coomy sends Jal for Dr. Fitter who lives a neighbouring building to attend to Nariman, but the doctor suggests they straight-away take him to a hospital. The sight of the dithering, gentle, deaf Jal irritates the old doctor who frets 'Demographics show we'll be extinct in fifty years. Maybe it's the best thing. What's the use of having spineless weaklings walking around, Parsi in name only' (50). Nariman is taken to the Parsi General Hospital, the ageing community's succour in Mumbai, where Nariman is diagnosed by Dr. Tarapore, a fellow Parsi, and a former student of Nariman's, as suffering from a fracture to his left ankle, complicated by osteoporosis and Parkinsonism. So his left leg is x-rayed and plastered by Mr. Rangarajan, a non-Parsi technician and the old man's bantering with him brings in the Shiv Sena's supposed infiltration of the post-offices and the non-delivery of letters addressed to Bombay and not Mumbai. Rangarajan also asks the one-time professor for advice on immigrating to the USA or Canada, as he does not wish to work in India anymore. Thus, Mistry ushers in the middle-class educated Indian's dream of immigration from an increasingly corrupt and extremist India to a Western country, which is not restricted to the Parsi community alone.

Dr. Tarapore's interaction with Nariman in the hospital is a clue for Mistry to discuss the displacement of English from the contemporary Indian university curriculum. When Mistry had studied for his Science degree at the University of Bombay in the early 1970s, English language and even literature had been a compulsory subject for students of all the faculties – Science, Commerce and Arts. Today, this has been scrapped for the Science faculty and only English for Business and General Communication is taught at a compulsory level to students of Commerce and Arts. Dr. Tarapore however had been taught more uplifting things like 'The Rime of the Ancient Mariner' and as he attends to his erstwhile professor, it is lines from that poem that run through his mind. Although the Parsi General Hospital by and large has an excellent sanitary record, Nariman's hospital stay and his acquaintance with the non-Parsi Rangarajan allows Mistry to bring in the topic of unhygienic Indian hospitals where rats run wild. The diasporic writer's 'newspaper research' technique is in evidence here once again as we are fed horror stories of new-born babies eaten by rats and of course the so-called plague outbreak in 1994, which was never confirmed, but created waves of horror in the West and led to the cancellation of all flights from the West to India in late September of that year.

After a two-day stay at the hospital Nariman is discharged. In a rather unbelievable manner Mistry lets Jal and Coomy withhold the news of Nariman's fall and hospitalisation from Roxana, so as to let himself have the twist in the plot where the step-children unceremoniously and without any warning dump the old man at Roxana's doorstep. However, they do try to manage themselves for a little while, till the logistics of giving the old man a bed pan and then when that was abandoned in favour of a bedside commode, the physical labour of hoisting Nariman onto it, defeats them. As his step-children wrestle with the smelly commode and their consciences, Nariman drifts in and out of painful delirium and the text slips into the next flashback episode. This one is concerned with the time when Yasmin used to hide his clothes so that he would not go down to meet Lucy who had taken to standing on the pavement and staring up at Nariman's window. Nariman would try to ignore her until his remorse would drive him down to see her and this in turn would upset Yasmin and the children, especially Coomy. After Nariman had left her, Lucy had given up her studies and since she had already been thrown out of her parents' home thanks to her relationship with Nariman, was living at the YWCA hostel. Nariman had countered Yasmin's ploy of hiding all his clothes, while he was taking his bath, by going down to meet Lucy wrapped just in a bath towel. This episode had driven a further wedge between Nariman and his wife Yasmin and also alienated him from Coomy.

Back to contemporary times, the narrative moves into another gear as Coomy defeated by the physical labour of taking care of the old man and now even bereft of her domestic help, who is driven away by the foul odours in the flat, convinces her brother to hire an ambulance and without any prior warning takes Nariman to Roxana's flat and leaves him there till the plaster is removed and he is mobile enough again to return to their flat. While the reader might be tempted to censure Coomy for this 'heartless' move, her action needs to be seen against the earlier mentioned scenario where there is no state help at all for the care of the old and infirm and the entire burden falls upon their not always willing to do so children.

Family Matters: About Happiness and Unhappiness

Nariman is nominally consulted on this move but he knows that he did not really have the right to veto it or even say: 'This flat is my home, and I put in in your names because I did not differentiate between you and Roxana. Would you now throw me out in my helplessness? They would probably laugh that I was getting dramatic' (83). So all that Nariman says is, 'Lying in bed, here or there, is all the same to me. But it will be difficult for them, in such a small flat' (83). Paucity of accommodation is the bane of the majority of family units in the congested city of Bombay and has ruined the happiness of families other than the ones in this text. So the ambulance is once again summoned and the hapless old man lifted onto a stretcher and as they take him out: 'He wondered if he was seeing the familiar faces [the portraits of his ancestors, which line the walls of the flat] for the last time. He wanted to tell the ambulancemen to make a tour of each room so he could examine everything, fix it in his mind before the door closed behind him' (85). Thus deprived of decision-making power by age and crippled by his fracture, Nariman is borne off to his unsuspecting daughter Roxana's little flat.

Roxana's idyllic little world in Pleasant Villa is described in detail by Mistry before it is hit by the catastrophe of Nariman's arrival. Included in this description is Roxana's almost obsessive concern with her sons' health, which entails keeping them at home at the slightest sign of a cold. On such days the younger son Jehangir would occupy himself with jigsaw puzzles and the reading of Enid Blyton books. As noted earlier the jigsaw puzzle has been used by Mistry as a leit motif and the fondness for Blyton's books, provides Mistry with an opportunity to bring in the attacks on these books by postcolonial and feminist critics who find them racist and sexist. So we have Yezad saying 'it did immense harm, it encouraged children to grow up without attachment to the place where they belonged, made them hate themselves for being who they were, created confusion about their identity. He said he had read the same books when he was small, and they had made him yearn to become a little Englishman of a type that even England did not have' (93). There is also Roxana though who says: 'But Enid Blyton is fun for children. It doesn't do any harm' (93). So the reader can take his/her pick as to which side to support in this argument.

In this utopian space Roxana is the guiding spirit, in the Romantic Wordsworthian mould. As she brings in the sun-dried clothes from her balcony, her little son hugs her and says: 'You smell like the sun, Mummy' (94). This is very like the idealisation of the character of Dilnavaz, the beautiful wife of Gustad Noble in *Such a Long Journey*. Much as she loves her father, much as he is adored by her little boys and much as her husband is fond of him, the fact remains that they live in what in Mumbai lingo is called a 1 BHK flat – one bedroom, hall kitchen. While Roxana and Yezad occupy the sole bedroom, the hall serves as their boy's bedroom at night and as the family's sitting-cum-dining room in the daytime. There is also the above mentioned small balcony where Roxana dries her clothes. When Nariman is dumped on them without prior notice, the Chinoys have to improvise even further to fit the immobile old man into their milieu. Roxana's world in Pleasant Villa also includes her neighbours, the violinist Daisy Icchaporia and the Matka-playing Villie Cardmaster. Matka being a gambling game which though run mainly by the Underworld, was patronised by even the middle-classes and upper-middle classes of Mumbai, till it was banned in an effort to weed out the influence of the Underworld and the clout it enjoyed. It is these two women who impinge in a major way on Nariman's life at Pleasant Villa – Daisy in a direct manner through her 'command concerts' for the old man and Villie indirectly by enabling Yezad to make a little extra money (needed to stretch the family budget to accommodate the old man) on the Matka game.

Thus the old man becomes part of the cramped but not initially unhappy little family of his daughter. Murad, the older boy, is shifted to the balcony under a plastic sheet provided by Villie Cardmaster and Nariman is settled on the couch in the sitting room which also serves as his bed. The younger boy, Jehangir, sleeps at night on the little pull-out bed that is under the couch during the day. Roxana, the home-maker exults in the fact that her little boy, who had been at home with an upset tummy when his grandfather was brought in, insists on hand-feeding lunch to his grandfather while his mother goes back to hanging up the clothes on the balcony, an activity that had been interrupted by the dramatic arrival of her father. From that vantage point Roxana was able to watch the scene, 'nine year old happily feeding seventy-nine...She felt she was witnessing something almost sacred, and her eyes refused to relinquish the precious moment, for she knew instinctively that it would become a memory to cherish, to recall in difficult times when she needed strength' (108).

The difficult times do arrive as Nariman's presence begins to irritate his son-in-law Yezad as he has to share his breakfast space with the smells and sounds of his father-in-law's desperately held back morning evacuations, that sometimes had to be let out even as the son-in-law was eating his fried eggs and toast. This might be low-key tragedy as compared to the greater horrors of castration and mutilated beggar children in *A Fine Balance*, but it is still very real indeed and even more moving because set in a more domestic and identifiable situation. As Ellen Seligman, Mistry's editor at McClelland & Stewart has said, in this book Mistry is dealing with 'issues of morality, making moral decisions in a complicated world. He's dealing with restrictions that this world places on the characters' lives' (quoted by Stacey Gibson in the *University of Toronto Magazine*, Summer 2002). Mistry himself has said that 'This book does not try to take on all the complexity of India as *A Fine Balance* did. It journeys inward into domestic life, just as profound a journey as far as the writing is concerned' (quoted in 'A Flavour of India', June 1, 2002, on www.smh.com.au). There are critics however who prefer the orientalist sterotypes of the horrorscape of India to the domestic canvas of *Family Matters*. Penny Huston is one of them and she says that 'Shrinking his canvas [from that of *A Fine Balance*], Mistry has produced a middle-brow novel straining to be "literary". Sometimes he makes us feel the pathos of his tragi-comic characters caught up in their confusing world, but in the end they seem to deserve the petty, miserable lives they lead' ('Scheming and arguing in claustrophobic chaos', June 24, 2002, www.theage.com.au). Ms. Huston is welcome to her views but the reason for her finding the world of Mistry's characters 'confusing' is a little difficult to understand as apart from their lives being led in the city of Bombay in India, there should be no confusion about resentful step-children and the universal problems of families unable to take care of ageing parents. Maybe Ms. Huston was having a bad hair day in her non-confusing, non-claustrophobic and non-chaotic world the day she wrote her snipy little piece and launched it into cyberspace. More space and words need not be expanded on such a review. After all as Nariman Vakil says, 'How can you force people? Can caring and concern be made compulsory? Either it resides in the heart, or nowhere' (116).

So the Chinoy family struggles on to care for Nariman and as the monthly budget becomes more and more strained, Roxana's men, each in his own way, attempts to supplement the dwindling pile of currency notes in the envelopes she has so painstakingly marked, butter, eggs, etc. and through which she tries desperately to juggle her monthly budget. Her elder son Murad in an honest, straightforward manner, takes to walking home from school and slips the saved bus fare into his mother's envelopes. Yezad and Jehangir are more adventurous and go in for bigger money. Yezad with the help of Villie, the Matka Queen, places at first small and later big bets on the daily lottery. Jehangir as the Homework Monitor works out deals with rich and not so clever boys in his class, whose unsatisfactory or even non-existent homework he marks as acceptable, in return for a monetary consideration. So Roxana's little envelopes mysteriously become plump again. But since they live in a moral universe, nemesis has to catch up with all of them, even though their misdemeanours were for a deserving cause. Of course as in all moral universes, it is more often than not, the good and the just who have to suffer and not the major offenders. This was so in *Such a Long Journey* and *A Fine Balance* too. This is the ancient paradox that had troubled even the Biblical Job, who like Mistry's characters had received no answers from High, to his impassioned pleas and complaints.

Yezad's little flutters on the Matka scene with the help of Villie makes possible the introduction into the text of hundreds of ageing Parsi single women like Villie, who eke out their lives looking after ageing parents and at times spice them with harmless little flirtations with men and gambling risks. Here at least Mistry has shown much more understanding and compassion towards such left-behind-on the shelf women, than he had done in his earlier texts -- for instance Miss Kutpitia in *Such A Long Journey*.

As for Nariman, in spite of the hardships of cheek-by-jowl existence in the tiny flat and his son-in-law's at times justified grumpiness, life is better than it was in his spacious flat where he had to contend with Coomy's sourness and Jal's helplessness. Here he had his grandsons' company and when he talked in his sleep, Roxana and Yezad rushed out of their bedroom to stand by and watch till he settled back into sleep.

The talking in his sleep is part of a flashback episode again. This time the jigsaw piece that falls into place is the one in which Lucy becomes a domestic servant at the home of the Arjani family who occupy the ground floor flat of the building in which Nariman lives. They employ Lucy to look after their grandchildren. Lucy takes on the job to be nearer Nariman, who no longer met her on the pavement after the bath towel episode. For the Arjanis this was 'an act of vengeance. Years earlier, around the time he had met Lucy, Mr. Arjani had been sued by Nariman's father for libel, and this was the reprisal, it became clear now' (125). At that time, Nariman's father had taken a stand through letters to newspapers on the issue of a Zoroastrian priest who was performing *Navjote* (investiture into the Zoroastrian religion) of the children of Parsi women and non-Parsi men -- the other way round already being legal. The elder Vakeel belonged to the Orthodox faction within the Parsi community, who frowned upon such moves. Mr. Arjani, his downstairs neighbour, who had no reason to like him, decided to join battle with Mr. Vakil and dashed off his own letters to the Parsi newspapers, supporting the Reformist agenda, that approved of such marriages and the acceptance of children of such marriages into the Zoroastrian fold. This incensed Mr. Vakeel and his letters became more vitriolic than ever and in them he called Mr. Arjani 'a prime example of the substandard mind whose cogitations were clearly worthless, unable to grasp the simplest tenets of the religion and the supreme significance of the Navjote' (127). Mr. Arjani in turn had sued him for libel. He had lost the case due to a technicality in the libel laws and years later had had an opportunity to wreak vengeance on the son through Lucy. So Lucy became a household drudge for the Arjanis. Nariman's conscience was once again aroused as he watched Lucy bent under the burden of school bags taking the Arjani grandchildren to school. He began helping her carry these bags. This naturally upset Yasmin and she threatened to take Roxana, the daughter they had had together, and leave him if he did not stop being 'the ayah's assistant' (129).

As the text weaves in and out of times past and present, it also pauses for a while to take in concerns dear to Mistry's heart and after this flash back it is the turn of immigration to be discussed. The agents for this discussion are Yezad and his sons. Yezad's life in Bombay like that of millions of other Bombayites/Mumbaikars is full of the stress and strain of a daily commute to work on overcrowded trains and the far from adequate salaries and insalubrious working conditions. Given this context it is not difficult to see why he should yearn for the dream of immigrating to Canada, even though he had been turned down by the immigration authorities many years ago. Ironically the man who had interviewed Yezad and Roxana and had turned them down, had been an ethnic Indian, in a crumpled kurta -- an act of reverse snobbishness? He had been extremely rude to them and at the end of the interview Yezad had let him have it back with, 'You sir, are a rude and ignorant man, a disgrace to your office and country. You have sat here abusing us, abusing Indians, and India, one of the many countries your government drains of its brainpower, the brainpower that is responsible for your growth and prosperity. Instead of having the grace to thank us, you spew your prejudices and your bigoted ideas. You, whose people suffered racism and xenophobia in Canada, where they were Canadian citizens, put in camps like prisoners of war -- you sir, might be expected, more than anyone else, to understand the more enlightened Canadian ideals of multiculturalism. But if you are anything to go by, then Canada is a gigantic hoax' (245). This is the first instance of anti-Canadian discourse in Mistry after the early critiquing of Canadian multiculturalism in 'Lead Kindly Light' and 'Swimming Lessons' in *Tales from Firozsha Baag*. However, it is not clear why it is a xenophobic second-generation Indian immigrant who is indicted, rather than a white Canadian. It can safely be presumed that there are many more of the latter variety than of the former. Is Mistry hedging his bets here?

If Canada is critiqued here, even if indirectly, Bombay in spite of all its shortcomings is clearly celebrated in this text. Her multiculturalism, notwithstanding the post-Babri Masjid riots is lauded by Yezad's boss Vikram Kapur, 'Bombay endures because it gives and it receives. Within this warp and weft is woven the special texture of its social fabric, the spirit of tolerance, acceptance generosity. Anywhere else in the world, in those so-called civilized places like England and America, such terrible conditions would lead to revolution' (152). Could it be that Mistry is here tongue-in-cheek poking fun at Salman Rushdie's eulogizing of the fabled tolerance of the city in his *The Moor's Last Sigh*, through Mr. Kapur's almost poetic praise of the city? What does one make of 'This beautiful city of seven islands, this jewel by the Arabian sea, this reclaimed and, this ocean gift transformed into ground beneath our feet, this enigma of cosmopolitanism where races and religions live side by side and cheek by jowl in peace and harmony...' (154). The sly insertion of 'the ground beneath our feet' only lends further substance to the suspicion that Mistry is needling Rushdie here. In fact, Mistry seems to be settling many other scores in this text. There is a not so veiled reference to Germaine Greer's attack on *A Fine Balance*, later in this text. A writer of course is free to be as self-reflexive as he chooses. But the point that comes to mind is that in the midst of the dignified tragedy of Nariman Vakil and the injury it does to the lives of his beloved daughter Roxana and his grandsons, does such trivial score-settling have any place? It is however, only Mistry who can provide an answer to such a question.

As noted earlier, Mistry is in many ways bearing witness to the last grand stand of the Parsi Zoroastrians in India. He had noted their rites and rituals and their eccentricities in his earlier texts, in this one he extends this to writing about the old myths and legends of ancient Iran. Using the device of oral narrature, Nariman Vakeel becomes the story-teller in this book and the audience who listen to his tales about ancient Iran are his young grandsons. With them the reader shares the story of the evil king Zuhak and the two serpents that grew out of his shoulders and needed to be fed the brains of two young men everyday.

This naturally meant that two men had to sacrificed to Zuhak's unnatural appetites every day. Finally this depredation is put to an end by the brave Faridoon who in a terrible fight defeats Zuhak but is unable to kill him, so chains him and buries him deep within a mountain. Thus evil is overcome by good. This myth reinforces the basic Zoroastrian tenets of the eternal battle between good and evil that rages within the soul of all men. Interwoven into this myth is the role of nature in the salvation of human souls. The evil Zuhak deep within the bowels of the mountain sucks on his chains all night and weakens them to the extent that he would be able to break them apart and thus let loose terror on the world again. But the cock who crows every morning to herald the dawn, also signals the end of Zuhak's aspirations and the chains grow strong again at the behest of the good angel Sarosh, who sends his messenger the spider to weave them whole again. Thus the bond between man and nature is renewed each day. This is archetypal myth-making and Mistry appears to be making the point that it is important for human beings to remember their origins through such devices.

Through these story-telling sessions, the bonding between Nariman and his grandsons, especially the younger Jehangir, becomes stronger and this irks Yezad who feels his sons are moving away from him. In the meantime Dr. Tarapore decrees that the ankle would take some more weeks to heal. As for Coomy, she has been busy creating a situation in which it would be impossible for Roxana and Yezad to insist that she keep to her side of the bargain and take her step-father back after the stipulated three weeks. In an extreme move she deliberately gets her brother to break open the plaster of the ceiling in Nariman's bedroom and so that it would not look suspicious, they also damage other rooms in the flat. She attributes the damage to water seepage from the overhead tanks on the terrace and in a cunning move engages her neighbour, Edul Munshi, a rather inapt craftsman to repair the flat. She does this secure in the knowledge that Edul would take an inordinately long time to do the work and this would give Nariman's ankle time to be fully healed before he would return to them. At one level this might appear an over the top kind of solution to the problem, especially as Nariman had turned his flat over to his step-children and they were damaging their own property, but if viewed in the context of Coomy's earlier behaviour, it would fall into place and only reveal the desperation with which she wanted to avoid becoming her step-father's nurse again.

So now Coomy refuses to take her father back until the flat is in perfect shape again and she also turns down Roxana's appeal to let her have a part of her father's savings to help balance their monthly budget. The bitter quarrel with Roxana and Yezad over this finally strains Jal's patience and he accuses his sister of not caring for the family and 'nursing your bitterness instead of nursing Pappa' (186). Coomy weeps at this but does not change her stand.

As for the sub-plots, Yezad's life at the sports-goods store and his coffee shop friends, gives Mistry the opportunity to berate the religious fundamentalists and indulge in secular-speak. However, this does tend to drag a bit and gets a bit tedious. What does provide a bit of spice to the tea shop gossip is the manner in which Mistry uses the opportunity to get back at Germaine Greer who had publicly said that she hated *A Fine Balance* for its portrayal of 'a dismal, dreary city', a city that did not match with the one she had found on a teaching assignment on which she had spent four months in Mumbai (quoted in 'A Flavour of India', June 1, 2002, smh.com.au). Greer is firmly put in her place by Yezad's friend Vilas who says that 'A while back, I read a novel about the Emergency. A big book, full of horrors, real as life. But also full of life, and the laughter and dignity of ordinary people. One hundred per cent honest – made me laugh and cry as I read it. But some reviewers said no, no, things were not that bad. Especially foreign critics. You know how they come here for two weeks and become experts. One poor woman whose name I can't remember made such a hash of it, she had to be a bit pagal, defending Indira, defending the Sanjay sterilisation scheme, defending the entire Emergency -- you felt sorry for her even though she was a big professor at some big university in England. What to do? People are afraid to accept the truth' (202–203). Mistry's defence of his book could have been undertaken in another forum I feel. Getting a character in your own book, to praise an earlier book you have written does leave a certain distaste in the mouth. Also, this way Mistry exposes himself to attacks from detractors who might find his own distance, in time and space, from the city and people he writes about as disenabling as he does the brief acquaintance of Greer with Bombay.

Mistry's own problems with a time-warp, common to most diasporic writers, and occasional lapse into nostalgia, surfaces in the chapters dealing with Jehangir's school -- St. Xavier's – not coincidentally also Mistry's own alma mater. Here there is plenty of scope to remember old school-teachers, pretty and female, as well as those who were male and priests. One wonders what the real-life Miss Alvarez, Jehangir's teacher, of the short skirts and shapely legs, now grown old, has made of Mistry's indirect accolades -- it would be as interesting to know, if not more than what Ms. Greer's reaction to Mistry's sniping is going to be.

Yet more images and memories and Mistry's old concerns with naming, already detailed vis-à-vis *Such a Long Journey*, appear here too in the form of Yezad's boss, Mr. Kapur's concern with the renaming of streets and buildings in Bombay and his collection of prints of colonial Bombay, 'From three pictures, so many memories. And this can happen with every single photo -- each one conceals volumes. All you need is the right pair of eyes…to unlock the magic' (221). The uncharitably disposed might attribute this interest in memory and imaging to Mistry's having come across such sepia-tinted prints while on one of his infrequent visits to the city. The latest of which was occasioned due to Mistry's *A Fine Balance* being chosen as the Book of the Month, by the Talk-Show Queen Oprah and for which he had accompanied her camera crew to Mumbai for the collection of images, to evoke the right atmosphere for her audience, who were unlikely to be familiar with the sights and sounds of Bombay.

Mr. Kapur's nostalgic praise of Bombay, is offset by Yezad's own memories, or rather his inherited ones, regarding the Bombay Docks explosion in 1944. This particular story is re-told to his sons in the context of the clock at home, which only Yezad winds. It is a special clock that was presented to his father and bore the legend 'In gratitude for an exemplary display of courage and honesty in the course of duty' (224). So Yezad now becomes the story-teller and tells his sons how their grandfather, who had been a cashier in a bank had safeguarded the bank's money in the midst of the chaos and destruction that had overtaken the city when a ship in the docks had exploded. This incidentally is a common memory shared by most Parsis of Mistry's age, through stories told by their fathers, who had in some way been associated with this explosion, which till the 12th of March 1993, when serial bombs exploded in the city, was the biggest explosion story in the city. As noted earlier in this chapter, it is intriguing how Mistry but for one reference in the context of the game of matka, almost completely elides this later bombing and replaces it with a much older incident. Is it because Mistry was wary of negotiating the involvement of the Bombay underworld and Islamic fundamentalism in this incident that shook the city? However, secular discourse cannot be one-sided and when you so strongly indict Hindu fundamentalism, in the shape of the Shiv Sena, you cannot in all fairness, ignore the other side. It is such writing that provides support to the anti-secular rhetoric of the Hindutva lobby, which accuses secularists of turning a blind eye to the antics of Islamic fundamentalists while attacking militant

Hinduism. Mistry needs to work this out in his subsequent writing if he wants to be taken as a serious political commentator on Indian affairs in his books. Maybe such a lopsided discourse is the result of the diasporic condition which as Nariman says, 'leaves a hole that never fills' (246). A hole that lets you fit in only some of the pieces in the jig saw puzzle that is Bombay.

Nariman's flashbacks are a relief from these aspects of the text. The next leap back in time concerns the time Nariman had taken Lucy home when his parents were out and had been observed by his neighbour Mr. Arjani. In passages of erotic prose rather rare for Mistry, we have Nariman undressing Lucy and even ignoring the doorbell while he worshipped her with his eyes and tongue. When he does open the door it is to find his parents and their friends having returned suddenly as his mother's blood pressure had dropped. Seeing Lucy there his father had been incensed, 'This son of mine has turned my house into a *raanwada*, bringing his whore here! It's the kind of immorality that is destroying the Parsi community' (259). To which Nariman had retorted: 'When you call the woman I love a whore, and our home a *raanwada* because I invite her here, you disgrace the role of father. And I despair for you' (259). Nariman's agitation over this memory, decades after the event, arouses concern in his younger grandson, who seeing his discomfort as he mumbles in his sleep, soothes him into slumber again. This tender scene is observed by Roxana who thinks of her son, 'What a beautiful boy...' (260).

The next flashback however portends the tragedy that is to ultimately blight Nariman's life and that of his step-children forever. Lucy who had been working as an ayah for the Arjani's grandchildren, was slowly losing her mental balance and had taken to going to the building's terrace and climbing down on to the outside ledge and threatening to jump. This meant that Nariman had to go up and coax her to return to safety much to the annoyance of his wife Yasmin.

As Nariman's discomforting memories make strong come-backs, his rational, till then almost agnostic son-in-law is increasingly drawn to religion as a mode of comfort from the hopelessness of his domestic and professional situation. He takes to slipping into the neighbouring *agiary*, the fire temple, on his way home from work. Mistry seizes the chance then to expound once again on the structure of an *agiary* – once more acting as a 'witness'. Nariman's ghosts in the meantime haunt him to a distraction, until finally he is forced to play out the final dreadful scene again, in which Yasmin had followed him to the terrace and had confronted the disturbed Lucy and before Nariman could save either, had plunged together with her rival to her death. Their final scream is echoed by Nariman who wakes up with a start and also startles young Jehangir.

In the wider, waking world too things begin to come to a head, as Yezad's source of extra income, the matka winnings, dry up thanks to the crackdown on the matka operators, 'rumour was that since those terrorist bombs had blown up the stock exchange and shattered Bombay, they had to do something about Matka. Even the crookedest politician didn't want Bombay to be the next Beirut' (263). This as mentioned earlier is the only reference, made in passing, to the cataclysmic bombs that had rent the socio-economic fabric of Bombay in 1993. What is elaborated upon is the cultural policing of the Shiv Sena and how thanks to Yezad's having lied about them demanding money from Mr. Kapur and then planning to use it for his own cash-strapped family, the whole thing blows up in his face. The real Shiv Sena goons do finally turn up and Mr. Kapur thinks they are there to demand money again – flares up in a fit of anger and dies. His death coincides with that of Coomy, who in a poetically just manner perishes along with her not so handy handyman, Edul, under the falling plaster in her step-father's room. Mistry now as in his other books, describes the Zoroastrian funeral rites, the towers of silence, where in the ancient Iranian tradition, the bodies of dead Parsis are exposed to the elements to be devoured by vultures and other birds of prey.

As for the shop, with Mr. Kapur, the idealistic worshipper of Bombay: 'Bombay is like a religion...Bombay makes room for everybody. Migrants, businessmen, perverts, politicians.... the city welcomes them and turns them into Bombayites...' (351), dead, his pragmatic widow shuts it down and dispenses with the service of Yezad. Now suddenly unemployed, religion becomes a full-time solace and he retreats into it to lick his wounds. However, instead of turning him into a stronger and better person, this *agiary*-going turns him into a bigot, the sort of man he used to despise.

Deprived of his regular income and with the matka earnings a thing of the past too, the Chinoy family and their unwelcome lodger, Nariman, would have been reduced to real poverty, if it had not been for Jal's idea that with Coomy gone, they should sell the Chinoy's flat and all move in together into Nariman's much larger flat. The Chinoy flat, although small, was very centrally located and would in Bombay's surreal estate world fetch a handsome price. So they would even after using the money from the sales to get the larger flat professionally repaired, still have enough left over to live on. And this is what happens. Old Doctor Fitter and the Parsi police inspector Mavawala, who had those many decades ago hushed up the twin deaths of Lucy and Yasmin, now help Jal and Yezad with the twin demise of Coomy and Edul. When Yezad goes over later to thank them for their help, he finds them discussing the issues that are currently obsessing both the Reformist and Orthodox sections of the dying Parsi community – the dwindling vulture population, as well as the low birth rate and the concurrent high death rate. 'The orthodox and reform argument? That's only one part of it. The more crucial point is our dwindling birth rate, our men and women marrying non-Parsis, and the heavy migration to the West. Vultures and crematoriums, both will be redundant...if there are no Parsis to feed them' (400).

So, the Chinoys moved in with Jal Contractor, in the flat that Nariman Vakeel had made over to his step-children. The new name plate on the door said it all, 'Mr. and Mrs. Yezad Chinoy, Mr. Jal Contractor, Mr. Nariman Vakeel' (441). The idea of the arranging the names, according to alphabetical order, had been that of Jal. The Chinoy's furniture is moved over in a truck to the old/new flat, Nariman still immobile is transported in an ambulance, like at the time he had first arrived there and the Chinoys themselves follow in a taxi and as it 'began to move, and Jehangir turned for one last look. Then a moth floated lazily out of the darkened interior of the stairwell. He watched it fly straight toward's the bird's open beak' (445).

This dark omen does not bode well for the family and the reader's apprehensions are unfortunately fulfilled as Mistry does not let his unhappy family finally bask in the comfort of a large flat and sufficient money. Instead in the epilogue appended to the novel, he describes their continuing unhappiness five years hence. The epilogue is entirely through the eyes of young Jehangir and in his own words too. It begins with 'Daddy and Murad had another fight today. They quarrel almost every day now' (449). Yezad's agiary-going has turned him into a full blown bigot who hates his son's association with non-Parsi girls with the same fervour once displayed by Nariman's father. So history repeats itself here but as Marx had said with reference to Hegel's stagement, 'History repeats itself twice once as tragedy and once as farce' (Marx, *Louis Bonaparte*). Nariman's tragic history is now being reiterated here in an almost farcical manner. What is of import however is whether this is intentional irony or else only one that strikes the discerning reader and not the writer.

So, the novel moves towards its end with the once rational Yezad turned into a almost comic raving despot. We are told that in the bedroom he shares with Roxana, the bookshelves are filled with 'volumes of Parsi history and Zoroastrianism.... Some of them belonged to Grandpa's father. His name is inscribed in them on bookplates: Marazban Vakeel' (451). His son Murad laughs at his excessive orthodoxy. What is not clear is does Mistry prescribe to Murad's belief that reading of religious texts leads to bigotry? For in the long list of Parsi scholars whose books line Yezad's shelves are erudite men, both Parsi and European, 'Zaehner, Spiegel, Darudhanawala, Dabu, Boyce, Dhalla, Hinnells and Karaka' (451) who can hardly be called bigots. Knowledge of any religion can enable and expand as much as it can disable and reduce.

The only saving grace of the epilogue is Jehangir's description of his grandfather's death, a year after his return to Chateau Felicity. No longer handicapped by lack of funds, the Chinoys had employed professional help to look after Nariman. But starved of the tender, personalised attention of his daughter he had developed bed-sores and died in considerable pain from them though he 'didn't make a sound despite the agony he was going through' (457). His death though had been beautified and dignified by the fulfillment of the promise made to him by his daughter's old neighbour, the violinist Daisy Icchaporia -- that she would come and play for him on his deathbed. When Jehangir, in spite of his parents' reservation, goes to fetch her she comes immediately. 'Daisy Aunty played for over an hour, till Dr. Tarapore arrived, as he had promised that morning. She ended with Grandpa's favourite song, "One Day When We were Young". When she finished she stood quietly for a moment, bowed again, then put away her violin' (462).

These beautifully quiet moments, filled with emotion and feeling are the forte of this book and make it worth reading, in spite of the shrillness, anger and spite that at times spills out of the pages. It appears that this is where Mistry is strongest and seems to have found a genuine mature voice. At the risk of inviting a snub of the kind that has flattened Ms. Greer in this text, one is tempted to tell Mistry to leave the settling of scores either with critics or the Shiv Sena alone and focus on what he is best at – family matters.

7

Conclusion:
Transcending the Self and the Other

The literary journey which began in 1983 with the winning of the Hart House Prize for the short story 'One Sunday', has progressed steadily through the collection of short stories, *Tales from Ferozsha Baag*, past the first novel *Such a Long Journey*, taking in the hugely successful *A Fine Balance*, to the latest *Family Matters*, which came out in 2002.

What has Mistry achieved in this journey of almost twenty years? Has there been a progression? Have the texts evolved conceptually as well as from the literary point of view? Has Mistry been able to transcend the narrow boundaries of the self and mere resistance against the other? Have his later texts moved into larger realms? Answers to these questions might be found if one were to look at these books collectively.

The short stories collection was an act of remembering, going back to the past left behind in order to understand the present and maybe through it grapple with an unknown future in a new land. This is the usual procedure of most diasporic writers. Yet it was not pure nostalgia that had fuelled the stories. The mature writer of *Family Matters* could be discerned even then in many of these stories. If there was scatological humour and broad farcical comedy in stories such as 'Auspicious Occasion' there was also deep compassion and caring. If conceptually the stories lacked weight, from the formal angle they were already experimenting with literary modes like the use of narrators -- Nariman Hansotia in 'Squatter' and Jacqueline/Jaakaylee in 'The Ghost from Firozsha Baag' -- and self-reflexiveness in 'Swimming Lessons'. Moreover, even as diasporic writing if the stories displayed the usual time-warp they also displayed the political awareness that became more pronounced in the novels to come. This was evident in 'Auspicious Occasion', where the coming to power of right-wing political parties and the apprehension this created in the minds of the minorities was in focus. Although these stories are ethnocentric and detail all the Parsiana, from fire-temples to towers of silence, they are not uncritical of the distancing of Parsis from postcolonial India and their hankering after the bygone status of a colonial elite. This comes through in almost all the stories, but more so in 'The Ghost of Firozsha Baag', where the catholic ayah Jacqueline, whose name is consistently mispronounced by her Parsi employers as Jaakaylee, complains that the Parsis 'thought they were like British only, ruling India side by side' (46). Jacqueline also notes the colour prejudice of the Parsis, 'Parsis like light skin, and when Parsi baby is born that is the first and most important thing. If it is fair they say, O how nice light skin just like parents. But if it is dark skin they say, *arre* what is this *ayah no chhokro*, ayah's child' (46). The Parsi nostalgia for the Raj is also found in 'Of White Hairs and Cricket'. Here the colonial game of cricket, which has become a postcolonial Indian passion, has been used as a motif for Parsi honour and vaour in an act of colonial conditioning. What has also come through in these stories, especially in 'Squatter', 'Lend Me Your Light' and 'Swimming Lessons' -- is the pathos and loneliness of ageing Parsis, whose children are in a Western diaspora. As for the Parsis in the West, they have to deal with being considered in the same league as other migrants from the Asian subcontinent, loneliness and alienation from their surroundings. The above mentioned stories also deal with this adverse aspect of migration to the West. Mistry has been very clear-eyed about the cost the migrating Parsis pay when abandoning the postcolonial Indian space, they fly off to the West, to supposedly live out their dreams of once more being an elite community -- dreams which rarely fructify. In fact most of these dreams end in nightmares of rejection and racism as seen in 'Squatter' or become guilt-laden nightmares that haunt in 'Lend me your Light'.

Mistry's first novel, *Such a Long Journey*, expanded not just his canvas, by taking in the wider Indian reality, but was also more carefully conceptualised and this was signaled by one of the epigraphs which he had pre-fixed to the book:

'He assembled the aged priests and put questions to them concerning the kings who had once possessed the world. 'How did they', he inquired, 'hold the world in the beginning, and why is it that it has been left to us in such a sorry state? And how was it that they were able to live free of care during the days of their heroic labours?'

This quotation from Firdausi's *Shah Nama*, the Iranian epic, which told the tale of the ancient Zoroastrian civilization, is of the dialogue the legendary King Jamshed had with Zoroastrian priests at his glittering court at Persepolis. The questions put by the King are a precursor to the ontological orientations of Mistry's book itself. *Such a Long Journey* is not a modernist text that is epistemological but is postmodern and seeks to understand the processes that have gone into the creation of the world -- here not just the Parsi world, but the larger postcolonial India.

This is what made *Such a Long Journey*, a very political book, a book that sought to understand how the Nehruvian dream of a secular India, degenerated into the real politik world of his daughter Indira Gandhi. Mistry has marked the beginning of this change in the last years of Nehru's rule itself -- the years after the defeat in the Indo-China war of 1962: "But everyone knew that the war with China froze Jawaharlal Nehru's heart, then broke it...Panditji...the unflinching humanist, the great visionary, turned bitter and rancourous...his appetite for philosophy and dreams lost for ever, he resigned himself to political intrigues and internal squabbles..." (11). This trend intensified under his daughter and in the novel sets off the chain of events that lead to the death of the factional character Major Jimmy Billimoria and puts in danger Gustad Noble, his family and his friend Gustaadji.

This first novel also continued to showcase Mistry's concern with bearing witness to a dying community. However, here along with the Parsiana on show is also the foregrounding of the city of Bombay and its fall from the pinnacles of cosmopolitan tolerance to the depths of regional and religious fascism. This is not surprising given the close connection of the Parsis with Bombay, a city they helped build and evolve to the status of *urbs prima* in India.

The book provides an 'insider-outsider' view of Bombay at a time when it was witnessing the erosion of its famed tolerance and secularism. The city began to change in the late 1960s with the rise of the extreme right-wing political party, the Shiv Sena. Thus began Bombay's engagement with sordid power-politicking, corruption at the highest level and the underworld-politician nexus that has since criminalised public life in the city.

Such a Long Journey also reminds its readers of other ethno-religious minorities such as the Christians who had helped develop Bombay. Such discourse naturally offers resistance to the monolithic view of Bombay propounded by political parties such as the Shiv Sena, which elides the contribution of minorities to the creation of wealth for all in Bombay. Malcolm is Gustad Noble's Christian friend who is a Manglorean Catholic whose antecedents go back 'over nineteen hundred years ago, when Apostle Thomas landed on the

Malabar coast among fishermen' even before the 'Parsis came in the seventh century from Persia' (24). This remembering of the past becomes even more vital in the current political climate that questions the rights of the minorities to live in India and demands that they 'prove' their Indianness. In this sense this novel and subsequent texts written by Mistry offer a potent challenge to the hegemonic discourse of nation initiated by the powerful extreme right.

Through this discourse Mistry has succeeded in transcending the boundaries of the Parsi self and moved into the wider arenas of the nation space. His text here is not just ethnocentric discourse but has become politically charged. This however, does not mean that there is no Parsiana in this book, there is, but the focus has changed. The Parsiana asserts itself through the depiction of the lives of Gustad Noble and his little family.

Even more importantly this novel marks the entry of a deep compassion into Mistry's writing. It is this compassion, honed to a fine art in *Family Matters*, which has ultimately enabled Mistry to rise above the usual postcolonial resistance to the other and surface into the deeper waters of humanism – though not deracinated or shorn of political concern. In *Such a Long Journey*, Gustad's humanism is what provides a wider angle to his love for his family. His humanism embraces not just his politically incorrect friend Dinshawji but also takes in the unlovable, and often incomprehensible, physically and mentally challenged Tehmul. The compassion also extends to the pavement artist who rescues the boundary wall of his building from the foul smells of urinating passerbys by converting it into the Wall of all Religions. It is this compassion which makes him travel all the way to Delhi to meet his friend the Major, even after he had endangered Gustad's family and made the ailing Dinshawji's last days miserable by involving them in the white-washing of illegal money.

Unfortunately, this compassion did not extend to the female characters in this book, who from the middle-aged but still lovely Dilnavaz, to the ailing little Roshan, to the eccentric spinster Miss Kutpitia all emerge as cardboard figures, one dimensional and with no depth. This makes this book very male-oriented and the women become mere recipients of male action. This is of course not just a 'crime' that can be laid only at Mistry's door, but rankles most obtrusively in the otherwise compassionate universe created by him. The soft, cuddly, pretty Dilnawaz and Roshan are as much stereotypes as is the acerbic spinster figure of Miss Kutpitia. In their inaction they also provide perfect foils to the male world. As Millet has sarcastically noted: 'If aggressiveness is the trait of the master class, docility must be the corresponding trait of the subject group'. So in a novel in which the central motif is that of journeying the female characters remain rather static -- they go nowhere and have no role to play on the wider political stage.

However, this lacuna was to a large extent redressed in Mistry's next novel, *A Fine Balance*. In this book, the female character Dina Dalal, is at the centre of the narrative and exhibits considerable agency. Unlike Dilnawaz, Dina journeys in this book from being a pampered daughter, to a stifled sister, to a happy wife, to a dependent widow, to an independent entrepreneur, back to being a dependent in her brother's home. Although Dina's journey might appear to be one which took her nowhere, this is not true. Mistry has recorded her evolution from a dependent female to an independent woman, even though she at the end has to bow down to circumstances and return to her brother's home. This return might be looked upon as a defeat but can also be seen in terms of continuing resistance as Dina clandestinely keeps up her relationship with her former tailors and in an act of subversion feeds the, now reduced to being beggars, men in her brother's best china.

Apart from this transcending of a purely male point of view, *A Fine Balance*, also moves into even wider circles of the

Indian world. If *Such a Long Journey* had expanded the scope of Mistry's Parsi Zoroastrian ethos to the world of Mrs. Indira Gandhi's political games, this book brings in more of the same, as well as the underbelly of metropolitan Indian existence, generally ignored by many postcolonial Indian writers in English. The fact that these characters do not always ring true and in many cases come across as cardboard figures is another story. However, it is one that Mistry will have to redress if he decides to write another book in which he deals with the have-nots of Indian society.

Notwithstanding these literary failings, *A Fine Balance* was a searing critique of India of the 1970s, especially the middle of that decade, which witnessed the nadir, of its postcolonial existence, during the Emergency declared by Mrs. Gandhi. The ebb-point of even this nadir was the declaration of the 20 Point Programme under the guidance of Mrs. Gandhi's younger son, Sanjay. Two of these twenty points impacted directly upon Mistry's underdogs. They were *Garibi Hatao* and *Hum Do Hamare Do*. While the former meant Eradicate Poverty, it often became eradicate the poor and Mistry's tailors found themselves in a beggar's camp, as in an effort to eradicate poverty, the poor, the concrete evidence of the existence of poverty, were airbrushed out of cities like Delhi and Bombay. The latter literally meant 'We Two, Our Two', but while control of India's burgeoning population had to be undertaken, it often resulted in officials, anxious to meet government set targets, sterilising unmarried men who had never had children. The tailors fell prey to this 'point' too. The fact that their sterilisation was prompted by age-old caste enmities is a reflection of the other important strand in this novel -- that of caste.

Caste though a paramount factor in Indian nationalist and postcolonial politics has not been tackled by too many Indian writers in English -- Mulk Raj Anand's *Untouchable* in the 1930s and Arundhati Roy's *God of Small Things* in the 1990s being exceptions. This has however been done by writers in Indian languages, notably the Marxist-Feminist Bengali writer Mahashweta Devi, the bi-lingual dramatist Girish Karnad and on celluloid by Shyam Benegal in films like *Ankur* (1973) and *Manthan* (1976). More obviously, the question of caste based inequalities and exploitation has been the center of Dalit writing by writers such as Daya Pawar and Narayan Surve in Marathi.

Mistry has very bravely taken caste head on in this novel. Unfortunately, his diasporic location in Canada and his pre-immigration Parsi *milieu* in Bombay, had cut him off from greater interaction with the lower castes in India. Hence, his tailors, who belonged to the mochi/chamar caste, do not have the material context that would have value added their existence. For men like Mistry caste-based atrocities were things you read about in newspapers, they did not impinge on your life directly. As a Parsi, who is outside the Hindu fold, contact with even upper caste Hindus would be very restricted given the Parsi isolation from mainstream Indian society and those with the lowest castes would be even fewer. As mentioned earlier in this book, this detracts from the value of this novel. However, the compassion Mistry extends towards his tailors and their other friends who belong to the subaltern sections of Indian society, such as the beggars, is very real. The compassion can be conjured and read as a 'postcolonial trauma' and makes this very centrally a text of import to postcolonial theorising.

Yet another divide Mistry has tried to bridge in this text is that between Hindus and Muslims. The Hindu-Muslim divide is a tragic othering that has been exacerbated by the partitioning of India in 1947. The bitterness left behind by the bloodshed on either side of the borders of the newly created nations of India and Pakistan, had been contained by Nehruvian secularism in the 1950s and early 1960s, but with the rise of Mrs. Gandhi and her unleashing of the beasts of communalism, in an effort to contain political rivals, resurfaced in the communal butcherings of the 1990s, which peaked after the destruction of the Babri Masjid and continues in the first decade of the twenty first century.

A Fine Balance has tried to balance the caste divide with cooperation and friendship between the lower caste Hindus and working class Muslims. However, there is nothing of the ideological in such a configuration and the relationship between the families of Dukhi Mochi and Ashraf Tailor in that sense exists in a universalist/humanist landscape, though in the context of first the independence of India and then the Emergency. The opportunity to comment on the irony inherent in the rampaging Hindu mobs during the independence of India, claiming the lower caste Om and Ishvar, as the self, while othering the Muslims, has not been utilised by Mistry. As noted earlier in the chapter on *A Fine Balance*, although Mistry writes of politics and politicians in his books, he does not have the ideological vision to move beyond the particular event and into the realm of understanding the wider issues that lurk behind them.

Hence, Mistry's "wretched of the earth" suffer but have no recourse to a future that might not include such degradation. The beggars beg, the beggar-master exploits, the politicians intrigue, Dina Dalal suffers, as do Om and Ishvar -- the status quo is thus maintained. To be fair to Mistry this is what often does happen in real life, but the treatment offered to tales of such rampant injustice is one of dogged, stoic acceptance rather than the anger, the sheer rage, one finds flaring through Mahashweta Devi's short story "Draupadi" or in her *Mother of 1084*. Very often the anger of Devi's protagonists do not lead to a reformation of the body politic and society, but it is a first step, as is the stone hurled by the young boy in Benegal's *Ankur*, or the inarticulate but articulated cry of yet another exploited being in Govind Nihlani's film *Aakrosh* (1980). What also needs to be comprehended is that in the case of Devi, given her grassroots work with the subaltern, the rage and anger are felt emotions. The proximity of Devi to the exploited people, an act of choice, gives her the praxiated space -- unavailable to Mistry, the diasporic writer.

With *Family Matters* the reader finds herself back in a vintage Mistry world -- but with a difference. The miniature Parsi world is there all right but is now enriched by the literary prowess and emotional maturity of a writer at the height of his writing talent. Foregrounded here are the problems of not just the ageing of Nariman Vakeel, but those of an ageing community. In that sense we could look at Nariman as a metaphor for a geriatric community on the brink of extinction. The Parsis in India have a zero birth rate today and hence the aged within the community do not have the support system provided by the young and able. Although, the Parsi trust funds do give financial support and run home for the aged, the burden of looking after the old does fall on the shoulders of middle-aged offspring or even nieces and nephews. As they themselves are more often than not single, from a psychological angle they resent looking after their elderly relatives, since the prospect before them is a lonely old age, leavened not even by grudging care-takers. This is the very real human tragedy that faces the Parsis today and it is with great sensitivity and compassion that Mistry has tried to portray this facet of the Parsis. Gone is the scatological humour and broad farcical characters. Used instead is a fine brush and delicate strokes. Also in evidence is a more sympathetic approach towards female characters. Unlike in *Such a Long Journey*, the ageing single women are not seen through the lenses of deviation and mockery. Instead, whether it is the "Matka-Queen" Villie Cardmaster or the aggressive, almost Machiavellian Coomy Contractor, Mistry has sympathy and more to spare for them. Villie's unrequited flirtation with Yezad Chinoy is not caricatured and Coomy's death under the debris of the ceiling in her stepfather's room almost assumes the stature of a tragedy, even though it is she who had deliberately broken the beams in the ceiling to keep Nariman from returning home.

This is yet another tragedy that haunts the Indian Parsi community – its lonely, single women – and although Mistry has not overtly taken cognisance of this subject, he has depicted one such woman in Dina Dalal in *A Fine Balance* and the gallery of similar women in *Family Matters*. However, not all such women are subjects of pity, the talented violinist, Daisy Icchaporia, also single, is talented and proves to be a saviour for Nariman. The beautiful music she plays for him wafts him away from the sordid and humiliating reality of bedpans and dependence, to a world of ethereal beauty.

Icchaporia is a very interesting character as Mistry does not usually portray strong women. His female protagonists generally belong to the category of the soft and pretty like Dilnawaz or Roxana. Dina Dalal as has been noted is strong but even she is ultimately dependent on male relatives. Daisy is talented and financially independent. It is she who has the upper hand therefore, when Jal Contractor is in a rather inarticulate way attracted towards her. As a single woman she did attract unflattering comments within Pleasant Villa, where she had the flat below that of the Chinoy's, but even these comments place her within the category of the 'to be secretly envied', rather than in that of the 'to be pitied'.

Daisy's dream was to be a soloist in the Bombay Symphony Orchestra, towards which end she practiced rigorously on her violin. Gossip had it that she did it in the nude like the famed Paganini. So the residents of her building sometimes called her 'Daisy-ninny...behind her back' (95) but Roxana defended her saying she had 'never seen Daisy in anything less than a robust brassiere and serviceable knickers, of a cut so generous they might as well have been blouse and skirt' (95). Jal however was smitten by her, but was too shy to express his admiration openly. Daisy's 'beauty' shines through brilliantly when having shaken hands with Nariman on the promise for a 'farewell concert', she abandons an important rehearsal with the orchestra to fulfill it, and rushes across the city, with little Jehangir, who had set out to fetch her. What makes her gesture even more gracious is that she dresses in her formal concert regalia, in the words of Jehangir, 'I will never forget what she was wearing: long black skirt, very beautiful, and a black long-sleeved blouse with something in the cloth that made it twinkle like stars. Her shoes were black too. A string of pearls clung to her neck' (460). It was dressed like this that she performed for over an hour, for the dying old man and made his last moments fragrant with grace and beauty as she played the *Serenade* by Schubert and ended with Brahms 'Lullaby'.

Family Matters is also a quintessential Bombay book -- very much diasporic discourse where from the bird's-eye view provided by the twenty-first century and the wide-angle secured by the location in Canada, Mistry has viewed life in Bombay in the 1990s. However, as he had left for Canada in the 1970s, this is a Bombay which is not so much re-created, as actually 'created', from newspaper reports, visits to the city and visiting friends and relatives from Bombay.

The political concerns are also present in the book and surface in the form of conversations Yezad Chinoy has with his friends in the Irani tea shops. Like the *addas* in Calcutta, the Irani tea shops used to be places where not just white-collar workers like Chinoy but also students, artists and intellectuals used to meet to discuss matters ranging from American Imperialism to the latest Hindi film. Such cafes have today and even in the 1990s become a fondly remembered memory, as they have been taken over by international coffee shop chains or become fast-food outlets. Here Mistry's diasporic time warp is in evidence when he places Chinoy's conversations on the Shiv Sena's continuing depradations, among other topics, in an Irani tea-shop.

Shattered dreams of immigration also haunt the pages of *Family Matters*: 'The immigration story used to have two parts: dream and reality. But over the years the dream -- of prosperity, house, car, CD player, computer, clean air, snow, lakes, mountains, abundance – had been renounced, since it was not going to come true' (240). A successful immigrant, though in the wake of the 9/11 catastrophe that struck the New York Trade Centre's twin towers, one angered by overt racism in the USA[1], Mistry has been sympathetic towards those who did not have the 'luck' he did.

Sympathy, compassion and humanity are in fact the keywords to the comprehension of this book. The compassion for the dalits and the other unfortunates first center-staged in *A Fine Balance* has come to ripeness in *Family Matters*, making it till date Mistry's finest novel. A novel in which the human touch, redeems the shortcomings noted in the chapter devoted to it in this text, and makes it a vehicle in which Mistry has indeed transcended both the self and the other. The self being both the persona of the writer and also his Parsi self; the other being the wider world. Here all three have come together in an epiphanic moment that speaks across national, ethnic and gender boundaries, with a voice that cannot be denied.

---

1. 'Long Journey of Humiliation Pains Mistry', *Times of India*, 4 November 2002.

Appendix

Biography: Rohinton Mistry (1952–)

Rohinton Mistry's birth and upbringing in Bombay makes him an eminently suitable writer for witnessing the last bright sparks of the existence of the Parsis in India, as well as for documenting the criminalisation of the city of his birth in the last three decades of the twentieth century. Mistry was born on 3rd July 1952 to Behram Mistry and Freny Jhaveri Mistry. He was the middle son of three and he also has a younger sister. The playwright and short-story writer Cyrus Mistry is his younger brother. His father worked in the field of advertising, while his mother was the home-maker. As Mistry has said in an interview, 'She was happy in that role doing the miracle that all mothers perform of making what was barely enough seem like abundance. We didn't have new clothes and shoes as often as we might have liked but were certainly better off than half the population'[1]

The relative prosperity can be corroborated by the fact that he went to two very good schools in Bombay – first to the Villa Theresa Primary School and then to the St. Xavier's High School. He also did not live in a Parsi Baag – housing estate – in Bombay, but 'had friends who inhabited these places and I had the opportunity to observe a little bit of it'[2]. When Mistry was in the fifth standard he wrote a story about a cricket bat – the

---

1. See interview with Angela Lambert, *The Guardian*, 26 April 2002.
2. See interview with Ali Lakhani.

autobiography of a cricket bat. However, as he has admitted this was as far as his youthful 'literary efforts went'[3].

Both he and the woman he later married, Freny Elavia, graduated from the St. Xavier's College in Bombay. As an Arts degree and especially one in English Literature was thought to be an indulgence for boys in those days as today in India, Mistry enrolled for a more 'worthwhile' course in Mathematics and completed his degree in Science in the year 1974.

By this time he was already involved in the music scene in Bombay, gave performances and was seriously contemplating a career as a folk singer. Freny who did not have the distractions that he did, had graduated a year earlier and decided to emigrate to Canada, where she had relatives. Mistry followed her a year later in 1975 and they got married there in that same year. That was also the year in which, as noted earlier, Polydor released an EP, *Ronnie Mistry*, on which he sang his own compositions and traditional folk songs. When he first joined Freny in Canada his ambition was 'to be famous in the music world there. I wanted to be a star'[4].

In Toronto however the teacher at the music school which he had joined bracketed him with absolute newcomers and this meant the end of his musical dreams. Freny already had a job there as a secretary and then as a school teacher, Mistry too took up a position as a clerk and accountant in the Canadian Imperial Bank of Commerce, where he stayed from 1975 to 1985. He worked his way up from being a clerk to being the supervisor of the customer-service department. The Mistrys lived in Brampton, a suburb of Toronto, for twenty years, where they had in relation to Bombay, a materialistically comfortable existence. A very private and reticent man Mistry

---

3. Interview with Stacey Gibson, *University of Toronto Magazine*, Summer 2002.
4. See interview with Adil Jussawalla, *Midday*, Sept.9th 1988.

and his wife have led a quiet existence in Canada and have no children. This way of life has continued even after his novels had gained international recognition. Visits to Bombay have been few and far in-between and very private again.

In 1978 Mistry and his wife took up evening courses at the University of Toronto, which in the case of Mistry were subsidised by his bank. He studied English Literature and Philosophy and got a second bachelor's degree in 1982. He wrote his first short-story, 'One Sunday' in 1983, when he was over thirty and it won him the Hart House prize that year at the literary contest of the University of Toronto. The decision to enter this story for the Hart House prize was prompted not just by the prospect of the cash prize it carried but also the fact that the winning entry would be bound in leather. Mistry won the Hart award two years running, the second time for 'Lend me your Light', but in an ironic twist, worthy of his own narratives, never got his winning stories bound in leather as the sponsors were facing a financial crunch.

This did not dampen his enthusiasm though and he went on to win more prizes. In 1985, 'Auspicious Occasion' won the contributor's award of *Canadian Fiction*, where it was published. The slew of awards resulted in multiple publishers showing an interest in publishing a collection of Mistry's short stories and in 1987 Penguin Canada published *Tales from Firozsha Baag*, set in a Parsi housing estate in Bombay, which was subsequently brought out in Britain and the USA under the title *Swimming Lessons and other Stories from Firozsha Baag*. This book was short-listed for the Canadian Governor General's Award.

Mistry's first novel appeared in 1991 and won a string of awards again. *Such a Long Journey*, which revolves around a Parsi family in Bombay, was short-listed for the Booker Prize and for the Trillium Award. It also won the Governor General's Award, the Smith Books/Books in Canada First

Novel Award and the Commonwealth Writer's Prize for the Best book.

His second novel, *A Fine Balance*, came out in 1995 and garnered some more awards for Mistry. It was once again short-listed for the Booker Prize and also again won the Governor General's Award and the Giller Prize. It also received the Royal Society of Literature's Winfried Holtby Prize and the 1996 Los Angeles Times Award for fiction. Although it took in a wider reality, it is also as noted earlier basically a Bombay book and re-fashioned from memory. As Mistry has said, 'Writers write best about what they know. In the broad sense, as a processing of everything one hears or witnesses, all fiction is autobiographical – imagination ground through the mill of memory. Its impossible to separate the two ingredients'[5]. He has also gone on record to say that it was his brother Cyrus who made him realise that it is not necessary to write about New York or Paris in order to be a successful writer. 'Bombay is as viable a city for fiction'[6]. Cyrus, the younger sibling, in fact was first off the mark in the literary stakes in the Mistry family and at the age of 22 had won the Sultan Padamsee Prize for his play *Doongaji House*. It was Cyrus who had introduced Mistry to the world of books when they lived together in Bombay and when he was in the full glare of media publicity after having won several awards it was again Cyrus who had lent him a copy of Cyril Connolly's *The Enemies of Promise*, which confirmed Mistry's instincts about staying aloof from the media and concentrating on his writing[7].

Mistry's admiring readers are spread across a variety of age groups and nationalities. His wide ranging appeal could be attributed to the fact that he is interested in human beings – 'I'm interested in what makes a human being, and I don't have

5. Interview with Lambert, *The Guardian*.
6. Interview with Indu Saraiya, *The Independent*.
7. Interview with Adil Jussawalla, *Midday*.

any agenda that I start out with'[8] and all he wants to do is 'tell a darn good story'[9].

In spite of his isolationist nature, Mistry is quite practical when it comes to prizes as they bring in more readers. When *A Fine Balance* was picked by the Talk Show queen Oprah Winfrey as the Book of the Month in 2001, the publishers ordered a huge number of extra copies, most of which were sold out. Yet when asked about this Mistry said that, 'I prefer not to talk about sales. I like to take the high road and talk about writing and literature'[10].

A slow and careful writer Mistry's novels have appeared after a gap of several years. Between *Such a Long Journey* and *A Fine Balance*, there were over four years and the latest in the list, *Family Matters*, has come out only in 2002. Mistry does not acknowledge influences on his writing and has said that when he is writing 'the only judgement he relies on is his own' but 'when its done my wife reads it first and I value her opinion'[11].

In 1996 the Faculty of Arts at Ottawa University awarded Mistry an honorary doctorate and the dream run of awards and honours continues. The immediate response to *Family Matters* has been very positive too. It was short-listed for the Booker prize but once again missed it. Other awards though have been realised – the seventh annual Kiriyama Prize for literature of the Pacific Rim and the South Asia subcontinent. Mistry feels he is 'blessed as I'm able to follow this line of work. I didn't grow up with the burning ambition to be a writer -- I never thought of it as a possibility. It seemed such a huge thing, it never occurred to me that I could aspire to it'[12].

8. Interview with Stacey Gibson.
9. Ibid.
10. From story on http://www.smh.com.au/articles/2002/05/31/1022569827526.html.
11. Interview with Angela Lambert.
12. Ibid.

So far, except for a couple of stories in the *Tales from Firozsha Baag* collection, Mistry has set his books in India – mainly in Bombay. He is not averse though to writing about Canada and has said that 'If a story comes to me with a Canadian setting, I will do it...I am quite open to it, in fact I would welcome it, it would be a new challenge and that ultimately is what makes me write'[13].

---

13. Interview with Dirk Bennett, on www.artsworld.com.

Bibliography

Primary Sources

The Works of Rohinton Mistry

Family Matters, Faber and Faber: London, 2002.

A Fine Balance, McCelland & Stewart Inc.: Toronto, 1995, The First International Vintage Edition: New York, 1996.

Such a Long Journey, Faber and Faber: London, 1991, Rupa & Co.: New Delhi, 1991.

Tales from Firozsha Baag, Faber and Faber: London, 1987, Rupa & Co.: New Delhi, 1993.

Interviews with Rohinton Mistry

Bennett, Dirk. 'Speaking Out', www.artsworld.com/books-film/news/rohinton-mistry.

Gibson, Stacey. 'Such a Long Journey', *University of Toronto Magazine*, Summer 2002.

Gokhale, Veena. 'How Memory Lives and Dies', *The Sunday Review, The Times of India*, October 27, 1996.

Hancock, Geoff. 'An Interview with Rohinton Mistry', *Canadian Fiction Magazine* No. 65, 1989.

Janet, Chimonyo. 'A Flavour of India', www.smh.com.au, June 1 2002.

Jussawalla, Adil. 'Writers Aren't Self-Centred', *Midday*, September 9, 1988.

Lakhani, Ali. 'The Long Journey of Rohinton Mistry', Interview at the Vancouver International Writers' Festival, publication details not available.

Lambert, Angela. 'Touched with Fire', *The Guardian*, April 26, 2002.

McLay, Robert. 'Rohinton Mistry Talks to Robert McLay', *Wasafiri*, No. 23, Spring 1996.

Saraiya, Indu. 'Luck Played a Great Part', *The Independent*, August 4, 1991.

Secondary Sources

Benjamin, Walter. *Charles Baudelaire: A Lyric Poet in the Era of High Capitalism*, Verso, London, 1992.

Bhabha, Homi K. 'Freedom's Basis in the Indeterminate', *The Identity in Question*, Ed. John Rajchman, Routledge, London, 1995.

--- *The Location of Culture*, Routledge, London, 1994.

--- Ed. *Nation and Narration*, Routledge, London, 1990.

--- 'On the Irremovable Strangeness of Being Different', *PMLA* 113, 1, January 1998.

--- 'The Vernacular Cosmopolitan', *Voices of the Crossing: The Impact of Britain on Writers from Asia, the Caribbean and Africa*, Eds. D. Ferdinand & Naseem Khan, Serpent's Tail, London, 2000.

Bharucha, Nilufer E. 'Articulating Silences?: Rohinton Mistry's *A Fine Balance*', *Critical Practice*, Delhi, Vol.V, No.1, January 1998.

--- 'The Charting of Cultural Territory: Second Generation Postcolonial Indian English Fiction', *The Postmodern Indian Novel in English*, Ed. Viney Kirpal, Allied Publishers, Bombay, 1996.

--- 'From Behind a Fine Veil: A Feminist Reading of Three Parsi Novels', *Margins of Erasure: Purdah in the Subcontinental Novel in English*, Eds. Jasbir Jain & Amina Amin, Sterling Publishers Private Limited, Delhi, 1995.

--- 'Imagining the Parsi Diaspora: Narratives on the Wings of Fire', *Shifting Continents/Colliding Cultures: Diaspora Writing of the Indian Subcontinent*, Eds. Ralph J. Crane & Radhika Mohanram, Rodopi, Amsterdam, 2000.

―― 'Inhabiting Enclosures and Creating Spaces: The Worlds of Women in Indian Literature in English', *ARIEL: A Review of International English Literature*, 29.1, January 1998.

―― 'Mixed Marriage, Mixed Bag – A Review of *Mixed Marriage and other Parsi Stories* by Mehr Pestonji', *Parsiana*, Mumbai, August 2000.

―― 'The Parsi Voice in Recent Indian English Fiction: An Assertion of Ethnic Identity', *Indian English Fiction 1980-1990: An Assessment*, Eds. Nilufer E. Bharucha & Vilas Sarang, B.R. Publishers, Delhi, 1994.

―― 'The Parsi Voice in Western Indian Literature and Journalism: 1820-1920', *The Parsi Contribution to Western India: The First Hundred Years*, Ed. Nawaz Mody, Allied Publishers, Delhi, 1999.

―― 'Reflections in Broken Mirrors: The Diverse Diasporas in Parsi Fiction', *Wasafiri*, London, 1995.

―― 'Resisting Colonial and Postcolonial Hegemonies: Bapsi Sidhwa's Ethno-Religious Discourse', *The Diasporic Imagination: Asian-American Writing*, Vol. 2, Ed. Somdatta Mandal, Prestige Books, Delhi, 2000.

―― 'Retreating into Tribal Mansions: Race and Religion in Plays written by Parsi Zoroastrians in India', *Contemporary Drama in English*, Vol. 6, Frankfurt, 1999.

―― 'Review of Boman Desai's *Asylum, USA*', *Parsiana*, Mumbai, November, 2001.

―― 'Review of Keki N. Daruwala's *Night River*: Poems', *Parsiana*, Mumbai, February 2002.

―― 'South Asian Novelists in Canada: Narratives of Dislocations and Relocations', *Literary Criterion*, Vol.XXXII, No.1 & 2, 1997.

―― 'When Old Tracks are Lost: Rohinton Mistry's Fiction as Diasporic Discourse', *Journal of Commonwealth Literature*, Vol.XXX, No. 2, 1995.

―― 'Why all this Parsiness?: An Assertion of Ethno-Religious Identity in Recent Novels Written by Parsis', in *Mapping Cultural Spaces: Postcolonial Indian English Writing*, Ed. Nilufer E. Bharucha & Vrinda Nabar, Vision Books, Delhi, 1998.

Bharucha, Nilufer E. & Sridhar Rajeswaran. 'A Critique of Postcolonial Reason: Gayatri Spivak's History of the Vanishing

Present', *Atlantic Literary Review*, Vol.2, No.3 (July-September 2001), Delhi.

Blumer, M. 'Race and Ethnicity', *Key Variables in Sociological Interventions*, Ed. R.G. Burgess, Routledge, London, 1986.

Bourne, Jenny. 'Homelands of the Mind: Jewish Feminism and Identity Politics', *Race and Class*, XXIX, 1, 1987.

Boyce, Mary. *Zoroastrians: Their Religious Beliefs and Practices*, Routledge & Kegan Paul, London, 1979.

Chimonyo, Janet. *Family Matters*, www.smh.com.au, June 6, 2002.

Cohen, Robin. *Global Diasporas: An Introduction*, UCL Press, London, 1997.

Davis, Rocio G. 'Revisioning a Homeland in Michael Ondaatje's *Running in the Family* and Rohinton Mistry's *Tales from Firozsha Baag*', *The Literary Half Yearly*, Vol. 1, No. 37, January 1996.

Derrida, Jacques. *Specters of Marx: The State of the Debt, the Work of Mourning and the New International*, tr. Peggy Kamuf, Routledge, New York, 1994.

Desai, Boman. *Memory of Elephants*, Andre Deutsch, London, 1988.

Dev, Amiya. 'Comparative Literature from Below', *Differential Multilogue: Comparative Literature and National Literature*, Ed. Gurbhagat Singh, Ajanta, Delhi, 1991.

Dhalla, M.N. *Zoroastrian Theology from the Earliest Times to the Present Day*, AMS, New York, 1914, 1972.

Dharan, N.S. 'Ethnic Atrophy Syndrome in Rohinton Mistry's Fiction', *Parsi Fiction*, Eds. Novy Kapadia, J. Dodiya and R.K. Dhawan, Prestige Books, Delhi, 2001.

Dodiya, Jaydipsingh. ed. *The Fiction of Rohinton Mistry*, Prestige Books: Delhi, 1998.

---- 'Literature of the Indian Diaspora in Canada', *The Fiction of Rohinton Mistry*, Ed. J. Dodiya, Prestige, Delhi, 1998.

Duignan, Kate. *Family Matters*, www.stuff.co.nz/stuff, 27 June 2002.

Enthoven, R.E. *Tribes and Castes of Bombay*, Government Central Press, Bombay, Vol.3, 1922.

Fanon, Frantz. *Black Skin, White Masks*, 1952, tr. Charles Lam Markmann, Pluto, London, 1986.

— *The Wretched of the Earth*, Intro. Jean Paul Sartre, 1961, tr. Constance Farrington, Grove, 1963.

Gilman, Sander L. 'Ethnicity-Ethnicities-Literature-Literatures', *PMLA* 113, 1, January 1998.

Gilz, Sabine I. 'How Ethnic Am I?', *PMLA* 113, 1, January 1998.

Godard, Barbara. 'The Discourse of the Other: Canadian Literature and the Discourse of Ethnicity', *Massachusetts Review*, XXXI, Nos. 2&3, Spring and Summer 1990.

Goel, Savita. 'Diasporic Consciousness and Sense of Displacement in the Selected Works of Rohinton Mistry', *Parsi Fiction*, Eds. Novy Kapadia, J. Dodiya & R.K. Dhawan, Prestige Books, Delhi, 2001.

Greene G. and C. Kahn. *Making a Difference: Feminist Literary Criticism*, New York, Methuen, 1985.

Greenlees, Duncan. *The Gospel of Zarthustra*, 1951, The Theosophy Publishing House, Madras, 1978.

Greetz, Clifford. 'The Uses of Diversity', *Michigan Quarterly Review* 25, 1986.

Guha, Ranajit. Ed. *Subaltern Studies 1: Writing on South Asian History and Society*, Oxford University Press, Delhi, 1982.

Hall, Stuart. 'Cultural Identity and Diaspora', *Identity: Community, Culture, Difference*; editor, Jonathan Rutherford, Lawrence and Wishart, London, 1990.

Hariharan, B. 'On the Road: Rohinton Mistry's *Such a Long Journey*', *South Asian Canadiana*, Eds. Jameela Begum and Maya Dutt, Anu Chitra Publications, Madras, 1996.

Hariharan, Githa. *When Dreams Travel*. Picador, London, 1999.

Heble, Ajay. 'A Foreign Presence in the Stall: Towards a Poetics of Cultural Hybridity-Rohinton Mistry's Migration Stories', *Canadian Literature*, Summer 1993.

Heidegger, Martin. 'Building, dwelling, thinking', in *Poetry, Language, Thought*, Harper & Row, New York, 1971.

Hueston, Penny. 'Scheming and Arguing in Claustrophobic Chaos, *Family Matters*', www.theage.comau/cgi-bin.

Huntington, Samuel. *The Clash of Civilizations and the Remaking of the World Order*. Viking, Penguin Books of India, Delhi, 1997.

Huston, Penny. 'Scheming and arguing in claustrophobic chaos', June 24, 2002, www.theage.com.au.

Hutcheon, Linda. 'Crypto-Ethnicity', *PMLA* 113, 1, January 1998.

--- and Marion Richmond. Eds. *Other Solitudes: Canadian Multicultural Fiction*, Oxford University Press, Toronto, 1990.

Isaacs, Harold R. 'The House of Mumbi', *Washington Monthly*, 3 December 1971.

Jaggi, Maya. 'Candidates for Compassion: Review *Family Matters*', www.chico.mweb.co.za/art/2002, June 14, 2002.

Juan, San E. Jr. *Beyond Postcolonial Theory*, Macmillan, London, 1998.

Kamerkar, Mani. 'Parsees in Surat from the Sixteenth to the middle Nineteenth Century: Their Social Economic and Political Dynamics', *Journal of the Asiatic Society of Bombay*, 70, 1995.

Kamerkar, Mani and Soonu Dhujisha. *From the Iranian Plateau to the Shores of Gujarat: The Story of Parsi Settlements and Absorption in India*, Allied Publisher Pvt. Ltd., Mumbai, 2002.

Kapadia, Novy, J. Dodiya and R.K. Dhawan. Eds. *Parsi Fiction*, Vols. 1 & 2, Prestige Books, Delhi, 2001.

Karaka, D.F. *History of the Parsis*, Macmillan, London and Bombay, 1884.

Kristeva, Julia. 'Woman's Time', *The Kristeva Reader*, Ed. Toril Moi, Columbia University Press, New York, 1986.

Kulke, E. *History of the Parsis: A Minority as Agent of Social Change* Vikas, Delhi, 1978.

Lanson, Guy. *A Fine Balance*, *Mcleans*, Canada, 1996.

Leahy, David. 'Running in the Family, Volkswagon Blues and Heorine: Three Post Colonial Post-Modernist Quests?', *Kunappi*, Vol.XIV, No. 3, 1992.

'Long Journey of Humiliation Pains Mistry', *Times of India*, 4 November 2002.

Luhrmann, Tanya. *The Good Parsi: The Fate of a Colonial Elite in a Postcolonial Society*, Oxford University Press, Delhi, 1996.

MacFarlane, Scott. 'The Haunt of Race: Canada's Multiculturalism Act, the Politics of Incorporation and Writing Through Race', *Fuse*, 18, 3, Spring 1995.

Malak, Amin. 'Images of India', *Canadian Literature*, No.119, Winter 1998.

—— 'Insider/Outsider Views on Belonging: The Short Stories of Bharati Mukherjee and Rohinton Mistry, *Short Fiction in the New Literatures in English*, Ed. Josephine Bardolph, Nice, 1989.

Marx, Karl. *On Colonialism*, Progress Publishers, Moscow, 1959.

—— *The Eighteenth Brumaire of Louis Bonaparte*, 1869, Progress Publishers, Moscow, 1934.

Meitei, Mani M. 'Modes of Resistance in Rohinton Mistry's *Such a Long Journey*', *Parsi Fiction*, Eds. Kapadia et al, Prestige Books, Delhi, 2001.

—— 'Rohinton Mistry's *Such a Long Journey* and its Critical Realism', *Fiction of the Nineties*, Eds. Veena Noble Dass & R.K. Dhawan, Prestige Books, New Delhi, 1994.

McGifford, Diane. Introduction, *The Geography of Voice: Canadian Literature of the South Asian Diaspora*, Toronto, Tsar, 1992.

Mishra, Chandra Charu. 'Two Cupboards: Transcultural Discourse', *Rohinton Mistry's Short Fiction, Parsi Fiction*, Eds. N. Kapadia, et al, Prestige Books, Delhi, 2001.

Mishra, Vijay. 'The Diasporic Imaginary: Theorising the Indian Diaspora', *Textual Practice* 10.3, 1996, 421–47.

Millet, Kate. *Sexual Politics*, Doubleday, New York, 1969.

Modi, J.J. *A Few Events in the Early History of the Parsis and Their Dates*, Fort, Bombay, 1905.

—— *The Parsees at the Court of Akbar*, Bombay Education Society Press, Bombay, 1903.

Mukherjee, Arun P. 'Whose Post-Colonialism and Whose Postmodernism?', *World Literature Written in English*, 30.2, 1990.

Mukherjee, Bharati. *Darkness*, Penguin Books India, Delhi, 1985.

—— *The Tiger's Daughter*, Penguin Books India, Delhi, 1972.

—— *Wife*, Penguin Books India, Delhi, 1975.

Murzban, M.M. *The Parsis in India*, enlarged, annotated and illustrated English tr. of Delphine Menant, *Les Parsis*, 2 vols., Bombay, 1917.

Myles, Anita. 'Thematic Concerns in Rohinton Mistry's *Such a Long Journey*', *Recent Indian Fiction*, editor R.S. Pathak, Prestige Books, New Delhi, 1994.

Naipaul, V.S. *An Area of Darkness*, Andre Deutsch, London, 1964.

Nair, Rukmini Bhaya. 'Bombay's Balzac: *A Fine Balance*', *Biblio*, March 1996.

Nandy, Ashis. *Intimate Enemy: Loss and Recovery of Self Under Colonialism*, Oxford University Press, Delhi, 1983.

Ondaatje, Michael. *The English Patient*, Bloomsbury, London, 1992.

— *Running in the Family*, McClelland and Stewart Ltd., Toronto, 1982.

Pal, Sumita. 'In Search of Roots: The Diasporic Dilemma in Rohinton Mistry's *Tales from Firozsha Baag*', *Parsi Fiction*, Eds. Kapadia, et al, Delhi, Prestige Books, 2001.

Parekh, Bhiku. 'Some Reflections on the Hindu Diaspora', *New Community*, 20 (4), 1994.

Parmeswaran, Uma. 'Let Us Sing Their Names: Women Writers in South Asian Canadian Literature', eds. Coomi S. Vevaina and Barbara Godard, *Intersexions: Issues of Race and Gender in Canadian Women's Writing*, Creative Books, Delhi, 1996.

Philip, Nourbese. *Frontiers: Essays on Racism and Culture*, Stratford, Mercury, 1992.

Pratt, Marie Louise. *Imperial Eyes: Travel Writing and Transculturation*, Routledge, London and New York, 1992.

Rajeswaran, Sridhar. 'Colonialism and Culture: Understanding Fanon, Locating Said', *Critical Practice*, Vol. VII, No.1, January 2000.

— 'Historicising the Colonial, the Postcolonial and the Diaspora of India — A Method', *The Diasporic Imagination: Asian-American Writing*, Vol. 3, Ed. Somdatta Mandal, Prestige Books, Delhi, 2000.

Ramachandra, Ragini. 'Rohinton Mistry's *Such a Long Journey*: Some First Impressions', *Literary Criterion*, Vol. XXIX, No. 4, 1994.

Rao, Damodar K. 'Ordinariness of Dreams, Longevity of the Journey: Story, Statement and Allegory in Rohinton Mistry's Such a Long Journey', *Indian Literature Today*, Vol. 1, Ed. R.K. Dhawan, Prestige, New Delhi, 1994.

Rawal, Anantrai. *Gujarati Sahitya*, 3rd Edition, Macmillan, Bombay, 1968.

Rennison, Nick. *Family Matters*, Amazon.com.uk Review.

Rushdie, Salman. *The Ground Beneath Her Feet*, Jonathan Cape, London, 1999.

— *Haroun and the Sea of Stories*, Viking Penguin, London, 1991.

— *Imaginary Homelands*, Granta Books, London, 1992.

— *Midnight's Children*, Jonathan Cape, London, 1991.

— *The Moor's Last Sigh*, Pantheon, New York, 1995.

— *The Satanic Verses*, Viking, London, 1988.

Safran, William. 'Diasporas in Modern Societies: Myths of Homeland and Return', *Diaspora* 1.1, 1991, 83–99.

Said, Edward. *Culture and Imperialism*, Vintage, London, 1994.

— *Orientalism*, Pantheon, New York, 1978.

— 'Permission to Narrate', *London Review of Books*, 16 February 1984.

Schermbrucker, Bill. 'Live from Khodad Building', *Event*, Vol.21 No. 1, Spring 1992.

Seervai, K.N. and K.B. Patel. *Gazetteer of the Bombay Presidency*, J.M.Campbell, Ed., Bombay, 1899, Vol. IX, II.

Shastri, Gopal. *Parsi Ranghoomi*, Gopal Shastri, Baroda, 1995.

Sollers, Werner. *The Invention of Ethnicity*, Oxford University Press, New York, 1989.

Spivak, Gayatri. 'Can the Subaltern Speak?', *Marxism and the Interpretation of Culture*, Macmillan Education, Basingstoke, 1988.

— *A Critique of Postcolonial Reason: Toward A History of the Vanishing Present*, Harvard University Press, Camb. Mass., 1999.

Spurr, David. *The Rhetoric of Empire: Colonial Discourse in Journalism, Travel Writing and Imperial Administration*, Duke University Press, Durham NC & London, 1993.

Tapping, Craig. 'South Asia/N.America: New Dwellings and the Past', *Reworlding: The Literature of the Indian Diaspora*, Ed. Emmanuel S. Nelson, Greenwood Press, New York, 1992.

Taraporewala, Irach J.S. *The Divine Songs of Zarthushtra*, 1951, Hukta Foundation, Bombay 1993.

Thomas, Nicholas. *Colonialism's Culture: Anthropology, Travel and Government*, Polity, London, 1986.

Vassanji, Moyez G. *The Gunny Sack*, Toronto, TSAR, 1989.

— *No New Land*, Toronto, TSAR, 1991.

Williams, David. 'What's in a Name?: Changing Boundaries of Identity in *Such a Long Journey* and *The Puppeteer*', *Postmodernism and Feminism (Canadian Contexts)*, Ed. Shirin Kudchedkar, Pencraft India, Delhi, 1995.

Index

Africanisation programmes, 20
Akbar, 30, 58
Ambedkar, B.R., 152
Anand, Mulk Raj, 203
Arya Samaj, 32
Atwood, M., 114

Bengal Renaissance, 32
Bennett, Dirk, 43
Bhabha, Homi, 22, 33, 46, 55, 59, 61
BJP (Bharatiya Janata Party), 52, 115
Black Feminism, 50
Blumer, M., 49
Blyton, Enid, 170
Bombay, 193
bourgeois elitism, 144
Bourne, Jenny, 50
British colonialism, 31
brown races, 20, 43

Cama, Bhikaji (Madame), 33, 54
Carter, Angela, 158

Chor Bazar, 129
civilisational clashes, 48
Cohen, Robin, 19
cosmopolitanism
   concept of, 62
culture, 139

Derrida, Jaques, 55
Desai, Boman, 26
Dev, Amiya, 63
diasporic, 22
Din-e-Ilahi, 30
Dodiya, J., 66

East India Company, 63
Eliot, T.S., 24, 120, 159
Emergency, 44, 45, 142, 155, 157, 188-89, 203
ethnic minorities
   in India, 51
ethnicity, 56-57
ethnocentricity, 58
ethno-religious discourse
   in India, 52

ethno-religious politics, 47
Ezekiel, Nissim, 52, 121

Family Matters, 168, 169, 170, 171, 182, 201, 206, 208-9
Fanon, Frantz, 20, 33, 34, 39
A Fine Balance, 142, 147, 159, 165, 167, 168, 181, 182, 183, 186, 190, 202-3, 205
Firdausi, 24, 119, 199
First World diaspora, 29
Forster, E.M., 161
Foucault, M., 144
fundamental freedoms, 45

Gandhi, Feroze, 44
Gandhi, Indira, 44, 120, 126, 137, 142, 157, 158, 203
Gandhi, Mahatma, 153
Gandhi, Sanjay, 155
Gibson, Stacey, 181
Gilman, Sander L., 54
Goddard, Barbara, 64
Gokhle, Veena, 143, 146, 167
Greer, Germaine, 186
Greetz, Clifford, 55, 56
Guha, Ranjit, 144

Hall, Stuart, 34
Hariharen, Githa, 103
Hindu fundamentalism, 190
Hindutva lobby, 190
House of Mumbi, 47

Huntington, Samuel P., 47, 48, 49, 61
Hussain, M.F., 157

IIT, 126
imaginary homelands, 113
imperial labour diaspora, 65
Indian Constitution, 45, 114-15
Indian diaspora, 19
    classification of, 21
Indian National Congress, 54
individual de-gooding, 76
Isaacs, Harold R., 47
Islamic fundamentalism, 190

Jeejeebhoy, Jamsetjee, 38
Jewish diaspora, 22
Jordanus, 30
Jussawalla, Adil, 72

Kabarji, Fredoon, 40
Kafka, F., 57
Kairos, 59
Kapoor, Raj, 154
Karaka, D.F., 34
Karnad, Girish, 204
Khalistan, 23
Khalistani movement, 23
Koma Gata Maru incident, 66
Kristeva, Julia, 57
Kulke, E., 31

labour diaspora, 19

Index

Lakhani, Ali, 141
Lawson, Guy, 144
Leahy, David, 71
literature of recognition, 59
Little Indias, 21
Luhrmann, T.H., 32

MacFarlane, Scott, 64
Malabari, Behram, 35-38, 56
Mandal Commission, 15
Marx, Karl, 31
McGifford, Diane, 68
Mehta, Pherozshah, 33, 54
Millet, Kate, 133
Millian, David, 128
Mishra, Vijay, 22, 27
Mistry, Rohinton, 19, 22, 23, 41, 43, 44, 45, 65, 68, 69-70, 72, 119, 141, 142, 167, 168, 177, 196, 197, 204, 210-15
Modi, J.J., 30
Mukherjee, Arun Prabha, 41
Mukherjee, Bharati, 68, 69
militant Hinduism, 53, 190-91
multiculturalism
  Canada's policy of, 62, 185

Naipaul, V.S., 19, 23
Naoroji, Dadabhai, 33, 35, 54
Narayanan, K.R., 115
Natives, 20
Nehru, Jawaharlal, 142
Nehruvian utopia, 121

OBCs, 115
Ondaatje, Michael, 68, 71

Parmeswaran, Uma, 66, 68
Parsis
  in India, 42, 53
Parsi diaspora, 27
  theorising the, 19-46
Parsi Hindu, 35, 42, 56
partition diaspora, 29
partitioning
  of India, 204
petro-dollar diaspora, 20-21
Philip, Nourbese, 64, 65
postcolonial economic and
  academic diaspora, 21
Pratt, Marie Louise, 36
Purdah system, 39

Ramayana, 165
Rao, Raja, 67
RAW, 129, 136, 139
Red Light area, 129
Richler, Mordecai, 23
Rivayats, 30
Roy, Arundhati, 263
Rushdie, Salman, 21, 22, 41, 67, 99, 103, 117, 121, 169, 186

Safran, William, 31
Said, Edward, 20, 34, 39, 57, 73, 144
San Juan, E., Jr., 48
sati, 37

Seligman, Ellen, 181
semitic people, 49
Shiv Sena, 115, 168, 190
show-window discourse, 74
slave mentality, 106
Sollers, Werner, 56-57
Sorobji, Cornelia, 38
Spivak, Gayatri, 144
Spurr, David, 36
Such a Long Journey, 119, 133, 134, 142, 146, 156, 173, 180, 183, 189, 199-201

Tagore, Rabindranath, 24, 120, 141
Tales from Firozsha Baag, 72, 73, 170, 176, 185
Tapping, Craig, 73
Tata, Jamsetjee Nusserwanji, 33
Tata, Jamshedji, 31

Thomas, Nicholas, 36
three-monkey principle, 98
two-nation theory, 40

vasectomy programme
    of Sanjay Gandhi, 155
Vassanji, Moyez, 70

Wall of all Religions, 135, 136
William, David, 128
Wilson, John (Dr.), 34, 35
world civilisations, 47
World Literature
    concept of, 60-62
world of civilisation, 47

Zoroastrian religion, 24
Zoroastrianism, 35, 53

US $30